DATE DUE

SEP 1 7			
MR 2 5 '93			
APR 1 2 1998			
GAYLORD			PRINTED IN U.S.A.

A teacher is many things

A teacher
is many things

EARL V. PULLIAS

and

JAMES D. YOUNG

Indiana University Press
Bloomington and London

371.1

DEDICATED TO

Calvin, Douglas, John, and Vicki,
four students who taught us much
and would have taught us more
had we but had the wit to listen better;
and to all our other students,
especially those who teach
or aspire to teach.

Contents

Part 1 Background

Part II *A teacher is many things*

Foreword

Before reading *A Teacher Is Many Things,* I held the same opinion as Margaret Mead, the anthropologist, who characterized teaching as "an art that has no appeal when it is described only in words."

The authors of this book, however, have succeeded for me in communicating both the significance and the substance of teaching. It is a unique book, since every chapter is a complete and fulfilling essay, yet at the same time, each chapter is but one facet of a portrait which subtly materializes in the mind's eye; and as the final paragraph is read, one mentally stands back to admire, to nod with satisfaction, and to exclaim, "Yes, this truly is teaching!"

The book is fashioned from the observations and experiences of two men whose lifetimes have been dedicated to the infinitely complex and delicate art of teaching. The "born" teacher will enjoy that rare experience which all humans yearn for, that burst of insight in which he recognizes himself, even fleetingly, in the context of the teaching process. Those who have been indoctrinated to wade through footnotes and percentiles in their professional reading may feel that the insights of the book are intuitive rather than scientific; yet they too must learn that the qualities of great teaching are no less real for being unmeasurable.

The truth is, that in this increasingly impersonal world with its concentration on the quantitative, we must come to grips with past failures to recognize and value good teaching, or it will become another lost art.

It is imperative in our society that young people of imagination and creativity be drawn into teaching, and, once in, that they receive the support, the guidance and the perspective to develop their capacities as teachers in the fullest meaning.

PAUL J. AVERY

Superintendent of Schools
Winnetka, Illinois

Introduction

Those who teach in the colleges and universities of the United States during the final third of the twentieth century will be a major factor in the making of the future. It will be their responsibility to discover and to assimilate an avalanche of information and to transmit it to a similar avalanche of students. Even more challenging, however, will be their responsibility to seek for themselves and to help others to obtain and apply wisdom enough to use our pyramiding knowledge for the preservation of man and for the improvement of his condition.

College teachers, in spite of their many past accomplishments, have no reason to be complacent. Neither past accomplishments nor present practices will satisfy the demands of the future. The college teacher cannot neglect the roles he must play and the responsibilities he must discharge. The college teacher cannot ignore the art of teaching.

The authors of this book have supported the thesis that there is a body of knowledge related to the art of teaching and that some ways of teaching are bétter than other ways. The authors give us hope that these ways of teaching—these elements of the art—can be identified and cultivated and improved. They bring to their task an unusual and a happy combination of insights and ideas. From a rich teaching and clinical experience one of the authors contributes a deep understanding of the nature of personality. From extensive teaching experience in speech and drama the other contributes a broad understanding of communication between teacher and learner and of communication within the classroom. Together, they bring a profound appreciation for their profession and respect for the students they serve.

Some readers of this book will turn away from teaching convinced that too much is asked of a teacher. Many will move more firmly and eagerly toward teaching knowing that no vocation is more worthy of man's best efforts. Reading this book makes this reader, who no longer teaches, wish that he might return to the classroom.

The authors have made complex relationships and elusive skills seem disarmingly clear and simple. You will find, however, that the relationships are not easily accepted and the skills are not easily applied. You will discover dimensions and demands you have not considered. You will be introduced to qualities of teachers long known to be necessary but seldom found. You will become aware of practices in teaching long known to be desirable but too seldom practiced. You will find that a teacher is, indeed, many things. Understanding that, you will develop a deeper pride in your profession and a greater purpose in your teaching.

Los Angeles City College　　　　Glenn G. Gooder, *President*

Preface

A few facts about this book may be of interest to readers, especially fellow teachers.

We faced and have continued to face the question, Why another book about teaching? Could we write something of special worth? We wanted particularly to speak to on-the-job teachers, to those in preparation for teaching, and perhaps to thoughtful parents and other citizens who have an interest in the teaching art.

What should we say? Our experience as classroom teachers and our close work with teachers over many years have led us to see that a large proportion of teachers begin their work with enthusiasm and high hope and gradually lose their way under the severe demands of the profession. We have struggled with this problem in ourselves. Simply stated, the theory of this book is that a clearer and more deeply based understanding of the nature and meaning of teaching as it takes place in the classroom helps the teacher to offset a destructive trend toward staleness and to continue his growth toward excellence: a clearer picture of what a teacher is and can be gives greater meaning to teaching and better skill to the teacher.

But how does one make the meaning and significance of teaching clearer to oneself and to others? A teacher is many things; teaching is many things. We have used the method of picturing what the teacher is and what he does. Through portraying important parts or phases of the teacher's work we hope that what he is and does as a whole will be enriched and made clearer.

Although teaching is varied and made up of many parts, it is also in a larger sense a unity. In the very nature of the book there is some overlapping in the chapters. Central or common themes appear again and again, but the purpose of each chapter is to present a distinct idea and a particular emphasis. If there are paradoxes and even apparent contradictions from chapter to chapter this fact illustrates the complex nature of the subject.

We are reasonably well acquainted with the great body of published research on teaching. We wish that all we have said could be substantiated by empirical evidence. Our training has taught us to look for and respect such evidence. But, in the main, clear research is not yet available on the issues we have discussed; thus, much of what we have said is in the nature of hypotheses: our present beliefs arising from the best general and specific evidence available, including our own experience. We have tried to escape the crippling query, What will this or that critical colleague think? We have tried to keep before us the greater questions: What, as we see it, is true about the teacher and teaching? and What, in the light of our experience and knowledge, might be most helpful to teachers?

The reader should know that both of the authors respect and cherish the great body of Judaeo-Christian and Greek values which have been the essence of Western civilization. These values underlie our views on numerous problems that arise in this book. We know that these values are at present under attack on many fronts so that it is somewhat out of fashion to speak of them openly. The basic problem of values is very complex and it is good that modern man should be examining his beliefs and premises. But the great issues rooted in values, such as the nature and potential of man, the nature and significance of truth, the worth of the individual, the meaning of freedom, the nature of the "good" or the "beautiful," are so urgent that they cannot be dodged—particularly by teachers. In fact, the gradual erosion of meaning and purpose from personal and communal life which probably results from confusion in values may be the most important fact of modern life. We are convinced that teachers inevitably teach what they believe and what they do not believe. Hence, values play a great part in this discussion of teaching.

The book is a work of partnership and cooperation. The authors have thought and worked together for about twenty-five years. The labor of actual writing was divided in this way: Earl V. Pullias, whose chief technical training is in psychology with special emphasis on personality theory and mental health and in education with emphasis on learning and teaching, was responsible for chapters 2-13 and chapter 24. James D. Young, whose chief technical training is in speech and drama with special emphasis on speech personality and drama as an educational means, prepared chapters 14-23. For the convenience of readers who might be interested, authorship is indicated at the end of each chapter by initials. In the main, we probably tend to see things alike, but each has been free to express his own views in his own individual style. The twenty-two roles came out of prolonged discussion together. Each author selected the areas in which he was most interested and was urged to develop the topics in his own way.

It should be noted that each chapter has been written to stand alone. The typical reader might find Part I helpful as a background for the subsequent chapters. The sequence in which the chapters are read or used as a basis of discussion is not important. However, the volume as a whole is designed to provide a tentative portrait of the complete teacher.

THE AUTHORS

Acknowledgments

We are greatly indebted to numerous people who have helped directly and indirectly in bringing this book into being. There are many who have assisted with the practical and very necessary tasks of typing, critical reading of the manuscript at various stages, checking references, proofreading, and all the other work that the production of a book involves. We appreciate all that these friends have done even though our defensive, almost irritable, reactions may have sometimes suggested otherwise. Their reward, if any, must lie in being a part of this project, for any words at this point would at best be empty.

Perhaps we owe most to our students, for what are teachers

without students? All or nearly all that is said in this book has been again and again put to the severe test of the classroom: that strangely open and fluid place where ideas are forced to descend from their safe ivory tower into the arena of critical, free discussion by alert minds and where theory is put daily to the test of practice. We have had the incomparable opportunity to work with a steady stream of sincere, alert, thoughtful, searching students, with many who had or almost had lost their zest for learning, and with not a few whom life had hurt and embittered nearly beyond healing and growth. *All* have helped us to learn. We are pleased to acknowledge here the great debt we owe our students.

And then there are others who have influenced our thought about teaching and learning and about the varied problems of life. How does one acknowledge the debt he owes to that host of persons who have been his teachers? In addition to classroom teachers, there are all the others known and unknown from whom one learns in a lifetime of experience and study. Thus we cannot attempt to trace out and mention even the dominant strands of influence that have formed our thought. We can say only that doubtless every thought in this book has its history and we appreciate the work of those who have made that history. Whatever the original source of these thoughts we must assume responsibility for the form they take in this book. As they appear here they are ours, and we gladly accept them as such.

We should like to thank the following publishers for permission to quote from works under their copyright: Wm. C. Brown Company Publishers; The Clarendon Press, Oxford; Doubleday & Company, Inc.; Harcourt, Brace & World, Inc.; Harper & Row, Publishers, Incorporated; Harvard University Press; Holt, Rinehart and Winston, Inc.; John Knox Press; The Macmillan Company; New York University Press; W. W. Norton & Company, Inc.; Peter Pauper Press, Inc.; Henry Regnery Company; Simon and Schuster, Inc.; The University of Chicago Press; The Viking Press Inc.; and we should also like to thank Mrs. Norma Millay Ellis for permission to quote from "Renascence" by Edna St. Vincent Millay.

For permission to quote from works under their copyright in the chapter epigraphs, we should like to thank the following: The Clarendon Press, Oxford, for the excerpt from "I love all beauteous things," from *The Poetical Works of Robert Bridges,* second edition, 1936; Harper & Row, Publishers, for the excerpt from Abraham H. Maslow's *Motivation and Personality,* 1954; Alfred A. Knopf Incorporated for the excerpt from *Markings,* 1964, by Dag Hammarskjold, translated by Leif Sjöberg and W. H. Auden; Atlantic–Little, Brown and Company for the excerpt from Jacques Barzun's *Teacher in America,* copyright 1944, 1945, by Jacques Barzun; The Macmillan Company for the excerpts from Alfred North Whitehead's *The Aims of Education,* 1929, copyright renewed, 1957, by Evelyn Whitehead; New Directions Publishing Corporation, J. M. Dent and Sons, Ltd., and the trustees for the copyrights of the late Dylan Thomas, for the excerpt from "Poem in October" by Dylan Thomas in *Collected Poems,* 1946; and W. W. Norton & Company for excerpts from *Three Greek Plays,* 1937, 1958, translated by Edith Hamilton.

A teacher is many things

Part I
Background

The most important day I remember in all my life
is the one on which my teacher, Anne Mansfield Sullivan,
came to me.
—*Helen Keller*

1
What is teaching?

A distinguished psychologist once said that there are three roles no sensible person should undertake: parent, statesman, or teacher. The relationships are so complex and often contradictory, the demands so inescapable, the stakes so high that a thoughtful person has a natural tendency to pull back from the responsibilities. Doubtless the great psychologist made the statement with tongue in cheek, knowing full well that something in man pulls him toward the greatest risks in life. Men and women seek the special demands, and risk the great odds for disillusion and failure, so often involved in community leadership, parenthood, and teaching.

We are concerned in this book with teaching, learning, and the teacher. In a sense, every person is a learner and teacher, for to live is to learn, and one's life inevitably instructs those who are touched by it. But our concern is with the formal process of education, particularly as it goes on in the schools. A crucial factor in this process is the teacher working with individuals in a classroom, within prescribed limits of time, the maturity level of the learners, and the specific goals of education.

The process goes on in thousands of classrooms in all civilized countries. What is teaching? What does the effective, skillful teacher do? What varied roles does he play as he teaches? What are the satisfactions and the disappointments of teaching? Why does one enter this profession? These are the questions that engage us.

Teaching is many things. The teacher is many persons. Teaching is sometimes instructing, explaining or telling, yet very little can be "taught" in this sense. Teaching is waiting, but there is a time for action. Teaching involves demands that externally imposed standards be met, yet the best standards are self-made. The teacher is "learned"—he should know more than his students—but he is aware of deep ignorance and is in essence a learner. The teacher is, in the nature of the teaching-learning process, an example, yet he is stumblingly faulty; he has feet of clay. A teacher should be objective and detached, but probably the best of teaching is very like a love affair.[1]

What then is teaching? What is a teacher? One is reminded of the ancient fable of the blind men and the elephant. One version goes like this:

A traveler from a far land brought a strange, almost unbelievable, animal to the capital city. The traveler permitted the elephant, as it was called, to be seen for a price and the ancient city was full of rumors as to the nature of the animal. Fantastic and often contradictory reports came to the king.

The king was curious to know the true nature of the strange beast, so he sent six of the wisest of the wise blind men of his court to investigate personally and report their findings to him. Each was to tell the king what the strange animal was most like. They went to the place where the elephant was kept and each in turn, beginning with the oldest, made his investigation. The first, in coming up to the elephant, felt his tail and concluded that he is most like a rope; the second caught a tusk and thought he is most like a spear; the third felt a quivering, moving ear and his conclusion was that this animal is most like a fan; the fourth came to the elephant's large and rough side and it was clear to him the beast is most like a wall; the fifth approaching somewhat differently grasped a sturdy foreleg and promptly thought the elephant is like a tree; the last man felt the squirming trunk and it was evident to him the animal is most like a snake.

Each man made his mental notes and the group returned confidently and eagerly to the palace to report to the waiting king. Beginning with the eldest each was asked to say what the elephant is most like. The oldest: "O King, the elephant is most like a rope" and detail was given of his evidence. And so on: "A spear"; "A fan"; "A wall"; "A tree"; "A snake." The six wise men fell into loud and abusive argument among themselves; the searching king was baffled, and mused, "What indeed is the nature of this strange beast?"

In a sense, we are like those blind men. We cannot hope to see teaching and the teacher in their complete fullness. Now one phase comes into view or clear focus, and then another. Like the blind men we are in danger of fastening upon one aspect, and in our great need to find a simple answer we may contend ardently and eventually believe that one limited aspect is really the whole. Thus a teacher tends to limit his teaching activities and his personality development in terms of his narrow conception of the nature of teaching and of the teacher. To him the "elephant is like a rope" and he strives to build his life in terms of his conception. This subtle psychological process probably accounts for the narrow stereotypes into which so many teachers fall.

Not unlike the most important things in life—love, faith, play, truth, meaning—teaching cannot be perceived directly as a whole in all its myriad qualities. Rather it may be like the Tao as described by the ancient Chinese philosopher, Lao-Tzu:

The Tao described in words is not the real Tao. Words cannot describe it. Nameless it is the source of creation; named it is the mother of all things. . . . Looked for it cannot be seen; it is invisible. Listened for it cannot be heard; it is inaudible. Reached for it cannot be touched; it is intangible. These three are beyond analysis; these three are one.[2]

In like manner, something of the nature and meaning of teaching is grasped not by intense attempts to define, delimit, and circumscribe but by observing its varied manifestations while taking care to remember that no single aspect is the essence or the whole. Fellow teachers will expect and understand that in the discussion of the teacher's roles there are apparent, and perhaps real, contradictions and paradoxes. Conceivably there may be a wholeness in all that the teacher knows, is, and does, but in real life the parts do not fit so neatly together. Perhaps one should work toward a wholeness where all the parts complement and supplement each other; yet we are not sure. There lingers in our minds a feeling that the most creative wholes (whether persons, processes, or institutions) are composed of apparent and real contradictions and paradoxes. Indeed the tensions produced by these may be necessary to growth.

What then do the authors propose to do in this book? The basic spirit of the book is that of a humble search for a fuller grasp of the nature and meaning of the teaching-learning process at its best. At present, certainly, there are no final answers. Indeed there are not likely to be. Teaching is so alive, so dynamic, so person-involved that fixed answers may not be possible. Crucial aspects of the teaching-learning situation are produced by the immediate factors in the process, and hence in their very nature may not be predictable or controllable. Such a view is unsatisfying and even painful to some scientists; but for the present we cannot escape this emergent quality of teaching—indeed of all human relationships. It may be that a principle suggested by Sir Winston Churchill is applicable to the complex work of the teacher. "It is a mistake to look too far ahead. Only one link in the chain of destiny can be handled at a time."

Yet teaching has meaning, purpose, and a degree of structure.

Teaching as conceived here is essentially a means of guiding students in securing the amount and quality of experience which will promote the optimum development of their potential as human beings.

The authors have special beliefs about the nature of man—his potential and his limitations. These beliefs are partially summarized in the following statement:

. . . man is conceived as a delicate combination of the physical and spiritual, perhaps unique in the universe; as a treasure of almost unlimited potential which proper processes can uncover; as a sensitive yet unbelievably durable instrument for the discovery, refinement and creative use of truth, beauty, goodness, and love; as a remarkably versatile and energetic thinker, knower, builder, seeker who can be guided by love and truth; as a sacred being still in the process of creation, a part of which can now be self-directed; . . .

We are not ignorant of the dark history of man, nor unmindful of his long record of inhumanity to his fellow creatures. We are painfully aware of his gaudy and proud empires built on human misery, suffering, and exploitation; of his armies of helpless and ignorant men that "clash by night"; of his wide-flung brothels that traffic in bodies and souls; of his storied, ostentatious wealth side by side with grinding poverty and deprivation; of his indignities and cruelties to women, minorities, and even his own children; of his puny pride in his accomplishment, bringing him dangerously near a self-destructive cosmic irreverence—the *hubris* that *nemesis* ever follows.

But the potential of man is judged most meaningfully by what he has thought and done at his best. These high-water marks, largely individually achieved, give the true estimate of the nature of man; they suggest what he can be. I refer not only to the high points reached by so-called geniuses but equally to the best each of us occasionally reaches in dream or action. These "peak experiences" throw a quickly passing but revealing light, like a flash of lightning on a dark night, on the real potential of man.[3]

To be the most effective, the teacher understands and respects this material with which he works, i.e., human personality, including his own.

The teaching-learning process involves a spirit of learning which includes in intimate, intricate relation the teacher (the presumably somewhat more mature learner), the student (the somewhat less mature learner), and the whole of life which as Whitehead suggests is the true subject matter for learning.

> The solution which I am urging, is to eradicate the fatal disconnection of subjects which kills the vitality of our modern curriculum. There is only one subject-matter for education, and that is Life in all its manifestations.[4]

This delicately fluid process goes on in the environment of a society, a school, and most immediately a classroom.

Teaching so conceived is both a science and an art.[5] Clearly there is much the teacher must know: the area of reality which he is responsible to teach (his subject); knowledge closely related to his subject; the nature of learning; human psychology including implications for self-understanding and the understanding of others; the social order in which the educative process goes on; etc. But he may know all of this and much more and not be an effective teacher, for teaching is an art that demands a delicate balance of many factors in actual performance: knowledge, skill, and traits of personality and character. A great physician must know much, but that knowledge alone does not make him a skilled healer; a good coach must know the game he coaches and must know much about people, but in action he must perform as an artist; a musician must know music ever so well, but this does not make him an effective concert performer.

The relation between science and art is complex and difficult to explain. Suffice it to say here that knowledge can be achieved by proper study; art involves personal style and is developed largely through purposeful practice, perhaps most effectively under a master guide. It seems that, in general, the best art rests upon a mastery of the appropriate science. So it is with teaching.

In writing these essays we have wished to avoid the extremes of easy, irresponsible sentimentality and of irritable, cheap cynicism. Teaching is a very demanding and risk-filled profession, but when reasonably well done it is a deeply rewarding one. There is no easy, painless road to full self-actualization through teaching. We do not wish so to emphasize the difficulties of the road that worthy persons seeking to enter it would be discouraged, nor do we wish to paint a picture that is deceptively attractive. In short, teaching is a great and deeply satisfying calling, but it is difficult and demanding, and tends to be destructive of both the teacher and the taught when poorly done.

The central purpose of the book then is to throw additional light on the nature and meaning of teaching and learning, and the relation of the teacher to this process. Although aspects of learning and teaching vary in terms of the maturity level and ability of the students and of the area or subject of study, it has been our desire to reach a level of principle that is equally applicable to all teaching from the beginning of formal school through the college years.

Our method is to portray as vividly as possible, in separate brief chapters, the varied roles the teacher assumes, the kinds of things the teacher does. There is no attempt at complete analysis; the purpose is to suggest paths of thought that may be taken rather than to make a full exploration of those paths.

We know full well that teaching is not merely or chiefly any one of the activities described, nor is it all of them taken together. Further, we know that no single picture of a role or activity really stands alone, but in actual teaching each relates to and involves all the rest of what goes on in teaching and learning. Although no one can see and fully comprehend the whole process, our hope is that looking closely and imaginatively (as with a special camera) at these perceivable parts or phases will in meaningful ways enrich and clarify the whole science and art of teaching. This hope is based upon the fact that such views have helped us and seemed to have helped some of our students who have entered teaching. Our great desire is that many who teach and plan to teach will be stimulated to thought, study, and practice that will cast still further light on the life and work of the teacher; that all who teach may enter the path of steady growth toward being the complete, the whole teacher, even though most of us will not reach the full goal.

Finally, why twenty-two roles or special activities of the teacher? There is no good reason for twenty-two over six or eleven or forty-two. The important point is that the list is not exhaustive but merely suggestive and illustrative.

E. V. P.

J. D. Y.

Questions and problems for dialogue

1 A thoughtful scholar and writer once said to his advanced students that an introduction usually should be written but then it should be be discarded. That is, the value of the introduction is largely that of "warming up" the writer. What do you think of this idea? In your judgment, does it apply to the introduction to this book?

2 Why is the fable of the blind men given in this introduction? What central point does it suggest?

3 In your judgment, is teaching more nearly an art or a science? Why do you think so?

4 Is it possible for a person to be highly skilled in a performance and not know the underlying science? Think of illustrations.

5 Would you be disturbed if some of the various roles or activities of the teacher seemed to be contradictory or in conflict? Why?

6 What is meant by the statement that often the factors in a teaching situation are emergent and hence unpredictable? Find illustrations from your experience as a student or as a teacher.

7 What are some of the values and some of the dangers of a teacher's studying all of the varied roles he plays? Is there a likelihood that he will become confused, like the centipede that was asked which foot he moved first?

8 What do you think of the suggestion that it is wiser for a teacher to conceive his task narrowly and hence more "realistically"? Give arguments for and against this view.

9 How do you react to the proposition that the same basic principles apply to all levels of teaching from kindergarten to graduate school?

In your judgment, would it have been wiser to have pointed the book specifically at a particular level of teaching? Why?

10 From your experience, what is the chief weakness of books about teaching? That is, as you see it, what is wrong with them? Try to decide if this book has these faults.

Exercises
for further learning

1 State in a paragraph what you consider to be the central purpose of this introductory chapter. Was the purpose achieved?

2 Examine carefully the table of contents of the book after you have read the Introduction. Attempt to imagine how the chapters do what the Introduction suggests that the book intends to do.

3 Interview or read about three or four highly skilled people (actors, doctors, coaches, statesmen, athletes, artists, teachers) in an attempt to clarify the most creative or effective relation between science and art.

4 Undertake to define in your own words the meaning of art and of science as the terms are used in this chapter.

5 On the basis of your reading this chapter state in a paragraph or two the central purpose of this book.

6 Make a list of not less than five and not more than ten things you would hope to learn from a book of this kind. What types of learning do you think would be most helpful for you?

7 Interview five experienced teachers in order to get their reaction to books they have read about teaching. Strive to get beneath surface feeling and cynicism to determine what their essential criticisms are.

8 Undertake to determine if doctors have a similar feeling about books on the practice of medicine or lawyers on books about the practice of law. Is there a difference? If so, why?

9 In the early days of the Land Grant college and the study of agriculture in this country, there was great resistance on the part of the farmers. They called the agriculture teachers "book farmers" and theory men. Analyze this type of resistance, looking for causes.

10 Make a brief list of the ways in which one's conception of the nature of his profession might affect his activity as a professional worker. Think of more than one profession.

> . . . to know
> That which before us lies in daily life
> Is the prime wisdom . . .
> —*John Milton*

2

Some obstacles
to growth toward excellence
in teaching

Throughout this book we think with you about the varied nature of teaching. We picture the teaching-learning process from numerous angles and perspectives in the hope that the nature and meaning of teaching and of education might be clarified and enriched. We have tried to escape both of two seriously destructive extremes: sentimentality and cynicism.

We do not pull back from picturing teaching in all its complexity and as it can be and often has been at its best. The standard used for evaluating "best" is simple but we believe valid: the most effective release and development of the potential in

14

human beings. What can man be? What do we want him to be? What are the opportunities and responsibilities of teachers in directing the process of education? These are the great questions that confront those who accept responsibility for education.

We come to this discussion from many years of classroom experience. We are aware of how far below the optimum we as practicing teachers usually fall. Our emphasis is (1) upon seeing teaching in its fullness and (2) upon the importance of *growth toward* what we perceive. We know something of the stubborn obstacles that are in the path of growth toward excellence. It is foolhardy to ignore these obstacles or to underestimate their destructive power.

Thus, as a part of our thought together about teaching, we mention and briefly analyze some of the major obstacles to growth that we have experienced and observed. These obstacles are not listed in a mood of alarm or censure but in a spirit of sharing what we have experienced and what seems to be the common experience of other teachers. These are some of the often subtle and frequently deadly enemies to optimum growth of the teacher. Let us look briefly at ten such obstacles.

1. Cynicism. Human beings are given to extremes. To avoid or counteract what has become a distasteful or dangerous extreme in one direction, we often go to another which may be equally distasteful and dangerous. Our age, in a real or pretended attempt to escape what is or seems to be sentimentality, is in serious danger of becoming chronically cynical. A sentimental world is maudlin, slushy, unrealistic; a cynical world is scheming, distrustful, sneering, unimaginative. The cynic is skeptical of all ideals and of most purposes. He is on the way toward losing faith in himself, in his fellows, in goodness, beauty, and truth, and frequently even in meaning. To speak in his presence of love, or unselfish action, of dedication, of sacrifice is to invite a sneer or ridicule.

But it would not seem wise to be merely critical of cynicism or the cynic. Understanding is much better, although hard to achieve. Modern cynicism is probably a reaction to a thin romanticism and often phony idealism prevalent in the nineteenth century. Perhaps more fundamentally, this tendency to cynicism is an attempted defense against the swift, deep, and broad transitions that are taking place in the twentieth century—particularly since the First World War—which shake the foundations of almost every phase of life. Cynicism may in essence be a reaction to deeply based and prolonged fear and general anxiety. The most pervasive questioning and upheaval are in the area of values. What matters most in life? Does anything really matter except immediate individually perceived personal advantage and pleasure? These are good questions and unbelievably complex. The cynic has a quick, "smart" answer to these and similar questions—an answer which threatens to erode meaning from individual and group life. Perhaps the most characteristic symptom of the cynic is that he feels little or no responsibility for the consequences of this erosion for himself or others.

This spirit is widespread and the teacher must work in it as a physician works in the midst of a deadly plague. He must avoid infection himself, for only then can he have a chance to heal others and perhaps eventually to discover causes that lead to prevention and to the promotion of positive health.

The best defense against the virus of cynicism is a clearheaded courageous offense. This offense is in essence a persistent search for the truth in a spirit of faith and hope that life can have genuine meaning and purpose. Without this offense, the best in man withers and dies; or, even worse, in desperation man espouses a false or partial faith that promotes a distorted and cancerous growth in individual and communal life. The Nazi period in German history was one of the most dramatic instances of such distortion in modern times, but history is replete with similar distortions and no one can feel smug about his own nation or culture.

But we are concerned with teachers—individual teachers in the classrooms. Why the emphasis upon historical cases? Simply because the principle is applicable to individuals: the loss of meaning and the desperate reaction to that loss, which is cynicism, are poisons at the very root of individual and group life. The results of this poison appear in every part of personality and behavior. Of course cynicism is not an all-or-none condition: like most diseases it has relatively simple and small beginnings; it may manifest itself little or much; it perhaps seldom goes its full course, presenting the full-blown cynic. Indeed, if the full symptoms appeared more often, the beginning signs might receive more attention.

Practically, what is this cynicism like? Essentially the cynical person is unable to see or to believe in any form of "good" in himself or others. He looks for and as a rule finds a hidden or ulterior motive behind a belief or an action. As the origin of the word suggests, he is like a "dog" with his nose to the ground in search of evil smells.

The typical young teacher probably comes to his work with strong positive beliefs about the high potential of human beings, the value of individuals, the purpose and significance of education, the meaning and importance of teaching as a life work, the joy and satisfaction in work skillfully done, the prime value in forgetting oneself in a cause considered worthy. If he takes the road of the cynic those beliefs are washed out of him and in general replaced by their opposites.

2. Narrowness. The demands of modern life require specialization. In order to know any one thing well, it seems that others must be neglected. This tendency to specialization is likely to grow stronger in the foreseeable future: each part of a complex whole coming to know and do his small duty better and better with less and less knowledge of or interest in other parts or the whole. Such specialization may be necessary to the highest efficiency and economy in a complex industrial society such as ours.

But we have fearful examples of the extremes of specialization in the social insects, particularly the ants and the bees. The hive or the colony carries on its work with remarkable efficiency. Its ways have very high survival value. Each part carries out its specialized work with admirable skill, but there is no reason to believe that the "purpose" of the colony, nor even its biological survival, has any "meaning" for the parts. Some students of modern society feel that we are moving inexorably in this direction: efficient, but sans purpose, sans meaning, sans individuality.

Clearly a chief concern of many individuals is to find some way not to become a meaningless cog in a huge, noisy, impersonal machine. We search, often almost frantically, for a foothold of integrity, of individuality and selfhood. Not that one would wish to be less efficient or specialized; rather that he might achieve the space and means to be a genuine self, as a specialized part of a specialized world. Teachers are no exception. The pressure toward a destructive narrowness is powerful and unrelenting.[1]

The teacher seeks for breadth of experience as an antidote for this narrowness. Each teacher must find his own best ways to desirable breadth, but we urge a conscious searching. The most useful avenues seem to be (1) wide reading outside one's special area, (2) cultivation of associates and friends outside one's specialization, (3) varied recreational and cultural participation, (4) travel, (5) a cultivation of broad interests, (6) a persistent relation with the world of nature, and (7) activity which lifts one out of self and narrow self-concern, e.g., service or worship.

3. Confusion about role and purpose. Education is one of man's chief endeavors. By nature man is largely unmade; by nurture he becomes man. Formal education (that carried on in a school) is a major means of that nurture. Such education is essentially a series of experiences planned in terms of ability and maturity level designed to bring the students to full development. The teacher is the organizer and mediator of this educative experience and as such is the key influence in the development of men by nurture. As such, teachers are potentially the most influential forces in a civilization, particularly an advanced civilization.

For various reasons the typical teacher does not clearly perceive the nature and meaning of his profession. Often he does not seem to have a clear conception of what education proposes to do, what the process is essentially, or the significance of his part in it. He sees a particular job to be done: a first grade to be taught, a class in high school algebra, a college course in literature or history or biology. Caught in the web of daily, immediate demands, the teacher may never have asked, or may have long since ceased to ask, what he is really attempting to do and why. In such cases meaning is leached out of teaching, the teacher ceases to be a self-respecting professional worker, and rapidly becomes a routine piece-worker, perhaps a time-server, with a decreasing concern for the quality of his work and an increasing concern for narrow self-aggrandizement.

The need evidently is for regular professional renewal, probably most effectively achieved through programs of in-service training, professional study, and planned leaves. We are in sore need of more skilled men and women who have a clear vision of the nature and meaning of education and teaching, who have special ability to communicate that vision with power and enthusiasm to teachers and who are not neutralized by a fear of the caustic cynic's ban. This is no plea for cheap, canned, insipid "inspiration" improperly related to knowledge, experience, and genuine concern. Teachers, we are confident, respond to genuine, informed, responsible educational statesmanship. They long for professional renewal in a world in danger of losing all purpose.

4. Distorted conception of the nature of people. The material with which teachers work is man. Just as a sculptor works in stone, a carpenter in wood, a horse trainer with horses, an agriculturist with plants and animals, a poet with words and meter, so the teacher works with human beings—*homo sapiens*. His knowledge and beliefs about this material are profoundly important for his work, his current effectiveness, and his future growth.

The teacher will see human beings at every level of development, in a wide variety of forms, and in many conditions. There is the young child new to school. Even this child will have had five years of complex and crucial experience which represents a biological and social inheritance of long ages (including physique, special talent, ability, energy level, etc.), and will have ways of dealing with the environment which are in the process of becoming a characteristic style of life. Or there is the high school student or the college senior perhaps manifesting greater variety than the five-year-old, for the varied influences of the environment have played upon him longer. The teacher himself is an example of this human material as made by the delicate and continuous interaction of heredity and environment. He can see or perceive the material with which he works only through the prism of himself—what he has come to believe and be.

Greatly influenced by practices and theories arising from man's long history and struggle, the typical person, including the teacher, is full of preconceptions about the nature and potential of people. For example, the mentality that created and sustained human slavery and related exploitations was characteristic of the societies of man until very recent times. Class feelings and a variety of folk notions about ability and talent are still widely prevalent and manifest themselves in language, writing, law, and custom.

There is a continuous and persistent attempt to study man by varied means to determine more objectively his nature and potential. But it must be faced that conclusions resulting from even the more systematic study of man are at this stage confused. Out of this welter of truth, half-truth, fiction, and tradition, how is the teacher to get a workable conception or theory of the material with which he deals? There is an inevitable tendency for his conception to be piecemeal, confused, reflective of the prejudices of his tribe or the "cave."[2]

Our point here is that every phase of the teacher's work and of his own development as a person will be crucially influenced by his beliefs about the nature and potential of people. What is the nature of this "raw material" with which the teacher works? What are its negative and positive possibilities? These are the crucial questions from which nearly all others in education receive direction and meaning. Thus ignorance, prejudice, and confusion in this area are major obstacles to full realization for the teacher.

5. Clutter and crowdedness. Almost everything in modern life

is cluttered and crowded. We seem literally hypnotized by the need to do more, see more, learn more, get more, until *more* becomes an obsession. This drive for more enters and influences every phase of life, including education.

We have been told again and again in recent years that knowledge is increasing at a phenomenal rate. How can we put all this new knowledge into the curriculum? There is more and more to know and limited human capacity to learn and limited time in which to learn. How can it be done? Learning machines? Television? Courses with more and more content? Longer and longer school days and school years? Night shifts? All of these may help some, but however we may crowd and clutter, there still will be more, clamoring to be included.

Should we not ask again the crucial questions: What knowledge is worth knowing? What really are the use and meaning of this personal and professional crowdedness and clutter? If we really decided and wanted to, could we not reduce and simplify—create and protect an area of psychological and physical living space around ourselves that is so crucial to wholesome growth? Must our lives—classroom and personal lives—have this frenzied quality which almost everyone bemoans? Is it necessary to be so rushed that almost nothing is done with grace and style? Perhaps we are so far along the road of crowdedness and clutter that we cannot even pause to ask these questions, not to speak of finding objective, intelligent answers.

6. Pedantry. The problem here is simple and can be simply stated; the solution is quite another matter.[3] The problem is that knowledge and understanding are condensed into language which in essence is a network of symbols. Originally this knowledge and understanding grew out of and were close to actual experience; the symbol—the abstraction which represents the experience—had the life and warmth of the original interaction between the mind and the immediate occurrences. With time, the distance between the experience and the symbol or abstraction increases until eventually the abstraction has little or no meaning to the learner. This is

a major danger in formal education—the danger of inert or dead knowledge, of pedantry.

The teacher works largely with abstractions or symbols. Through them he is able to provide the vicarious experience which is the chief means of education. But if these abstractions are allowed to lose their living relation with reality, as they strongly tend to do, they no longer educate, no longer reach the learner as the experience from which learning can arise. Further, the teacher as he becomes more and more a pedant may become so enthralled with his neat set of abstractions—with his dead or dying knowledge—that he is unaware of their lack of relation to reality. He is "learned" in a quaint way and may be tolerated by those who need the live, fresh knowledge necessary to genuine education, but he becomes less and less their teacher. A study of the great teachers of history suggests that an almost childlike elemental quality of directness, of nearness to life, is the quality most common to all of them. In modern times, Albert Einstein is a moving example.

7. Dullness or failure of imagination. A few days ago we asked two friends who are now in the sixth grade how school is this year. Their response was brief and clear: "Dreadful." "What is wrong? Last year you said things were wonderful." They replied, "Our teacher this year is dull, every day the same, no life or new ideas or special things going on. That teacher last year was great. Always something interesting and different. You really wanted to go to school."

Talk to a child or adult now in school or ask older people to tell you about the best or the worst teacher in their school experience. Again and again this quality of imagination and enthusiasm will come to the fore. Dullness coupled as it often is with a fractious meanness of spirit will be near the top of the characteristics of the worst teachers; imagination and its close associate, enthusiasm, will very nearly head the list for best teachers.

It may be objected, Is not imagination a natural quality of the personality? Can imagination really be cultivated or dullness avoided? Doubtless some people are naturally more imaginative than others (at least this quality seems natural when they are mature); and some seem to have almost a talent for making even very interesting and exciting things dull. Still common sense and other evidence suggest that by giving a little care and thought at least the simpler forms of imagination can be nurtured. Simple variation in pace, the changing of routine, a searching for new ideas, trying new things now and then, listening more deeply to younger people—any of these things may help to break the crust of dull sameness.

This obstacle is especially important to the teacher because, on the surface, much of teaching has a sameness about it: year after year another second grade, another English class, another graduate seminar. Sameness is easy and in a way inviting but tends to produce a stifling dullness.

There is, of course, the danger that the teacher trying to escape dullness will rush into silliness, perhaps more repulsive to young people than dullness. Dullness may be expected and accepted in us as teachers, but phony attempts to be imaginative and enthusiastic may be more difficult to overlook. However, there are *genuine* imagination and zest and they are very nearly the finest qualities of human personality. The teacher seeks to cultivate their roots as the most effective defense against dullness.

8. Routine. A major portion of life is composed of hard, recurring, relatively dull routine. These demands may be called the "profane" aspects of one's life. There are also the deeper, more satisfying aspects, as a rule composing the smaller portion of a person's activities. These may be called the "sacred." These terms should carry no value connotations; they are used merely to help us understand a profound principle. That is to say, in the practice of life, sacred and profane activities are equally important and equally good. They are different but to conceive of the profane as particularly undesirable or bad and the sacred as desirable

or good would be to miss the central point of this discussion. In proper proportion and proper relation each contributes toward making life what it is.

An illustration may help to give meaning to this concept. A young lawyer, especially if he is ambitious and tends somewhat toward the idealistic, may allow himself to become enchanted by one part of the nature and practice of the law. Fastening upon a picture of a famous trial lawyer or the life of a renowned Supreme Court judge, his vision of the law may be dominated by the "sacred" aspects of its study and practice: great moments before a jury, the writing of briefs that may influence the development of the law, great opportunities for service, and other high moments.

Then he passes the bar and attempts to settle down to the practice of the law. The flood of routine or "profane" demands may almost destroy him and his vision of the greatness of his profession. Hours of detailed research for every moment in court, long waiting periods while the ancient procedures drag forward, rent and overhead to be met and clients coming ever so slowly, and similar often dull cases appearing again and again. In short, a life largely of routine, dry work day in and day out. Is this the law of which the student dreamed? It is an aspect of that law, but certainly not all of it. These activities are the basic means to the achieving of the deeper, the sacred, satisfactions of a life with the law. They are not evil things imposed as it were by a devil and which under better circumstances might not need to be done. They are hard work, oftentimes drudgery, but in human life a living and necessary part of the larger whole.[4]

The teacher's situation is similar. There is the recurring, back-breaking, daily, weekly, yearly routine; there is the deeply satisfying, even exhilarating, guidance of learning: seeing the fulfillment of one's work. It seems that these "sacred" peaks in life are achieved only at the price of doing with reasonable skill and abandon the "profane." Perhaps at best, although this is very hard to accomplish, the routine, the drudgery so to speak, is enlightened and given meaning by being related by thought and imagination to the larger goals it serves and perhaps makes possible.

A fine perspective is needed to place and keep these two aspects of life in proper relation. The exhausting, mounting routines will tend to defeat and destroy a parent, a physician, a statesman, or a teacher who does not have this perspective. Armed with a good perspective, the teacher may use even the most severe of routine demands as a means of growth.

9. Pace unsuited to temperament. Every person tends to develop special ways of carrying on his work. At best, these ways work into an effective pattern which fits and satisfies the deeper needs and temperamental rhythms of the individual. Speed of work, intensity or degree of concentration, span of effort, need for variation or recreation, energy supply, and specific work habits are some of the factors that are involved.

In terms of his nature (innate or acquired) and the particular requirements of his calling, the teacher or other professional worker gradually develops a highly personal style of work and of living. Such a style enables him to do that which his work requires with a maximum of effectiveness and a minimum of needless strain. In a word, an appropriate style enables the person to work in a way and at a pace appropriate to his nature and the demands of the job.

A failure on the part of the teacher to develop a style that is suited both to his temperament and to his work becomes a serious obstacle to relaxed growth toward excellence. In such a case, his work is a constant strain which tends to undermine joy and zest in work and eventually destroys the worker's general health. He becomes then like an engine pulling a load beyond its capacity or trying to make a grade in the wrong gear. Thoreau expressed the principle:

Winter has come unnoticed by me, I have been so busy writing. This is the life most lead in respect to nature. How different from my habitual one! It is hasty, coarse, and trivial, as if you were a spindle in a factory. The other is leisurely, fine, and glorious, like a flower. In the

first case you are merely getting your living; in the second you live as
you go along. You travel only on roads of the proper grade without jar
or running off the track, and sweep round the hills by beautiful curves.[5]

It should be remembered that style cannot be wisely copied. It
must be developed in the heat of action and is a deeply individual
matter, probably greatly helped by a growing understanding of
the key aspects of the self, both limitations and strengths.

10. Fatigue and illness. Sickness rapidly undermines all of the
desirable processes we describe in this book. To grow toward excellence as persons and as teachers, we must be reasonably well
in a world that is not very well, and this applies to body, mind
and spirit. A few simple suggestions may help teachers to deal
more effectively with this major obstacle.[6]

(a) Strive to learn the limits of your personality. A person is
not unlike a bridge in the sense that there is a limit to the weight
it can bear. Most students of this subject agree that each personality has a breaking point—a point beyond which, if the pressure
continues, the personality will begin to develop symptoms which
are often merely inappropriate and desperate defenses against un-
bearable demands. The problem here is for the teacher to learn
to reduce demands well before the breaking point is reached. In
health, especially in mental health but perhaps in all phases, there
is a "point of no return" beyond which there may be great suffering, and a restoration of health may require prolonged professional care.

(b) Practice regular and systematic withdrawal and renewal.
The wise teacher develops his "great good place" (to use the
phrase of Henry James) to which he goes bodily and psychologically to recreate and restore himself. Perhaps the "place" is not
so important as a place, but rather as the atmosphere which renews
—which takes one out of himself if only for a short period, which
gives the glorious feeling of freedom from demand, which is a real
moment of respite between that which has been completed and
that which has not yet begun. Each individual must find his own

most helpful means of withdrawal and renewal; and the good means are as varied as life.

Modern individuals, especially those in cities, need regular and close contact with nature. Few things are more healing and refreshing than interaction with forest, land, sea, desert, stream, or the open sky. Also, there are music, the quiet walk, reading, sports, the theater, meditation, unrestrained talk with friends, worship, and many other activities.

(c) Develop a few mental and spiritual intimates. In a sense, as the English poet Donne said, "No man is an island . . ." but in another sense, equally deep, every person as an individual is alone, or at least often feels alone which is not very different. Mounting evidence seems to indicate that modern technology which in many ways has brought men closer together in physical proximity, crowding them in cities and on freeways and on battlefields, has in reality made satisfying nearness more difficult among human beings and between people and nature. Therefore, a characteristic of modern persons is loneliness with an undertone of anxiety. The teacher who wishes to bring his best to his art—who, in a word, hopes to be well—must find constructive ways of overcoming this aloneness.

Almost no one can deal with the demands of human life alone. It is a great help to health to be able to share the experiences of life in mutual respect and full confidence. But the relationship must be right, or it will add to the burden. Few relationships are of such quality as to permit uninhibited sharing of triumphs and joys, of frustrations and sorrows. Yet it is the uninhibited expression of these feelings that is vital to the soothing healing of wounds and the satisfying process of growth. Strangely enough, such release and positive expression of concerns contribute to the well-being of all three large phases of personality: body, mind, and spirit.

Unfortunately, the conditions and processes of work of nearly all teachers are fraught with friction and tension. An atmosphere of good will, mutual trust, and common joy in achievement would contribute immeasurably to the teacher's health and effectiveness, but such conditions are rare in the framework of modern life. Thus the wise teacher attempts to develop a few intimates with whom he overcomes the gnawing loneliness so common, especially in current professional life.

These ten obstacles illustrate the many and varied ones teachers encounter. They may serve to put the teacher on guard against forces that can defeat and destroy him. More important, through presenting this list we intend to suggest that these and most other obstacles the teacher will meet, if properly approached, can be a means of continuous growth.

E. V. P.

Questions and problems for dialogue

1 Does the discussion on obstacles seem to you to have a pessimistic or an optimistic tone? Did the reading of this chapter tend to encourage or discourage you? Be ready to say why.

2 Which of the ten obstacles mentioned seem to you to apply about equally to all professional work and which are particularly applicable to teaching?

3 Are older or younger teachers more subject to cynicism? Or does age seem to be a factor? If the typical modern person is afraid to be considered idealistic, why do you think this is true?

4 In your judgment, would a discussion of these and other obstacles be of more interest and value to young people who are preparing to teach or to teachers with some experience? Why?

5 How much danger is there that a discussion of obstacles will discourage young people from entering teaching? How would you deal with this danger?

6 Of the ten obstacles mentioned in this chapter which two are likely to be the most serious for you personally?

7 Who in the school system, in your judgment, has the responsibility to keep the role and purpose of the teacher clear and growing?

That is, from what point is good leadership most likely to be effective?

8 Is a teacher's conception of the nature of people (their potential and limitations) really so important for his work? If so, why?

9 In your judgment, can the individual teacher do much about the obstacles? Are they so much a part of modern life that he cannot overcome them? To what extent are they so much a part of the civilization that he cannot hope to escape them?

10 In teacher training as you have experienced it, at what point is the prospective teacher prepared to deal with such obstacles as are discussed in this chapter? Where and how could this preparation be best done?

Exercises for further learning

1 Go over this list of obstacles with five teachers who are in the first three years of their teaching experience and with five teachers with ten or more years of experience. Try to discover if there is any observable difference between the two groups as to how they perceive the obstacles.

2 As you talk with teachers undertake to put them on a scale of cynicism or freedom from cynicism. List three to five of what you have found to be fairly reliable symptoms of cynicism.

3 Keep careful notes on the next four or five educational speeches you hear. Evaluate the talks in terms of your standard of educational leadership. Note with care the criteria you use.

4 Suppose you were asked to reduce this list of obstacles from ten to five. Indicate the five you would retain as being most significant and indicate why.

5 Assume that you were asked to add another five to the list, bringing it to fifteen. State briefly the five you would add.

6 State in your own words in a paragraph or two the meaning of "sacred" and "profane" as the terms are used in this chapter. Give some thought as to the optimum relation between these two aspects of life. Search for illustrations from your own experience.

7 Try to determine if there is an obstacle that in principle seems to you to be crucial to all the others. Or to put it positively, is there an effective defense against all these obstacles and if so, what is it?

8 Get together a small group of prospective teachers or teachers on

the job and use these dangers or obstacles as points of discussion. Note with care the attitudes expressed.

9 Interview two or three experienced teachers that seem to you to have fine imagination. Try to discover what has kept that imagination alive and growing. Do the same with two or three teachers that seem to you to be dull. Look for principles.

10 Interview (a) three doctors, (b) three lawyers, (c) three nurses, and (d) three teachers of approximately the same age and experience. Strive to discover their basic conception of their work. Do you find any observable difference in the four groups?

Part II
A teacher is many things

Thou art my master and my guide;
thou alone art he from whom I
learned the good style that hath
done me honor.
—*Dante to Virgil*

3

A teacher is

a guide

The teacher is a guide on the learning journey. As a guide, on the basis of his experience, his knowledge of the road and of the travelers, and his keen interest in their learning, he assumes major responsibility for the trip. He sets the goals, establishes the limits of the trip in terms of the students' needs and abilities, determines the way to be taken, enlivens and enriches every aspect of the journey, and evaluates progress. All of this is done in closest cooperation with the fellow travelers, but the teacher will be the chief influence in every aspect of the journey. Perhaps he should not seem to be the central factor, surely he will in no sense be domineering or even dominant, but he will be and should be a guide and thus accept a guide's privileges and responsibilities.

The figure of the odyssey or journey has often been used in literature and history to represent the life of man or some phase of that life. Usually the term does not mean merely physical travel but the deeper and more complex mental and spiritual searchings and wanderings. Homer's ancient tale of the ten-year journey of Odysseus from Troy to his home island of Ithaca is much more than an account of the wanderings of the old warrior; it is doubtless a symbol of man's psychological and spiritual exploration. The modern Greek poet, Kazantzakis, made his *Odyssey: A Modern Sequel* strictly a symbolic journey. Also, Lillian Smith's insightful *Journey* is largely spiritual and psychological exploration. So was Goethe's charming *Wilhelm Meister's Travels*. There are many other such journeys that may interest and stir the imagination of the thoughtful reader.[1]

The term journey is especially appropriate to the process of learning, whether it is a single class, one's entire formal education, or the whole of life. The analogy of the journey gathers into itself almost everything that is involved in learning and teaching. A journey has purpose or a destination unless the traveler is pushed merely to wander by accident, curiosity, or necessity, and even then the nature of man seems to demand that he create goals. Plans are made, the trip is taken, and from time to time there is a pause for looking back and assessing the nature and meaning of the odyssey to this point.

A teacher meets a class of kindergarten children: new to formal school, afraid yet eager to push out to new experience, equipped with all the senses, with the incomparable human central nervous system, and with the basics of language, but with few of the technical tools of learning. There are perhaps thirty of them to be in the class a half-day session for a year. Since birth, chiefly in the home they have made five years or so of what will normally be a seventy- or eighty-year journey. They are beginning their formal education which in our society will last from eight to twenty years; in the future this will likely be twelve to sixteen years for almost everyone. What is this first crucial nine months' segment of the trip to be like?

Or a teacher meets a class of advanced doctoral students at the university. There are twenty-five or thirty of them. They have traveled much more of the journey than have the children; their average age is thirty. They have had a minimum of seventeen years of formal education, through the Master's degree; they have had dozens of teachers; they have succeeded and failed in the varied endeavors of life; they have well-developed styles of life—often rigidly fixed ways of dealing with themselves and others; they are full of the wounds and scars of life's struggle. They and the teacher have a semester (about four and one-half months) or a quarter (about three months) to travel together—to go psychologically from here to there. What shall the journey of these graduate students be like? What are the teacher's special privileges and responsibilities for the journey?

In between the kindergarten and the advanced graduate or professional school—the experiences which we have used as examples —lie all the particular legs of the journey that in general we call elementary school, secondary school, and college or the undergraduate part of the university. The point is that the analogy of the journey or odyssey applies equally well all along the scale. The details will vary greatly, but the basic principles involved in the learning journey, with the assistance of an effective guide, are essentially the same. Teaching conceived in this way is put into a different and more meaningful dimension, is lifted out of the dead routine that makes much of teaching and formal education a destructive, cramping process both for teacher and learner, or, to continue the analogy, for both the older and younger travelers on the journey.

A warning must be inserted here against an unrealistic concep-

tion of this journey. The experienced teacher is painfully aware
of the difficulties involved in being a guide for learning. He knows
the seriously negative results of bad teaching practice both on the
teacher and on the taught. He is not ignorant of the harmful
effects of the loss of purpose and meaning; of the petty, self-
centered irritableness of commercialism; of the near despair of
awkwardness and lack of proper skill and style in the presence of
the demands of a complex and delicate art; of the disintegrating
fatigue of endless work that leaches out the very last of one's
energy; of the pedantry and cynicism that come from dealing too
long with inert or dead ideas.

But that experienced teacher knows also that these dangers can
be overcome and that the journey, even with growing, restless children and youth, can be a joyous adventure. My theory is that
the way teaching is conceived makes a difference, perhaps the
major difference, as to what it is, what it becomes, and what it
does for both teacher and student.

What then does an effective guide do and what does he not do?
What must he know and be in order to do his job well? These two
questions are intricately related but for analysis let us examine
them in order.

The guide on the learning journey is highly skilled in doing four
things:[2]

1. He plans the objectives of the learning endeavor.[3] This means
that he decides what this segment of education or learning can
most profitably or wisely include. There are literally thousands of
places to go or, if you will, things to be learned. The teacher's task
is to decide in each class (as formal education is now organized)
what the travelers are ready for, both in terms of their background and ability, and what they need to learn on this part of
the trip in view of the various goals that lie before them. The
teacher, to plan the objectives well, in a sense sees the whole journey from birth to death. For example, the quality of one's life will
depend in considerable measure on an ability to read well[4] and to

express one's thoughts clearly in the mother tongue, to mention only two critical objectives of all learning. What can and should this segment of education contribute to those large but very practical objectives?

These are problems of what we technically call curriculum which wisely or unwisely are often handled in general by people other than the classroom teacher, even sometimes those so far away from the learner as the legislature or various boards. As representatives of the public, with a vital interest in education, these people have a legitimate concern in the learning objectives, but they can in no wise sense displace the teacher who is the immediate guide of the learning process. The objectives must be his own in that he has carefully thought them through and concluded that they are the best possible objectives for this part of education. Further, the teacher as guide so interprets the objectives that they have life and meaning for the learners—in a word, so they are accepted as meaningful, alive, interesting goals for them. There are few things more foolish than the common tendency of teachers to fail, or refuse, to make clear both their specific and general objectives. Above almost anything, the human mind rebels at not being informed, at being forced to travel blind like a slave, at meaninglessness. Here perhaps is the reason that so large a portion of the teacher's time is taken up with quelling rebellion (or with discipline), as seems so often to be the case.

A major aspect of the task of planning objectives is the problem of economy.[5] Only a limited amount can be grasped by the human mind in a given time. And time is limited in the extreme. Within the limitations of the human mind and of the time available what should be attempted? To lift our minds out of a classroom situation where we are so bound by stereotypes of action and thought, let us imagine for a moment that you have the opportunity to guide twenty-five seniors in college through the Greek Peninsula and the Greek Islands. They have a certain background of history; you know well the Greek lands and their relation to man's efforts at civilization; you are reasonably clear as to what an educated person should know, understand, feel about these lands; you have only three months for the trip.

Evidently there are innumerable decisions you would need to make, but just now center on the problem of economy. What can be wisely done in the three months? Where will you begin? Perhaps in Athens? If so, how long will you stay in that city of Athena with its buildings, ruins, language, customs, legends, all reaching back to the roots of Western civilization? If you stay a month there, you may have to cut the time short at Delphi, or on Rhodes or Crete. But if you do not spend proper time in Athens perhaps the experience at Delphi will not be meaningful. The three months' period is short, the human mind is limited, and what to see, to understand, to appreciate is unlimited. The informed, responsible, experienced guide cannot and should not escape the major decisions.

Some one suggests a solution to that problem. Let the interests of the travelers decide. If they like Athens and want to spend the three months there, then why not? This question relates to nearly all the problems of formal education. Practically, the suggested solution would have its complications, but there is a deeper level of consideration. This is not a recreational trip although it may have recreational values. This is a very expensive trip financed at public or private expense and designed to make the very best contribution to the development of the travelers. The teacher or guide is engaged because presumably he knows how this journey can best be made. He may enjoy the trip—probably he must if he is to be a good guide—he may be paid well for his services, he may have fine conditions of travel, but really these are all side issues to the main purpose of the trip. The purpose is maximum educational experience; the guide should be skilled in planning it to that end.

Now shift to a second grade, or a high school physics class or a graduate seminar. The problems of economy are essentially the same; the same type of basic decisions must be made; the teacher as guide has the will and wit to make them, else the journey will flounder and fail.

2. The teacher as guide sees that the students take the learning journey. The finest plan one can imagine is not a trip; even an embossed and illustrated map is not a journey. Most fundamental of all, the students must themselves take the journey, not in body, but deeply engaged psychologically. Or to use other words, the learners, whether first grade or graduate school, must be led to have the experiences from which the objectives will be achieved. This principle is equally applicable to the learning of elementary mathematical processes or the most subtle philosophical principles. In each case, the learner must learn and in order to learn he must have the experience (engage in the activity, mental or otherwise) which produces learning. Nothing is more fundamental in learning and teaching, for there is a strong tendency for the teacher to believe that *his* activity is the crucial factor in learning. What the teacher does is important, crucial in a sense, but only as a means, and its significance is to be judged chiefly by its effect upon the student. Perhaps the apparent simplicity of this principle causes many teachers to overlook its fundamental importance.

Great skill is required to get the students to take the journey: to return to our illustration, to get them to see, react, analyze, discuss in sufficient amount and depth to achieve the objectives of the three months' visit to the Greek lands. The problem is the same in any class. Assuming that we know what experiences or activities are likely to produce learning, it is our task to see that the students get the experiences or engage in the activities.

Only one further word can be said about this task. For a long time, teachers have been inclined to depend upon threat of failure or, at best, the achievement of a symbol of success (a grade) as the major method of getting the students to have the experience. In practice, one supposes, the teacher uses almost every resource available to him, but surely most would agree that artificial arbitrary rewards and threats of failure are not the best means of motivation. We seek to make the process of learning more and more its own reward, its own motive power. Probably nearly all mean-ingful achievement comes from this type of inner motivation. The teacher as guide is constantly working to bring the student to this level of interest and activity. Whatever the means, the student must get the experience that brings learning: he must take the journey in all its fullness.

3. Perhaps the most subtle, difficult, and important of all the tasks of the teacher as guide is that of giving life and meaning to the learning journey. The trip may be well planned, it may be taken in all its detail (every place visited, every part of the subject cov-ered with conscientious, dogged persistence) but the experience may lack relevance, life, imagination. In such case, there will be little learning, and such as there is will be "book learning" in the worst sense of that phrase. It will not become a meaningful part of the student's life and thought; in some strange way it remains separate or unavailable and, in the main, inapplicable to the problems of life. Probably the often-noted failure of much of formal education to profoundly influence character arises from the fact that much of ethical, moral, and philosophic learning re-mains thus unrelated to the learner's deeper thought and practical life.[6]

The teacher is constantly in search of ways to give the imme-diacy and life of direct experience to the student's learning. His success as a teacher will perhaps depend more on his ability in this area than on any other single thing.[7] For an illustration of this principle, Professor Whitehead uses fish.[8] He says that learning, like fish, does not keep well and hence to be the best must be fresh from the sea. That is, it must be closely related both for the teacher and the student to the direct experience which gives it meaning. Probably because my background is different, another analogy is more powerful for me. In the country where I grew up, fresh corn on the cob was a great delicacy. It was said that to capture its ultimate flavor one should have a boiling pot between the rows of corn and the freshly pulled ear should be dropped immediately into the boiling water. The truth is that immediately

after the ear is pulled a subtle chemical change begins to trans-
form the precious sugar into tasteless, stale starch. So it is with
much of formal learning. Most of it was pulled a long time ago and
comes to us as tasteless starch. Perhaps there is little wonder that
students have always sought the sweet sugars of more direct experience—as thin and harmful as some of it may often be.

4. The fourth large task of the teacher is evaluation.[9] Like the
other major tasks of the teacher as guide, this one is worthy of a
chapter or even a separate book. The questions here are: How
are we getting along on this learning journey? To what extent
are we achieving the objectives? If we are succeeding, why, and
if not, why? What can we do on the next trip to make it better?
Most important of all, are the learners coming to evaluate their
own progress to the end that they may become self-directing?

The attitude of the teacher is all-important here. The effective
teacher strives to make the evaluation a part of the learning process, and an endeavor of mutual interest to both teacher and learner.
Evaluation thus escapes being a cruel, uneven game or even a war
between teacher and student and becomes a sincere effort in partnership designed to find an accurate answer to the question: What
progress are we making toward our mutually accepted goals?

This task of the teacher as guide is easiest and most natural in
the early grades and for very complex reasons seems to become
more difficult as formal education goes forward. Often in the
beginning grades the learning and the evaluation of progress are
so intimately related as to be one process. Then the teacher and
the taught work toward common goals and nothing is more
natural than a mutual friendly interest in progress toward these
goals. Gradually the learning situation becomes more formal, more
arbitrary and even more artificial, and in many cases the teacher
and the student cease to be partners in search of meaningful
achievement. They are now more or less antagonists, each dominated by the symbols of learning rather than the exhilarating process itself. We are face to face here with a major enemy of effective
education. Every teacher as a guide will be wrestling with this

enemy throughout his career; failure at this point may sour every aspect of teaching.

The optimum qualifications of a guide are implied in the tasks he performs. Thus a mere mentioning of some of the more evident of his skills will perhaps suffice. He knows the territory to be covered. Evidently the trip to the Greek lands will be an unsatisfying hit-or-miss affair if the guide does not know something of what is there and of the relation of the things to be seen to the goals or objectives of the trip. There has been much ridiculous discussion of which is more important, knowledge of the subject or skill in teaching. Both are fundamental. Not that one ever knows any subject fully, but he knows more than his fellow travelers (his students) and, most important, he himself is learning. Not that anyone has optimum skill in the subtle art of teaching, but he has a style and is steadily refining it.

Also, he must know well the travelers for whom he is guide. The better he knows their backgrounds, abilities, maturity levels, strengths and weaknesses, special talents and interests, the better he will be able to guide them. He then is able to relate in numerous ways his knowledge of the country being traveled (his subject) to the special needs and interests of the travelers (his students).

A guide on a learning journey has the respect and confidence of those on the trip. They believe in him because of his knowledge, experience, and skill but also because of his intense and sincere interest in the meaning and significance of the journey for himself and for the other travelers. Most of all they believe in him for what he is, wishes to be, and is becoming.

One of the most serious dangers to the effectiveness of a guide is staleness and its close kinsman, cynicism. If the journey has gone sour or stale for the guide, how can the other travelers feel the fresh direct experience of a trip as if first taken? The trick seems to be to retain the genuine quality of adventure for every separate odyssey: the essence of that zest for life which fathers meaning. The sharp tang of adventure remains and the teacher avoids making the journey into the small, misshapen, fear-filled image of the cynic; rather, the spirit of the guide fits the living adventurous spirit of youth.

E. V. P.

Questions and problems for dialogue

1 Why do you think literary artists have so often used the journey or the odyssey as a vehicle for their thought? Why does this figure seem to be so appealing to man?

2 Of the four large tasks that the teacher as a guide must do, which *one* do you believe is most important to effective teaching? Why do you think so?

3 In what senses is teaching a course or a grade *not* like taking a journey? That is, at what point does the analogy break down?

4 It has been said that students inevitably study as they are tested. Have you found this to be true in your experience? If so, what are some of the implications for teaching?

5 Discipline (keeping simple order) seems always to have been a severe problem in formal education and still is. Why is this the case? How could it be made less so?

6 What do you feel are the primary requisites of a good guide? Name three to five attributes that would seem to be crucial.

7 Is it necessary or possible that the guide be genuinely interested in the journey? What are the principal differences between the teacher as a guide and a commercial guide giving his daily "spiel" about Montezuma's castle or St. Peter's cathedral?

8 As you think of yourself in the role of a guide (a teacher) what do you believe is your chief *strength* and your chief *weakness*? (The thing most likely to carry you through and the one most likely to drag you down.)

9 What do you feel are the chief differences between a "pleasure" trip and an "educational" trip? Should an educational journey be pleasurable? Why? Why is an educational journey not more often a joy?

10 Think of the most effective guide you have had either in school or elsewhere. What means did he use to give the journey special life? Do you believe this skill can be learned or cultivated?

Exercises
for further learning

1 Make a list of other terms or figures that might have been used in the place of "guide" to symbolize the nature and meaning of teaching. If you think some term more descriptive than guide, give reasons for your opinion.

2 Give careful thought to the four large tasks of the teacher described in this chapter. List aspects of the teaching process that are not included in these four tasks.

3 Bring to mind four or five of the best teachers you have encountered. Evaluate on a four-point scale their skill in each of the four large tasks.

4 Do the same for four or five of the poorest teachers you have experienced. Take care to note patterns. Does any *one* of the tasks appear to be crucial or a key to excellence in teaching?

5 Interview four or five teachers in order to determine which of these major tasks they consider to be most difficult in practice.

6 Assume that you are going to take a group of individuals on a journey (to Mexico or to some large city). Make as full list as you can of the decisions you would need to make in planning the trip.

7 Undertake to plan objectives for a specific course you might wish to teach. Develop both general and specific objectives.

8 Make what you consider to be an effective test on a unit of learning. Strive to test for specific objectives. Use various types of items.

9 Make arrangements to observe a teacher or two who has the reputation of making learning come alive. Note the various things that these teachers seem to do that contribute to their skill.

10 Make a list of the symptoms of staleness in a guide. What are some specific indications that the guide has lost his zest for the journey?

For he is good at finding a way out where there is none.
—*Aeschylus*

4

A teacher is

a teacher

The teacher teaches in the age-old sense of teaching. He helps the developing student to learn things he does not know, and to understand what he learns. A misunderstanding of the function of some modern devices has tended to bring this aspect of teaching somewhat into disrepute. Books are abundant and relatively inexpensive. Duplication has become almost a way of life. There are radio, television, all kinds of moving and still pictures, and more recently programmed learning. These are all in the tradition of the book, the slate, and the blackboard. Such developments have raised the question in the minds of some as to whether there is still a place for what is usually conceived as teaching: the individual classroom teacher informing, explaining, making clear.

Another line of thought has tended to undermine teaching as teaching. There is a sense in which no one can teach anyone anything: the learner must do the learning. This point is well taken, but does not mean that the teacher cannot assist that learning. This attack on teaching, based on an element of truth, arose as a reaction to an old emphasis which conceived of teaching as merely, or at least chiefly, "telling" or "teaching" with little or no regard for the student's part in the teaching-learning process. Surely there has been too much of this monotonous droning-on, called teaching, in the front of countless classrooms at all levels of instruction. The attack was needed and justified.

But to attempt to discredit all personal teaching (the aspect we are examining here) is to go to the other extreme. There is an important place for the ancient process of teaching: explaining, clarifying, and even informing. Our task in this chapter is to make that place clear and meaningful. The process we want to analyze is similar to that of a mother teaching a child how to tie a bowknot, or how to make a bed; of a teacher showing the relation between abstract numbers—1, 2, 3, etc.—and the things they can symbolize; of his making clear the structure of a sentence or a paragraph; of his opening up the meaning of a literary or philosophic passage; of his clarifying a principle in physics; and perhaps most important, of his explaining and demonstrating an effective way to do something, i.e., to approach a task. This aspect of teaching is so near to us, so much a part of learning, that we can hardly examine it objectively; it is difficult to pull away and look at the process.[1]

The student will not always learn from such teaching. Whether or not he does learn will depend upon many factors, probably chief of which are (1) his motivation and readiness to learn, (2) his maturity level in relation to the task to be learned, (3) his relation to the teacher, (4) his ability to learn through words, (5) the degree of his freedom from fear, and (6) the teacher's skill in communication. If these conditions are reasonably favorable, then, through teaching, the student can learn much that is significant. Probably a skillful teacher knows almost intuitively when the situation is right for this kind of teaching and teaches then.

A rural friend of mine who had only five or six brief sessions of country school became a leader in his community, astute in legal and business matters, and in general a thoughtful citizen. Knowing my interest in schools and teaching, he often told me that he had only one teacher who was of any value to him. Without this teacher my friend believed that he would have had no education of worth. This "Professor," as all men teachers were called in those days, had the precious skill of explaining and making things clear, particularly of getting at the principles involved. Until this man came along, mathematics had been a meaningless group of symbols and problems or, at best, combinations to be rotely memorized. Under the tutelage of this one teacher, numbers and their relations took on a meaning and even a fascination that remained with my friend through life. Apparently the same was true of ideas or thought, particularly on legal and historical matters. The point is that this country teacher chiefly by the process of what is sometimes criticized as "mere" teaching enabled this ignorant boy to learn and, what is much more important, by the clarity of his explanations—his teaching—opened up a way of learning for him that enabled him to continue his education on his own.

Really we do not know what can and cannot be taught in this direct way—perhaps much more than we are inclined to think, if the teacher is clearheaded, skillful in communication, and keenly sensitive to the learning readiness of his students. To let a ready student flounder when he wishes to learn by direct teaching may be a severe waste. This emphasis, of course, does not suggest any neglect of the student's crucial part in all learning.

A significant but complex point must be mentioned here, although its full analysis would lead too far afield. Perhaps the greatest single hindrance to learning from simple explanation or teaching is fear. Because of improper pressure or unfortunate previous experience with a subject, students often feel fear which, if intense, amounts almost to panic in the presence of a new learning situation. Persistent failure or difficulty in an area may make the fear chronic. In counseling people over the years, I have again and again come upon these deeply embedded fears that make normal learning very nearly impossible.

I recall an acquaintance, who is old now, who said that because of negative experience with arithmetic when she was a child in school she feared and almost hated numbers all her life. To mention any problem requiring even the simplest mathematical processes was to block her whole mind. Otherwise, she was quite an able person. Others hate writing for much the same reasons. So the wounds of previous experience manifest themselves and must be healed before direct teaching will be very effective.

The teacher as an explainer—as one who makes obscure things clear—strives to become increasingly skillful in certain activities or processes which seem to contribute to making difficult, complex things meaningful. Here we can only list the more evident of these means to clarity. Teachers wishing to understand this phase of teaching more thoroughly may wish to extend the list and analyze each process. These are some of the things the teacher does as he teaches.[2]

1. Illustrates: essentially relates the thing to be learned to something the student knows, and at the same time gives him additional experience.

2. Defines: puts the thing to be learned into clear and simple terms—what the problem really is, in terms within the learner's experiences and understandings.

3. Analyzes: takes the problem apart piece by piece or, as someone has expressed it, "cuts the learning into chewable bites."

4. Synthesizes: puts the parts of a problem together so that the whole makes sense, the relation of each part to the whole is clear, and the whole of the problem at hand relates to still larger wholes.

5. Questions: asks meaningful and penetrating queries in order to clarify the thing to be learned. This process is as old as Socrates, and probably was old when he used it.

6. Responds: reacts to questions arising out of the interest and concern of the students. Teaching is perhaps most effective when it is in response to questions by the learner.

7. Listens: allows the student to make his difficulty in learning clear to the teacher and also to himself.

8. Creates confidence: goes through a process to be learned with the student while he gets the feel of it and the confidence that results from a success.

9. Provides varied views: looks at the thing to be learned from many angles—sees the problem in many combinations.

10. Provides assimilative material: gives a variety of experience or learning material related to the thing to be learned.

11. Adjusts method: adapts the method of explaining (language, complexity, etc.) to the ability and maturity level of the learner and relates new learnings to things already known.

12. Gives emotional tone: makes the learning meaningful and alive through enthusiasm and zest. It seems that much of the almost magic skill of a man like Professor Agassiz was that his explanation of matters that were usually dull was lighted by enthusiasm.[3] The same was true of Dr. William R. Harper teaching Hebrew or teaching John D. Rockefeller, Sr., the true nature of a university.

This list may sound technical and perhaps needs further discussion or study. In teaching we do many of these things by habit, almost as second nature. It may be that by taking some thought as to the nature of what we do we could improve our skill quite as one might improve his posture or his golf stroke or his clarity of expression.[4]

The things we do in teaching described briefly above depend largely upon language. Language is abstract symbol: the words are not the things they represent. At best, the student has had the

direct experience needed to give the symbol a reasonable degree
of meaning. Often, however, the distance between the symbol
(the words) and the reality which they represent and out of which
they have grown becomes so great that meaning is lost. For this
reason much of formal education, probably from about the middle
elementary grades, becomes an increasingly empty game of ma-
nipulating symbols that have lost their proper touch with reality.
In a word, formal education is plagued with pedantry. The story
is told of a bright student who said that she was grown and out of
school before she understood that the large blue line down the
middle of her geography book which symbolized the Mississippi
River was the same river as the one that backed up to her house in
winter floods.

Overabstraction is a major obstacle to meaningful explanation
and clarification. The clearest presentation one can conceive will
not do the job if the language used is outside the experience of the
learner, or is so remotely related to that experience as to lose its
freshness or immediacy. Even illustration or allusion will misfire
if it has no rootage in the learner's experience. This point should
in no sense be taken as a deprecation of symbols or language as a
means of learning. Skill in the use of language is a major strength
of the human mind. But the teacher seeks ways of keeping the
language close to its corresponding reality.

One of the most enlightening illustrations of this principle is
the encounter of Jesus with the young lawyer who in the course of
an interchange of thought asked, "And who is my neighbor?" A
less wise teacher would have been tempted to enter into a long
abstract dissertation on this subject. But Jesus told a story which
has become a part of the heritage of man, that tied the abstraction
"neighbor" to the realities it was designed to represent.

The teacher's advanced knowledge may also be a hindrance to
effective teaching. Of course there are many advantages to knowing in great depth and breadth what one is teaching, for then one
feels safe to explore beyond the edges of the learning and has the
knowledge to do so. Yet there is a danger in advanced knowledge.

It is extremely difficult for a teacher who has taught a subject for years, who knows the fundamentals thoroughly, and who has the habit of constantly learning beyond those fundamentals to remember how hard a new subject is. Facts that are commonplace and relations that are evident to the teacher are unknown and difficult to perceive by the early learner.[5] A teacher takes special care not to be impatient, and particularly to avoid arrogance. Now and then every teacher should undertake to learn some basically new thing—a language, or music, or the ways of computers. Such experiences might help us to be sensitive to the problems of the new learner.

There is an even more subtle obstacle to teaching in the sense that the term is used in this chapter. A thing explained again and again over the years of teaching may become stale to the teacher. He may be teaching his students a principle in plane geometry. This is the twentieth or thirtieth class he has led through this experience. Years ago when he learned and perhaps when he first taught this theorem he felt the thrill of its logic and the cleanness of its proof: the teaching of it was like an enchanting road freshly traveled. But through the years the freshness has worn off; the experience has become stale to the teacher and equally stale to the learner.

How do we keep original freshness and sincerity in an experience often repeated? There probably is no one best way, but evidently the loss of these qualities is a serious threat to good teaching. True, this may be the hundredth time a teacher has been asked this same question by students seeking their way to understanding, but to the students it is new and perhaps urgent. This may be the seventy-third wedding ceremony a minister has read, but for the young couple it is the first time over this road. This may be the three hundredth time a teacher has helped a young student to see the structure of the living cell—the building block of life—but for the student it may be like an astronaut's first view of the earth from outer space.

In order for teaching to have its maximum power, the growing teacher seeks continuously for some means to retain and even enrich the enthusiasm and zest he had as he first learned what he now teaches. Probably the best means is for the teacher himself to be constantly learning and relating that new learning to the old he now teaches—old learning which to the students is new.

The teacher as explainer or clarifier—as teacher—has clear objectives. He decides on the basis of his experience and study what the student can be reasonably expected to know and to understand, and what skills this segment of learning demands. He has these clearly in his own mind and he makes them as clear as possible to the students. Then he teaches to these objectives and the learning becomes an endeavor in partnership: tasks to be accomplished and obstacles to be surmounted by the somewhat more learned and the somewhat less learned working together. One of the strangest things to be observed about much of formal education at all levels is the vagueness of the objectives to be achieved; even more strange is the tendency of many teachers to consciously or unconsciously keep the objectives from the learners. It is somewhat as if a group were going on a hunt for something, and what was to be sought was kept vague or a secret. One suspects that we as teachers are often not too clear ourselves about the objectives.

Perhaps the most important factor in this aspect of teaching is the relation of the teacher to his students. Among other things this relation involves how the teacher perceives his students and the teaching of them, and how the students perceive the teacher. It would be interesting and enlightening for us as teachers to know how our students often view us. And it is wise to remember that the problem is equally acute from the early grades up the educational ladder to graduate and professional school. It might be equally revealing to us if we carefully and honestly examined how we feel toward the students and toward the process of teaching.

Deception in this area of the teacher's work is almost impossible. If the interest of the teacher in teaching and in his students is not genuine, it will be recognized as the phony thing it is. The teacher as teacher likes explaining, making clear, demonstrating, and even likes the sometimes dreadfully trying learner. There is always the tendency for the whole process to become stale and then, however learned and experienced a teacher may be, the teaching situation goes sour. Ideally, perhaps, when this happens a teacher should in honesty seek other work, but that would not be easy. It is much better to keep alive and growing although we may be a little gnarled by time, the seasons, the weather, and the special demands of the teaching art.

E. V. P.

Questions and problems for dialogue

1 To what extent and in what way do the new devices and media (programmed learning, television, tape recording, etc.) replace the teacher?
2 One distinguished teacher of our time left formal teaching because he was convinced that "no one could teach anyone anything of importance." What do you think of this idea—that all learning is self-learning?
3 What are the justifications for the frequent criticisms of teaching as "telling"? Think of examples.
4 When can a student profit most from teaching in the narrow sense—as explaining, clarifying, etc.? Think of examples in your own learning experience.
5 What are some of the causes of fear in students in learning situations? How can such fear be overcome?
6 Is it of value for the teacher to be conscious of what he does as he teaches or will he be freer and more effective if these things are relatively unconscious? Give reasons for your response.
7 How can a teacher know when his language has become too abstract for effective teaching—too far removed from the reality it symbolizes?
8 What would be the advantages and disadvantages of a teacher's

undertaking to learn something distinctly new at regular intervals? What types of things would you recommend for such learning?

9 What is the basic difference between an amateur and a professional? Is it possible for the professional to retain the freshness and enthusiasm of the amateur? How?

10 Is it really true that to be most effective the teacher must be genuinely interested in the learner and learning? If so, why? If not, give examples of effective teachers who did not manifest such interest.

Exercises
for further learning

1 Write a brief paper setting forth your thought as to the best use of the new teaching devices and the new media. Strive to state guiding principles or a philosophy.

2 Make a list of things you feel can be taught simply by teaching— by explaining, etc. Also, make a list of things that probably cannot be taught in this sense.

3 Think of the best teacher you have had. Did this teacher seem to be effective in teaching in this narrower sense? Make a list of examples of good teaching in the sense that it is used in this chapter.

4 Develop a list of fears that have hindered your own learning and that of your friends. Analyze the origin and the overcoming of such fears.

5 Study carefully the list of activities that a teacher uses in teaching as given in this chapter. Think of examples of each activity. In which are you strongest and in which weakest?

6 Try your hand at learning something new and strange to you. Report your experience to class or friends.

7 Recall a skilled professional person (teacher, minister, doctor, etc.) who seemed to retain the zest and freshness of an amateur. Analyze what was involved.

8 Observe carefully as you attend weddings or funerals, see other people teach, visit your doctor, or attend a concert to determine to what extent the performer seems to have gone stale in his performance and to what extent the activity has real meaning for him. Analyze the influence of the performer's attitude on the whole situation.

9 Make a list of common nouns ranging from those whose meaning is

relatively concrete to those that are more abstract. In each case, ask yourself what meaning the term has for you. How near is the symbol to the experience from which it grew?

10 In specific cases, think of ways that abstract terms can be given more meaning—can be related more closely to reality, to experience.

There are few efforts more conducive to humility
than that of the translator
trying to communicate an incommunicable beauty.
—*Edith Hamilton*

5

A teacher is

a modernizer: a bridge between generations

The teacher translates the experience of man into terms
that have meaning for the student. There is a broad chasm between generations.[1] This gap gets wider as time passes. The experience and language of our parents (though distant) have more
meaning to us than that of our grandparents, and theirs more than
that of our great-grandparents and so on back. A student learning now is psychologically a great distance from a large portion
of the experience of man, which, however, he must apprehend, assimilate, and even incarnate in behavior if he would be educated.
The teacher must bridge that gap for students, else they cannot

partake of the learning that will release their potential. Our task as we view this aspect of teaching is to understand what this gap is and how the teacher can most effectively bridge it.

The central point is that ideas and the way they are expressed (not only the vocabulary but the whole tone and quality of expression) are shaped by the mode of the time in which they are set down. Evidently language with all its subtleties is the vehicle or carrier of these thoughts. You or I have a thought or an experience or make an observation. Unless the thought or action or observation is recorded it exists only in us, in our memory. When it is put into words, particularly into written words, it is a record or an account of that thought or observation. The same is true of the thought or experience of Moses or Plato or Shelley or Schweitzer or Camus. These records of thought and experience expressed in language chiefly, but also in the various forms of man's accomplishments (buildings, works of art, inventions, institutions), are the residue of man's long experience that is left to us—what is often called the heritage of man.

The concept may be summarized in this way: the experience and achievement of man on this planet are available to us only through the records that have been left; these are largely in books, although to a lesser extent in other records of man's experience; this recorded body of experience is the material or means of the education of man, but this great wealth of learning cannot be used or grasped by young students because its form is such as to be largely incomprehensible to the new generation; the teacher as a bridge must make this "foreign" matter comprehensible. The process and meaning of formal education are encompassed in this principle.

A single life is short and extremely narrow. It is true one has the incomparable privilege of direct experience with all reality he can touch—all that exists about him. At best, however, this direct individual experience will be small indeed. We can hardly begin to fathom how small it actually is, for the wider experience of man begins to come to us and influence us from the cradle, again chiefly through language. The earliest words (songs, stories, simple teachings) of mothers or nurses embody the experience of the race, and so we begin to partake of that experience long before formal education begins. Our small, narrow, personal experience is thus extended through language, artifacts, and institutions to include the whole experience of man: in a word, education begins.

The most remarkable aspect of man is his ability to learn from the experience of others. We cannot go into the abilities that make vicarious learning possible. Doubtless the complexity of the human nervous system has something to do with it, and language, as we have mentioned, is fundamental, but basically we do not know what in reality is crucial to this essentially human quality. We know that every normal (that is, undamaged) human being is capable of education. And this means that given the proper opportunity he can partake of the thousands of years of experience, learning, and achievement of man and embody the best of it in a unique personality in a single lifetime. Or to put it in another way, he is not limited to his personal experience or even that of the associates of his generation, but he can partake of, actually embody in himself, the experience of all time and of every culture. In this way he can stand free, at the height of his time, a debtor to all that man has experienced and learned, including all that has been revealed to man through prophets, seers, and poets.

A teacher who is not sensitive to this quality in human beings is blind to the meaning of the profession of teaching. This unique ability of man to be educated gives the central meaning to the teacher's work. Here is the heart of the process in which he is engaged. Every student he encounters has this potential to be educated or, more accurately, to be in the process of being educated that can and should be lifelong. Doubtless most teachers do their job, and some quite effectively, without analyzing the process. However, if they understood and felt more fully what they are doing as teachers, probably teaching as a profession would be greatly enriched, the individuals in it would be more effective, their work would be more satisfying and have more meaning.

A brief aside may help to give depth and meaning to this idea. Throughout the history of man and down to this present day only a few people have been allowed to engage in this process which would have educated them—which could have educed their un-measured potential. Most have been kept illiterate which simply means that they were largely cut off from all means of education except that of their own individual immediate time and culture-bound experience. Professor Arnold Toynbee states the tragedy succinctly:

During these first five thousand years of the history of civilization, one of the most characteristic, and most ugly, features of this new way of life has been the monopoly of its amenities, spiritual as well as material, by a small minority of the members of societies in process of civilization.[2]

Here then is the tragic condition of man: unrealized potential. The tragedy is compounded when in large measure the means for full realization are deliberately withheld. Perhaps every teacher should at regular intervals read Edwin Markham's "The Man with the Hoe," although this extreme picture may blind us to the more common tragedy of *every* man. The point is simple but deeply significant: the literature, the philosophic and religious thought, the art and music—all the various records of the experience and learning of man which are the necessary means of an individual's full development (his education)—have been and still are unavailable to most men on earth. Thus the incomparably rich fields of human potential lie uncultivated, fallow, wasted. Another figure comes nearer to expressing the full truth involved: the powerful waters of human potential build up behind outmoded dams and thus unreleased and unchanneled not only are wasted but threaten all in reach with their possible violence and destructive power.

Back now to the central thread of our thought about the teacher as a modernizer or bridge. The experiences of man are recorded in the language and thought fashion of the time in which they occurred or the time of the individual recorders. It is the nature of everything mortal to grow old and out-of-date. The senior Oliver Wendell Holmes expressed the principle quaintly but memorably in these lines:

> Little of all we value here
> Wakes on the morn of its hundredth year
> Without both feeling and looking queer.[3]

Not only is this true of "one-hoss shays," cars, trains, clothes, but of the modes of thought.

Although this phenomenon of aging is common knowledge, a few illustrations will help to clarify the point and relate it to learning and teaching. It is very interesting and instructive to look at old school yearbooks or old mail-order catalogs. If one starts at the present—the now—and examines, let us say, school yearbooks, moving backward in time, he will notice that after a period the clothes and even the people's faces begin to look strange; there is a point when they are no longer *modern*. For reasons it would take much research to discover, after a certain period of time the pictures and the reality they represent appear to be of the past. They are in a deep sense foreign. It should be noted that the change is much deeper, broader, more pervasive than mere difference in clothes—for example, length or shape of dresses. There are probably many factors working in a configuration that makes for oldness or out-of-dateness.

I first noticed this principle at work in the realm of thought or ideas in classes in psychology. I was constantly looking for books that expressed clearly and vividly the central principles the students needed to grasp. In the late 1930's I discovered an insightful book by Professor William E. Hocking entitled *Human Nature and Its Remaking*.[4] Students read the book with keen interest and profited greatly by it. That is, the book "spoke to them" with great power. Then after a few years the book began to be less useful. More and more students did not like it and could not read it with profit. It was beginning to be out of date for them. Other more up-to-date reading material had to be found for these psychology students. Does this mean that the ideas in this book were outmoded by research or new thought? Essentially not. The thoughts were still sound in the 40's; in fact, they are still, in the main, sound; but for reasons not yet clear the book was no longer readable by students with essentially the same ability and preparation as those who had previously found it very readable and helpful.

The same is true of most novels that were popular when they appeared. For example, the novels of Sinclair Lewis, which in the 1930's were especially interesting, sharp, and powerful, in the late 1960's are hard to read and appear quaint and even shallow to the modern reader.

The use of the Great Books as a chief means of education is another illustration. Try your hand at reading these great books and you will find that unless you have a special scholar's interest in them and considerable training in a related field you cannot read them. They will speak even less to a college undergraduate or to a high school student. Of course, the great ideas of man are in them but they must be taught or "translated" in order for the modern student to grasp them.

Through the years the principle has been driven home by experience: books or other assimilative learning materials that instruct, thrill, and inspire this year, ten years later will leave a group of students cold. Doubtless the same is true of oral illustrations. Our very best stories may cease to speak to the youth we teach.

It is important to remember that more than the mere change and deterioration that usually accompany the passing of time is working here. Imagine an old lady, let us say eighty-five years of age, by some miracle of transmutation made again nineteen or twenty years old. What would she be like as a sophomore this year in her college? She would be young, full of life, intelligent, perhaps beautiful, but almost totally a stranger, lost, and out of place among young women of the present. She is out of mode or fashion—not merely in clothes, manners, values, but deeply, subtly out of date—unless her education to this point had begun to lift her into a universal level. More of this later.

The central thesis of the discussion in this chapter is that this principle of modernity applies not only to books, the chief means of education, but to all the records of man's experience. The teacher's task then is to translate this wealth of wisdom and experience into modern terms—into terms that speak to the students of today. In fact, all of man's thought must be constantly restated in each generation by all the various kinds of teachers, including those who aspire to write. Surely in a sense it is true as was said by the ancient preacher that "there is no new thing under the sun," but the teacher and writer may take heart in the fact that the old ideas need to be put in new mode, in new dress, and in this process they may seem to be, and sometimes may really be, new. At least they will be new to our students and our reading audience.

What does modernizing imply or demand? It is not done by putting Shakespeare into modern slang. The problem is infinitely more subtle than such an easy expedient would suggest. Nor does this translating require a watering-down or simplification of the language or thought. The students of today are as intelligent and well-informed as the audience of Shakespeare's or Plato's or Lincoln's time. They are simply different: they are modern, and they can no more accept, and make their own, the modes of thought of those times than they could accept and wear to class their grandparents' clothes.

This modernizing seems to demand above everything else a restatement of the ideas, perhaps chiefly through illustrations that relate them to the experiences of the student. By this and other means the skillful, sensitive teacher builds a bridge from where the student is across to the recorded experience that will educate him, for example, to Shakespeare's sonnets. In this way, the sonnets retain all the power of their thought and music but by means of the bridge built by the teacher partake of the *Zeitgeist* (the now) and thus have meaning for the student.

There are records of experience (literary pieces, art objects, principles) which seem to partake of the universal. They thus tend to be timeless and cultureless—they speak to all generations in all times and all places. Perhaps the extent of genius can be most meaningfully measured by this quality of universality. Yet even when the thought or feeling is universal the mode, the language, the forms in which it is expressed may obscure the universality of the deeper aspects.

Now we come to the very heart of our thought. In order to do well the job we have been describing in this chapter the teacher must be himself universal or at least be moving in that direction. He must be at home in the learning and spirit of the various pasts through which man has gone and he must be equally in tune with the present, and even with the emerging future. On first thought, this requirement may seem overwhelming to the teacher —too much to ask or hope. Of course, in practice no one ever completely escapes his tribal cave. The thought and behavior of the time and place in which he lives, especially that in which he was reared, become embodied in every aspect of his life. But one of the central purposes of education is to free the human mind of its various fetters, particularly those of tribal or provincial origin. Then the student can be started on his way toward first the understanding and later the embodiment in behavior of the truths that are universal—that transcend time, space, and local culture—and on to the thought and experimentation that lead to the continuous discovery of new truths. Thus genuine education causes the person to be less and less tied to a particular time, and consequently less a slave to mode or fashion whether in the material or less material realm.

Essentially he begins to grasp the deeper principles and is not swept about by surface turbulence. Modes or fashions are probably the surface manifestations of the deeper needs and ways of man that partake of universals. The man that is in the process of this kind of education escapes the trap of the surface manifestations of his time and hence is free to participate in the modes of

today and of tomorrow with wholeheartedness enough to understand them without being enslaved by them. He knows that
mode and fashion are a necessary part of life; that they serve as a
surface means of expression. At the same time he rises above
them and reaches the level of universal principle where these
time and culture differences lose their significance. For example,
a genuinely courteous person probably would not find it difficult
to be courteous in any culture, however different the local customs
might be.

The teacher as a bridge between the old and the new, as a
translator of experience, must be or must be becoming such an
educated person. There is a great tendency for a teacher or any
person to fasten upon the fashion or mode of the time when he
was at the zenith of his powers. This then becomes his reference
point, and often he clings to it however evident it may be that the
point was personal or provincial. Equally potent and perhaps more
subtle and dangerous is the tendency to get stuck in the ways of
a particular culture or civilization so that the modes or fashions
of that culture seem to be the voice of God—an expression of the
"nature of things." Whatever may be the nature of things it
will not manifest itself wholly in one particular civilization. The
teacher aware of these two great dangers may be able to escape
them in his journey toward freedom and truth.

A final point needs to be made. It was suggested earlier that
the experience of man left to us in varied kinds of records is
the crucial means of education. This does not mean that knowing
about (learning) this experience of man is education. Participation in the experience of man is only a means (albeit a necessary
means) to education. Such knowledge very easily and rapidly
becomes dead or inert knowledge, not only useless but cluttering
and harmful. The whole point of this essay is that the effective
teacher enables the student to so partake of the experience of the
past that it is alive and meaningful for the present. There is a
great difference between learning experience and learning from

experience. The former is a stultifying end in itself; the latter is a means of release and continuous growth.

E. V. P.

Questions and problems for dialogue

1 A thoughtful modern writer has suggested that the gap between generations is wider now than at any time in the past. Do you believe this is the case? If so, why? What are some of the implications for teaching and learning?

2 Is it possible for a person to be educated through his own personal experience? What are the strengths and the limitations of individual experience for education?

3 What is the basic nature of vicarious experience? How does it work to develop the potential of man?

4 Why, in your judgment, has formal education been largely reserved for a small minority throughout the history of man?

5 What do you feel are the major factors that cause anything to be out of date? Try to discover four or five things that seem crucial.

6 What do you feel is the psychology basic to the power of fashion or mode? Why is it so painful for a person to be out of fashion?

7 What seems to you to be involved in making modern the things (clothes, cars, ideas, etc.) that are out of date? Is the out-of-dateness of ideas largely a problem of language or are there deeper factors?

8 What essentially is the process by which an idea or a principle becomes universal? Is it possible that an idea can express such truth and be so stated as to be always current, to never be out of date? To what extent will the most universally applicable ideas need to be restated, interpreted, or taught to each generation?

9 What is the difference between "learning" an experience which has been passed on from other people and "learning from" the experience of other people? How are the two related?

10 In what senses is the mind freed by education? In what ways is it fettered or bound by education?

Exercises
for further learning

1 Secure two or three of what are called the "great books" in an area
   that is of interest to you. Try to read one or more of them. Report
   your experience carefully. How do they appear to you?

2 Get a list of the best-selling novels of the 1930's, 1920's, or earlier.
   Read one or two of them or read the first parts of them. Strive to
   grasp the difference between them and a current novel.

3 Study a series of school yearbooks or of mail-order catalogs. Examine them with the purpose of determining when (at what distance
   from the present) they begin to seem quaintly out of date. (A
   family picture album if reasonably complete may serve the same
   purpose.)

4 Have interviews with people a generation (or, if you are young,
   two generations) older than you are. Discuss some topic and
   strive to discover the differences between you and them. Try to
   locate specific, meaningful differences.

5 Select a literary passage, a philosophic statement or some other
   piece of work that means a great deal to you but does not "speak"
   to a younger or older friend. Analyze carefully how you would
   "modernize" or make the experience meaningful.

6 Find something (a scriptural passage, a bit of poetry, a piece of
   prose, etc.) that seems to you to be universal—timeless and cultureless—in its appeal. Then find a person who is not well acquainted with this work and see if it is meaningful to him. Think
   of other ways of testing the principle of universality.

7 Talk with one or more persons who are illiterate or nearly so.
   Strive to determine what means (since they cannot read) they
   have used to extend their personal experience.

8 Do a little research (reading and direct observation) into the
   psychology of fashion. Search for underlying principles.

9 Recall the people (especially teachers) you have known that
   seemed to approach being universal or timeless. What seemed to
   make them so?

10 Make a list of what might be called "fads" in education as you
   have experienced them or read about them. Try to discover the
   "universal" need that was involved in the fad.

6

A teacher is

a model: an example

The teacher has many roles. One of the most basic is that of being a model to his students and to all who think of him as a teacher. There is a strong tendency to feel uneasy about this role, to resist, and even to reject it. Thoughtfulness, common modesty, laziness, or fear, separately or all together, may cause one to think or say, "If I must be an example or be considered as a model, then teaching is not for me. I am not good enough in any sense to be an example, and besides I want to be free to be myself and not forever feel the responsibility of being an example for others. If students must have a model, let them find it somewhere else; I must be free."

This reaction is understandable, perhaps in a sense commendable, but it overlooks or denies a fundamental aspect of the nature of teaching and learning. The central thought of this chapter is that being a model is a part of teaching that no teacher can escape. Being an example arises out of the very nature of teaching, and when a teacher refuses to accept and constructively use this role he seriously reduces his effectiveness; what may be even more important, he refuses to face the reality of his situation as a teacher. This role properly conceived need not be a burden nor be, nor appear to be, presumptuous. Accepted and used with skill and humility this role greatly enriches the meaning of teaching. To be sure, there are dangers and later we must examine them with care.

There is a certain cynicism which threatens to poison the soil from which great teaching grows. This attitude often reflects itself in a desire to have the rewards and satisfactions of teaching without accepting the special responsibilities that are an integral part of this profession. It may be that the strong desire often expressed in modern times to make teaching just another job that pays well and that can be done when one is on the job (as is the case with many kinds of work) with little or no reference to the self as a whole is a central threat to our profession. Surely teaching is many things and the teacher has many skills and plays many parts, but as teacher, since the times of old, he has been a very special person. Rather than in partial understanding, selfishness, and fear trying to escape this part, we might be wiser to comprehend, appreciate, and wisely use this heritage and its power. Here is a key test for a teacher who would grow toward excellence: Does he understand and accept with enthusiasm the fact that in the very nature of his work he is an example?

But we must ask, Why is this so? Why must a teacher be special? May it not be that social custom has fastened this special "burden" on the teacher without sound reasons? Can he not be a worker that does his job with skill without assuming this special role? These are natural and good questions. They must be faced squarely.

A brief answer is very difficult, for the problem demands both knowledge and feeling. To ask what is the optimum relation between a student and his teacher is to ask a question that demands an education rather than a brief answer.[1] Whatever the level of learning or the kind of learning, teaching involves a very special relation between the learner and the teacher. In some recent very insightful literature the relation is described as having much of the intensity and emotional tone of a love affair.[2] This figure may not be the best to use since it is often laden with special and sometimes distorted connotations, but it properly emphasizes the essence of the relation so crucial to the best learning.

The teacher is a mediator of the varied experiences that are the means of learning for the student. For example, the words, thought, and music of Shakespeare as they flow through the prism of the teacher are given special life and meaning; they are not merely the writings of Shakespeare. In like manner, every experience in the classroom and often those out of it are seen by the student in relation to the teacher. Performance on an athletic team, in a play, in solving a mathematics problem, in writing a composition, is not an isolated event, but takes on a particular meaning and quality because of its relation to the teacher.

Much of what has gone on and goes on now in the name of teaching and teacher falls far short of this high standard. The dead and deadening process, the dull trafficking in inert ideas and dead knowledge (to use Whitehead's phrase) should find another name and thus leave the ancient terms of teacher and teaching for the live, imaginative, healing, growth-producing process that the student-teacher relation properly is.

Perhaps here lies the basic cause for a feeling of uneasiness on the part of many teachers at the apparently increasing enthusiasm for the "teaching machine."[3] In one sense, the term embodies a basic contradiction; one had as well speak of a love machine, or a friend machine, or a worship machine. This is not to say that machines are to be shunned or feared or rejected; there are things they can do and do well. They are especially useful for the student in learning facts and skills with efficiency and with important savings for teacher and student. There are things they cannot do, and teaching in the sense in which we are speaking of it is one of them.

Two brief quotations about learning and teaching may help further to clarify their nature and suggest the relation of a teacher, as a person, to them. The first is from Professor Whitehead and relates to college and university teaching and learning, but the principle applies equally to all levels of learning:

This atmosphere of excitement, arising from imaginative consideration, transforms knowledge. A fact is no longer a bare fact: it is invested with all its possibilities. It is no longer a burden on the memory: it is energizing as the poet of our dreams, and as the architect of our purposes. . . .
Youth is imaginative, and if the imagination be strengthened by discipline this energy of imagination can in great measure be preserved through life. The tragedy of the world is that those who are imaginative have but slight experience, and those who are experienced have feeble imaginations. Fools act on imagination without knowledge; pedants act on knowledge without imagination. The task of a university is to weld together imagination and experience.[4]

The second is from Professor Hocking:

The state can build schools, equip them; engage a teaching staff; organize and supervise instruction. And in these systems, education usually takes place: it takes place through the personal qualities of teachers who have in them what the state can neither pay for nor command. Vachel Lindsay, the Illinois poet, . . . put the matter to me in this way: "In every primary school of, say, a dozen teachers, there will be one who wakes the children up. And that is enough—for, once wakened, they *stay awake!*" This comment exhibits my point: into the net of the political requirements there happen the genuine spirits who educate.[5]

The quality and power of the teacher's example vary in terms of the nature and effectiveness of the teacher. This variation is complex. In a sense, the more effective the teacher the more powerful he is as an example. The traits and qualities that make him skillful in the teaching-learning situation—those that give imagination, life, meaning—are the very ones that give power to example. They tend to establish the open, emotion-toned relation that makes possible, and even promotes, the flow of feeling and thought between persons, especially the younger and the older, that is basic to influence.

It may be equally true that the very bad teacher (not to be confused with the merely poor or inadequate) also is an especially powerful influence as a person, as an example, and essentially for the same reasons that hold for the excellent teacher. His very bad-ness—sarcasm, pettiness, mean-spiritedness, arbitrariness, favorit-ism, cruelty, defensiveness, lack of sympathy, etc.—is sufficiently alive to have great power, though often negative. A thoughtful friend of mine suggests that perhaps most students set up a special defense against such overt badness and hence are not hurt much by it either by patterning after the negativeness or by reacting against it.

On the surface, it would seem that the dull, detached, mediocre teacher would be a less potent influence than either of the two other extremes. The student may not be pulled toward such a teacher nor repelled nor hurt by him. If this is true, perhaps there is consolation in this fact since doubtless many of us are often, or under the hammer blows of life become, a part of this middle group: neither very good nor very bad, and hence our example is weak and thus does not do much apparent harm or good.

Yet in a deeper sense little comfort can be found in this thought. For however dull and inoffensively ineffective we are, still we are examples. Probably for the growing learner searching for life, whose personality is in the making, whose mind longs to be stimulated and released, whose whole being yearns for mutual-ity, such dead-level dullness and meaninglessness may be the most stiflingly harmful of all. The thought is painful, but may embody much truth.

Thus it may be that if the *best* learning-teaching is much like a love affair the truly worst may not be most like a "hate affair" but rather like Orwell's *1984* cold, professional "no affair." In the world of the faceless no affair, perhaps the great power of example is transmuted into the slow poison of inertia and dying interest. In this process, it may be, lies the tragedy of a large portion of formal education: a slow loss of the imagination and the intense interest in learning so natural to man and so characteristic of the undamaged child. This problem is worthy of much more consideration than we can give it here. But the teacher can be encouraged by thought in two brief lines from Charles Lamb:

> A waking eye, a prying mind,
> A heart that stirs is hard to bind.[6]

Now let us turn to what may appear to be more immediate and practical concerns.

What are some of the principal avenues through which example expresses its power? As has been said, all that the teacher is and does teaches, but an illustrative list of areas of behavior that seem to have special power may be helpful. Each of these areas might be discussed at length by interested teachers, but a bare sketch will suffice for our present purpose.

1. Basic attitudes: the psychological posture taken toward important problems, e.g., success, failure, teaching, learning, human ability, love, truth, human relations, minorities, religion, work, play, the self.

2. Speech and diction: the use of language as the chief vehicle of thought.

3. Work habits: the style with which one does the work which composes so large a portion of every person's life.

4. Attitude toward experience and mistakes: an understanding of the relation between breadth of experience and the inevitableness and value of mistakes.

5. Dress: the material extension of the self that is a vital part of that self and is a continuous and revealing expression of the whole personality.

6. Human relations, especially under stress: the quality given to all human intercourse—social, intellectual, moral, aesthetic. Particularly, how do you behave when the students misbehave?[7]

7. Thought processes: the way the mind works when it is faced with problems.

8. Neurotic behavior: defenses which are habitually used to protect the personality and often used to hurt others.

9. Taste: the system of preferences (likes and dislikes) which persistently and subtly reflect a person's values.

10. Judgment: the rational and intuitive skills used in evaluating all kinds of situations.

11. Health: the quality and tone of the body, mind, and spirit which reflect themselves in energy level, perspective, poise, enthusiasm, and a genuine zest for life.

12. General style of life: what one believes about every aspect of life and the way in which those beliefs are incarnated into large and small actions; the amount of truth one has learned and the extent to which truth guided by love and inspired by beauty has permeated behavior.

This list is merely illustrative and is in no sense exhaustive. Every teacher could add other aspects of behavior that are forever presenting the teacher's way of life to the student. But the purpose here is to underscore the varied ways the example of the teacher expresses itself in day-to-day work.

To this point, our thought on the teacher as an example suggests some disturbing questions. Let us examine three of these questions. (1) Does this emphasis upon the teacher as an example or model mean that the teacher's whole life, personal as well as professional, must be lived in terms of his work as a teacher? In a sense, yes. There is a tendency for many teachers and perhaps their organizations to urge that if teachers are examples at all they are so only on the job; that it is right and fair that they be free in their personal lives outside the classroom. This contention has much appeal and certainly some merit. Few of us would want to be in the position of opposing freedom, especially personal freedom. If freedom is reasonably informed and responsible, the more the better. But the position that the teacher is free, except when he is on the job, to behave as he wishes without regard to his role as a teacher does not hold up either in practice or in theory.

In practice, for example, when I went on my first teaching job as a junior high school English teacher in a small mill town, I went as a teacher of the children of that community. Nothing could divorce me from that role. Neither can I escape the fact that I am now a member of the faculty of a university. I may have the legal right to engage in bizarre behavior on my street or at a ball game, but my actions will be, and will be considered to be, an example of a teacher at my university. I am a teacher there and no distinctions I may attempt to draw about time and place can change that fact.

In theory, this forever being an example is an integral part of being a teacher. That is, to be a teacher is to have the responsibility of being an example. Indeed, every profession has its special demands and to refuse to accept them is to deny the profession. The very vital and special role of the teacher in the education of the young places special demands upon him. These demands in reality reflect the depth and breadth—the essential significance—of the teacher's work. Properly viewed, they do not circumscribe, constrict, or distort his life. Such demands enrich and ennoble the teacher's whole existence by urging him to live up to the best standards he knows. Contrary to much of the sophisticated thought prevalent in our time, young people and older ones not too far along the road to cynicism will respond to this kind of an example as they do to any demanding endeavor, such as the Peace Corps.

(2) Does it follow that the student should consider the teacher as a model to be copied? Not at all. The teacher's behavior will greatly influence the student but every student should be encouraged, even urged, to develop his own personal style of life. In doing so, he evidently cannot escape the influences around him

as he develops, and will be touched especially by those whom he loves and admires: those who are truly his teachers whether in the classroom, or in the home, or in literature, or on the street.[8]

(3) Should the teacher present the best example of behavior (intellectual, moral, social, aesthetic) that he knows? What a hard question this is: One supposes that every sincere person has a set of values and wishes to live in terms of them. To do less is to be somewhat less than man at his best. Yet every individual is more or less faulty. In actual behavior he constantly falls short of his goal or standard for himself. A good teacher is aware of this gap between what he would like to be and what he is; he recognizes his faultiness.

So we face a serious situation, one that has significant implications for mental health and for optimum growth. The teacher simply because he is a teacher is expected by his students and by his society to be an example or a model. Presumably, he is expected to be and wishes to be a good example, but being human he is full of faults. He will be angry when a wiser man would have laughed; he will lie, or shade the truth, when a wiser man would have faced the facts; he will be harshly critical when a wiser man would have been more patient and kind; he will encourage, out of weakness, when to be frankly critical would have been fairer.

This tragic gap between what we would like to be and what we are, in a deep sense, expresses the very nature of human life. Fortunately, the degree of faultiness in the teacher, in my judgment, is not crucial to his effectiveness, provided (and this is a huge provision) he is sincere and is steadily growing toward the scholar and the person he wishes to be. In fact, where one is along the journey toward fuller wisdom does not count so much as the direction one is traveling and the attitude one takes toward where he is and where others are. Browning expressed a closely related point in this encouraging line: ". . . 'tis not what man / Does which exalts him, but what man / Would do!"[9]

So the teacher as model or example need not be dismayed or discouraged by his unworthiness to be a perfect example. He cannot be such, of course, and perhaps it would not be well if he could. Indeed, his faultiness can be a means of growth for him and for his students. He and they, engaged in this subtle life process, may become genuine partners in a central endeavor of life: the development of the full potential of each individual person. Teaching is truly many things. In a sense, this being an example or model involves all the other roles of the teacher that are discussed in this book. This role brings us face to face with the hypothesis: A teacher can be no greater as a teacher than he is or is becoming as a person.

Since what we are as persons profoundly influences our work as teachers, it might be helpful as we pursue this study to keep in mind that prayer of Socrates offered at the end of one of his most incisive dialogues:

. . . give me beauty in the inward soul; and may the outward and inward man be as one. May I reckon the wise to be the wealthy, and may I have such a quantity of gold as a temperate man and he only can bear and carry.[10]

E. V. P.

Questions and problems
for dialogue

1 Perhaps neither the term "example" not the term "model" conveys effectively the central thesis or thought of this chapter. What term would you suggest as possibly better?

2 How free do you believe a teacher should be in his personal life? Why and in what ways are the demands to be an example greater upon the teacher than they are upon members of other professions?

3 In theory, is a teacher's whole personality (all of his behavior) more related to his work than the personalities of people in other professions? If so, why?

4 What are some of the major dangers or hazards in a teacher's being considered or considering himself as example to his students?

5 In your judgment, at what level or levels of education is the power of the teacher as a model or example greatest? Elementary, secondary, college, graduate, or professional school?
6 Is the role of being an example easier for the younger, inexperienced teacher, or for the older, more experienced and more mature teacher? Why?
7 What aspects of a teacher's behavior have the most profound influence on his students? Thought processes? Personal habits? Methods of doing work? Human relations? etc.
8 Is there a contradiction between the two ideas that the teacher is an example or model for his students and that students should never be encouraged to copy or follow blindly their teachers? How can these positions be reconciled?
9 In what sense is a poor, weak or ineffective teacher a powerful influence as an example on students?
10 If a teacher is by the very nature of his work a model or example, does it not follow that faultiness in the teacher's personality or character will reduce the teacher's effectiveness? If the answer is "no," how can this apparent paradox be reconciled?

Exercises
for further learning

1 Recall and write down the names of the *five* teachers in your experience as a student that, all things considered, were your best teachers. Examine in what ways and to what extent you thought of them as models or examples.
2 Make a list of the kinds of behavior that seem to you should be left "free" for the teacher—that should not be influenced by the fact that he is a teacher. Be ready to defend your list.
3 Examine with care the list of types of behavior given in this chapter in which the teacher will have special importance as a model. Put them in the order of their power of influence. Are there some you would eliminate from the list?
4 Bring to mind the achievement in your life which you consider your best. List the ways your teachers influenced the development of this achievement.
5 Observe people in the various activities of life: in traffic, at restaurants, at work, at play, on the bus, etc. Would you expect a

teacher's behavior to be different from that of the majority of people? Why? Examine your attitude as honestly as you can.

6   In reading biography and in talking with people directly, seek to discover the extent to which examples or models influence the lives of people. As a rule, who are these heroes and why are they chosen?

7   If you find that in your own life or the lives of your friends, teachers have not often served as influential models, undertake to discover the reasons why this is true. Analyze the factors involved.

8   Describe in some detail and with as much psychological insight as possible the student-teacher relationship that promises the most desirable and significant influence.

9   Recall three or four of what you consider to be your "worst" teachers. Try to determine if they had significant negative or harmful influence on your development.

10 Interview a few teachers at various levels of education. Try to discover and understand their attitude toward the notion of a teacher's being an example or model. Keep careful notes on your findings.

Curiosity is one of the permanent and certain
characteristics of a vigorous intellect.
Every advance into knowledge offers new prospects,
and produces new incitements to greater progress.
—*Samuel Johnson*

7

A teacher is

a searcher: one
who does not know

The teacher is a seeker or searcher. He knows not and
knows that he knows not, in the words of the ancient proverb, and
hence is himself a fine subject for teaching and learning. For many
teachers this role may be the most painful of the many they play,
for having long and fondly played the part of an authority, of one
who knows, it may seem unbecoming a teacher to be one who
seeks, one who does not know. For others, the growing teachers,
this role is the most satisfying of all: to be one who is forever
searching for truth and understanding makes him a genuine phi-

losopher in the deepest meaning of that term. Plato expressed this
state in these words:

Wise, I may not call them; for that is a great name which belongs to
God alone,—lovers of wisdom or philosophers is their modest and be-
fitting title.[1]

The need to know seems to be universal in man. In the older
person it becomes more systematized, more channeled, expressing
itself in specialized pursuits such as the trades or professions, or
in the more general searching of the scientist, the poet, and the
seer. The higher learning (or university) is this endless search
organized into an institution, a community of scholars.[2]

In the very young, the seeking to know—to extend oneself by
knowing—is general and unrefined. In this state it is more easily
observed, for nothing is more evident than the healthy child's persistent urge to know. His curiosity is all-embracing. Before he has
mastered much of the symbols of language, and even when his
mobility is limited, his eyes follow every moving object and his
hands are into everything in reach. With the development of language, as every mother knows, the chorus of "what's" and "why's"
is unending.

The child's need to know is so natural and pervasive that there
is no hint of shame or hesitancy about its expression. The child
is no more ashamed of his hunger to know or of the fact that he
does not know than a healthy, hungry man is ashamed of his
hunger for food, or the energy-filled organism for movement. It
would be a fascinating subject for research to determine when and
how the edge is taken off the natural intensity of the child's urge
to know.

> Who made him dead to rapture and despair,
> A thing that grieves not and that never hopes,
> Stolid and stunned, a brother to the ox?[3]

It would be better still to learn how this pristine curiosity might
be kept alive and growing, perhaps to the very end of life.

The teacher as seeker is a sincere seeker—he does not pretend to seek because seeking is supposed to be a work of the teacher. The nature of life, perhaps especially civilized life, seems to dull man's natural need to know, so apparent in the burning curiosity of the child. Thus the teacher often finds himself becoming disillusioned about the significance and joy of knowing. But his very profession, his life work, is enmeshed in the knowing process. What can he do?

Two very destructive roads are frequently taken. He may pretend an interest in knowledge, in learning, in research (depending upon his level in the work of teaching) and develop an artificial attitude and manner of speaking in an attempt to manifest a keen interest in knowing. Then he becomes the stereotype of the dead or dying teacher (he may be twenty-five or seventy-five, for chronological age has little to do with it) and his speech and manner are like a record or a pantomime. Perhaps most of us can recall when we have been like this and disliked ourselves for it.

The other defense is that of cynicism. In this case the teacher, no longer curious or interested in learning and having achieved a kind of status, makes no pretense but considers the whole education effort as a sort of game. These people often refer to teaching as "this racket" or "our racket." They are bitter toward the young or older teachers who are afire with a natural enthusiasm for learning, for these living people are a constant reproach to those who have lost the sharp edge of interest. They frequently say "You will soon get over that," and many, perhaps most, do get over it.

We must not linger too long over this negative side. Surely many teachers remain alive and growing—they remain genuine seekers as long as they live. These teachers have a never-failing source of life in them. The zeal to know and to understand becomes such an intense longing to extend the borders of the known, to push back the boundaries of ignorance, that it partakes of the uniting process of love: the true scholar is said to love knowledge or to be in love with learning. In fact, the learner—young or old—is pulled to penetrate and mingle himself with the unknown, and thus to break down the walls between himself and the reality beyond him.[4]

So for the teacher, as one who does not know, the state of not knowing is a ground or reason for the search. It is, in a sense, a thing to be thankful for rather than to be ashamed of. For if one were full, if he had no hunger, how could he enjoy a good meal? If one had arrived, how could he anticipate the journey? If he were at the top of the mountain, how could he look forward to the climb? Fortunately, the area of the unknown is so great that there is no real possibility of its reach being exhausted by a teacher or by anyone else.

Nevertheless there is a danger that must be mentioned that can bring the search to an end somewhat as if all had been found. Just as there is a strong tendency in man to be forever seeking, there is an opposite tendency to tire of the search and to pretend to himself and others that he has arrived. Now and then I suppose (this need may increase with age) all of us long to pitch our tents and say "Here is the place. Let us cease this urgent pushing on and on and settle here." After the ten years at Troy and the ten years of trials on the sea we long for an Ithaca where we can walk among our flocks and herds and be at rest. The point is: we have had our share of seeking new answers; the old ones are good enough for us. If only the eternal young would stop their questioning we could be at peace, perhaps. It would be so easy to teach the old things we know so well in the old ways that are now so comfortable. We have heard enough of the new morality, the new math, the new grammar, the new hairdo, the new anything. Let us hedge in and enjoy our beloved Ithaca.

The teacher resists this tendency, for his world is another world. It is the world of the seeker—the restless, throbbing, urgent search of the human mind. There may come a "1984"[5] or something like it, but as yet nothing has been able to quench that thirst to seek, perhaps to find.[6]

In fact, it seems that in the case of both societies and individuals, the more that is known the stronger the need to know more becomes. Instead of becoming surfeited as one might expect, this need feeds on itself, as it were. As the borders of the known become larger the area of the unknown they touch becomes correspondingly larger. Thus the things that are not known increase as more is known. An observation of man's behavior since the Renaissance suggests that the same progression works to increase the intensity of man's need to know.[7]

The same principle applies to the individual and especially to the teacher. As he knows more in general, or about his specialty, the area of the unknown becomes larger (or at least he is aware of more of it which, in practice, is the same thing), and so the more learned he becomes the more he is aware of himself as one who does not know. On the surface, this condition would seem to be discouraging and disillusioning, but really it is one of the chief sources of the teacher's strength and renewed life. If he has the courage to face this fact squarely and with interest, he remains always as one who does not know, hence a perennial student, and in this very important sense like, and very near psychologically to, his students. Further, this dynamic relation between the known and the unknown increases the intensity of the need to search, so that as the natural need to seek, characteristic of the child, wanes or is dissipated a need created by his previous knowledge takes over and develops from the relation between the known and the unknown.

The attitude or spirit of not knowing and of searching which accompanies it is contagious. The teacher's constant seeking to know assures the student that not knowing, so widely characteristic of the student, is natural to life, and is a means of growth rather than a hindrance or handicap. The student does not know music or arithmetic or history; his teacher likewise does not know many things. Instead of being rivals and competitors they can become cooperating partners in a mutual search. Certainly the teacher knows much compared to the student; the student knows little compared to his teacher. But the teacher helps him to an appreciation of the relative nature of all knowledge. This awareness acquired early in his development provides the student with the best of all safeguards against pedantry and false pride in his learning. Also, this lesson well-learned may stand him in excellent stead if he goes on to special expertness in some field of knowledge, and if transmitted to the culture of which he is a part may save it from stagnation or the dangerous pride of *hubris*.

The teacher as a seeker, as one who does not know, keeps the spirit of inquiry alive and growing. He is in a genuine sense an investigator. The purpose and methods of his investigation will vary in terms of his interests and the maturity and ability level of his students. But whatever the subject of his interest or the level of his students, a special approach will characterize all that he does: the spirit of the investigator or the researcher. He may be teaching relatively elementary facts or processes in the early grades, but these facts or processes cease to be "inert ideas" when tinged with the spirit of investigation. Their history and meaning are subjects for research. By this means, most of learning takes on the enlivening quality of discovery for the learner.[8]

Training in careful observation is perhaps the best background preparation for more systematic investigation. The teacher as seeker will be a perceptive observer, and will help students by example and direct teaching to form the habit of continuous and careful observation.[9] In this way, the habit of seeing widely and deeply may be cultivated.

This ability and inclination to see is not only an excellent foundation for more systematic investigation, but it is a significant source of personal enrichment and joy. A large portion of the world escapes us because we have not learned to see. As a rule, we walk insensitive among the most interesting things because we have not the ability to perceive them. You may have noticed city children on a day in the country. Often they sit bent over their transistor radios, or color a picture book brought from home, or sadly observe there is nothing to do here that is fun. The varied things around them in abundance simply do not exist for them. Of course, the fault is not theirs; they have not learned to see.

Perhaps a more difficult habit to form is that of making notes on one's observations. Although many children and young people take a special pleasure in keeping records, they may need assistance in developing this skill. A careful account of interesting things observed, of changes noted, and particularly of striking phenomena is also a step toward the attitude and technique of the investigator, as well as a personal satisfaction. In these and similar ways the teacher as seeker, from the very beginning of formal education through to advanced graduate study, leads the student toward the spirit and skills of thoughtful inquiry.

The teacher as searcher brings the investigating spirit to every aspect of the learning effort. Under the tutelage of such teachers, the student comes to embody the investigative approach and bring it to all his problems. Thousands of citizens so educated may be the requisite for progress toward a more thoughtful civilization. In such a world, respect for evidence, honesty in application, earnestness in seeking the facts, and appreciation for their limitations might become almost as natural as breathing or seeing. The teacher as seeker is a principal hope for movement toward such a world.

Thus a teacher as searcher, like the unspoiled, keenly curious child, is full of questions. He is not afraid of the questions characteristic of childhood or the even more disturbing ones of youth; he sees them as the essence of the learning process. Nor is he afraid of his own questionings and even deeper doubts. He perceives these as an evidence of his close kinship with the universal child, the unquenchable need to know and understand. Now and then the questions and doubts having remained too long unanswered may threaten him with the "night view"[10] and cause him to doubt that life has meaning, or that there is truth. Many in our day (and perhaps in every day) become marooned in this dark land and like the blind man in Buddha's fable deny that seeing is possible.

There was a man born blind, and he said: "I do not believe in the world of light and appearance. There are no colors, bright or somber.

There is no sun, no moon, no stars. No one has witnessed these things."
His friends remonstrated with him, but he clung to his opinion: "What
you say that you see," he objected, "are illusions. If colors existed I
should be able to touch them. They have no substance and are not
real. Everything real has weight, but I feel no weight where you see
colors."[11]

Another problem arises for the teacher as a seeker that is so
complex and threatening that one hesitates to mention it. Honesty
demands that we examine it briefly. Can one be a sincere, open-
minded seeker and at the same time have the clear and meaningful
commitment so necessary to effective living?[12] The problem is
essentially this: on-going life at all its stages from early childhood
to old age requires that one live in terms of what he knows or
what he believes to be true. Decisions must be made; actions must
be taken. The urgent situation does not allow the gathering of
further evidence or the waiting with judgment suspended. In a
word, the individual is more effective in this practical part of his
life if he has clear commitment which is based upon the evidence
he has and the beliefs he holds. Suspended judgment confuses
action and reduces the power that comes from more centered
energy.

The adult community (the elders or fathers) sense the relation
between strong commitment and effective action. They perceive
the danger of the seeking, questioning spirit which to them seems
not only to threaten individual stability but also to undermine the
ancient community wisdom and even the voice of God upon which
all their values are based. Consequently they may be critical of
the teacher as seeker, and in times of fear may seriously circumscribe his freedom to search, and thus threaten the heart of his
vocation.

We as teachers should remember that the concern of the community is not wholly unjustified. The concern reflects a real danger. A core of certainty, of stability, and of commitment is necessary to wholesome growth and to effective seeking. The instinct
of the organized commuity is right on this point. The delicate

and difficult task of the teacher as seeker is to protect, respect, and further build this core of knowledge and value while he and his students engage in the process of seeking and refine the methods of seeking.

Thus it may be said that the proper balance between that which one knows and believes and that which one does not know and is seeking to know enables the individual to have the stability and commitment of sure knowledge and the flexibility and freedom needed for growth. The core of knowledge and commitment serves as a necessary base of safety from which exploration and experimentation can be launched. No balance in life is more difficult to achieve or more important for the quality of human life than this one. The teacher as seeker will keep it always before him as a goal.

E. V. P.

Questions and problems for dialogue

1 Are you or do you wish to be a philosopher? What is the meaning of the term philosophy? Is a teacher a philosopher?
2 Is the need "to know" common to all men or is it largely limited to those of a special frame of mind?
3 As you have observed teachers, what conclusion have you reached as to the cause of many teachers' becoming somewhat cynical, i.e., when they refer to teaching as "our racket" or ridicule the enthusiastic teacher?
4 What is meant by the statement that a true scholar is "in love with his learning"?
5 Do you feel the need to find an "Ithaca" and settle down? If so, why?
6 Is the spirit of search, of inquiry, applicable to all levels of learning? Is it principally applicable to college and university? Why?
7 What experiences in your education from early grades through to

the present did most to sharpen or stimulate your investigative spirit? Be specific in your response.

8 Can the teacher "not know," be a continuous seeker, and still hold the respect of his students? If so, what seems to be the key to doing so?

9 What are the values and the dangers of the feeling of the fathers of the organized community toward commitment—their fear of commitment being destroyed by too much seeking? Is there a genuine conflict between seeking and commitment?

10 In what sense is it true that the more we know, the more there is that we do not know?

Exercises
for further learning

1 Try to find the distinguishing characteristics of what we call elementary, secondary, and higher education. Note especially the overlapping functions and those that seem to be special to each level.

2 Find some opportunity to observe directly the behavior of small children (from birth to four or five years of age). Note especially their manifestations of curiosity. Then observe older children or adults. Note carefully the principal differences.

3 Over a period of a few weeks keep a record of instances when young people and adults indicated that they were ashamed of "not knowing." Try to determine causes of this feeling.

4 Interview four or five experienced teachers with the purpose of putting them on a rough scale as to their enthusiasm for learning. Do you find clear differences in attitude?

5 Undertake a small bit of investigation of something that interests you. Observe carefully and report concisely the results of your observation.

6 Try keeping a daily record of your search for ideas and of things of special interest that you observe.

7 Make a diagram that might help to make clear the relation between what one knows and what one does not know. That is, try to demonstrate the proposition that the more that is known the more there is that is unknown.

8 Observe with care a group of city children in the country or rural

children in the city. Try to account for their strange inability to "see."

9 Search your memory for individuals you have known who tended to retain a childlike zest for learning. Try to analyze what gave them this quality.

10 Interview a few people who have special responsibility in the community (councilman, school principal, church board member, etc.) to determine their attitude toward old truths and commitment and the search for new knowledge.

Let people realize clearly that every time they threaten
someone or humiliate or hurt unnecessarily or dominate or
reject another human being, they become forces for the
creation of psychopathology, even if these be small forces.
Let them recognize also that every man who is kind, helpful,
decent, psychologically democratic, affectionate, and warm,
is a psychotherapeutic force even though a small one.
—*Abraham H. Maslow*

8

A teacher is

a counselor: a confidant and friend

The teacher is a counselor[1] and confidant for his students and oftentimes for their parents. He may not have special
training as a counselor and, in a sense, may not wish to counsel
people. Many teachers tend to feel that counseling is too much
like trying to run other people's lives and so they are uncomfort-
able in this role. Yet to be a teacher at any level is to be a counselor
and confidant. The very nature of teaching puts one in that position. The learner is forever faced with the necessity of making
decisions; he will turn to his teacher for help in making them.
The learner will find himself lonely and baffled and perhaps self-

condemning; he will turn to his teacher as a confidant. The more effective the teacher is, the more students will turn to him for such counsel and such confidences.

The decisions will vary greatly, ranging from what may seem trivial to the adult to the most profound problems of life: whether or not to accept an invitation; how to respond to apparent snubbing; why friends are so hard to keep; what subjects to take; whether to go to college and, if so, where; whether to join a social group; how important are grades; what to do about a wrong committed; the meaning of life; the choice of a calling; and so on and on. A learning situation is the very soil out of which the questions of life arise. A teacher who pushes them aside will not be much more than a textbook or a film or a learning program. It follows then that the developing teacher will wish to understand this aspect of his work and be able to do it well.

The hazards of growing up are very great, probably increasing with the increasing complexity of a civilization.[2] We are inclined to assume that the journey from infancy to a reasonably self-directing, self-repairing maturity is almost automatic; that except for a few who develop serious pathology the trip is a relatively smooth one. The opposite is nearer the truth; growing up in a civilized society is full of dangers. The pathologies that develop in childhood, apparently as a result of childhood wounds, are evidence enough for one who is sensitive to human problems. These, as bad as they are, seem relatively unimportant, however, when compared to the almost universal tragedy of unfulfilled potential. In an attempt to deal with problems that are too much for us we develop ways of dealing with them and other problems—we develop a style of life—that may thwart our progress in almost every phase of life.

In order that the teacher as confidant and counselor may appreciate this problem in greater depth we must go aside a moment into the psychology of personality and of mental health. The human being is unique among living things on this planet in that his nature does not result primarily from simply growing up. What he becomes is influenced greatly by his experience—by what is commonly called his education. Man is not geared "to go" or to respond effectively to his environment by nature, by the mere process of growing up. The other animals through the higher forms are largely what they are because of their internally determined nature (what has often been called instinct) but man must learn a thousand things in the process of growing up. He must become a self. This openness, this unmadeness, makes possible both the glory and the shame of man: his chief strengths and his major weaknesses.

A distinguished anthropologist states the principle somewhat technically:

The behavior patterns of lower animals are, at least to a much greater extent, given to them with their physical structure; genetic sources of information order their actions within much narrower ranges of variation, the narrower and more thoroughgoing the lower the animal. For man, what are innately given are extremely general response capacities, which, although they make possible far greater plasticity, complexity, and on the scattered occasions when everything works as it should, effectiveness of behavior, leave it much less precisely regulated. This, then, is the second face of our argument: Undirected by culture patterns—organized systems of significant symbols—man's behavior would be virtually ungovernable, a mere chaos of pointless acts and exploding emotions, his experience virtually shapeless.[3]

It is this open quality in him that accounts in large measure for man's extremes. At his best (well made in terms of his potential) so like a god, except doubtless better than most gods we have heard about, so much above any other living form; at his worst (badly made in terms of his potential) horrible both to himself and his fellows, strangely lower than any animal, as expressed by his behavior in war, slavery, torture, etc. This openness or unmadeness or ungearedness gives education its real meaning. An animal limited by his relatively fixed nature can be trained somewhat; only man can be educated in the genuine sense.

This emphasis should not be taken as a denial of the power of heredity. The human being inherits that which makes him man, even the openness we are considering. Much that he is depends upon the unfolding of his nature through growth and development. Heredity sets limits and influences greatly the way the individual takes his environment. This relation between heredity and nurture is one of the most complex of all problems. Yet the fact remains that the unique self, the personality and character, is in the main the result of experience. This incomparably complex process of personality-making begins at birth, is most important during the period to physical maturity when the personality is most flexible, and continues to some degree throughout life.

The point for us here is that in its very nature this process of growing up, of building the personality, is replete with hazards. The reason is complex and yet simple: in the main, the "decisions" that a bee, a whale, a horse, or a Canada goose must make as he grows into his maturity are made by Nature; the decisions of the growing child and youth are made by his culture, by his parents, by his teachers, and eventually deeply by himself. This is the essence of man's great freedom, but evidently it is a risk-filled freedom, one that man has often wished he could escape, as a society or as individuals.[4] But there is apparently no way to go back to Eden, as comfortable and safe as that might seem to be. In a word, we have the limitless opportunity of education; or, if your mind tends to run toward cynicism, we are stuck with education.

Since this process of personality development is so complex and so full of risks it is perhaps inevitable that all are wounded along the way: some so badly as to be destroyed; many enough to be handicapped and stunted; some relatively little, and they offer a vision of what man can be and eventually may be.[5] The teacher who meets a class whether at kindergarten or at graduate school faces a group of individuals who are the result of the experience so far, and he will find them full of wounds from the living of life or bearing scars from such wounds. To speak more prosaically, in the process of growing up they will have fastened upon ways of dealing with their needs and the demands of life that are inappropriate and often even destructive. That is, to get something they want very badly, because of wrong turns or hurts in the past they use methods that do not get what they want but often bring the very opposite. However, these intriguing problems of mental health cannot be discussed in detail here.

There is a further complication that must be mentioned. The teacher who meets the class also has lived life to this point and bears in his personality the wounds and scars of that experience.[6] He comes to the teaching responsibility as a personality who also has developed a style of life, a way of dealing with his needs and the demands of the environment. It is hoped that special study and training, growth in self-understanding and perhaps in wisdom will have healed some of the worst wounds and produced a style of life better than that of the less experienced students. Of course, this is not always true. Many of us bring to our work as teachers badly distorted personalities which may grow steadily worse under the severe demands of teaching. The very best of us will bring only a "growing toward" what we would like to be as teachers. We will inevitably be faulty in many ways but the important thing is that we be growing in self-understanding, knowledge, and wisdom. This we all can do. Be that as it may, we bring ourselves to the educative situation. Evidently the freer we are from complexes that distort perception and behavior the better job we can do.

Our students who are in the process of being educated will be in constant need of counseling and will often desperately need a confidant. To put it another way, they come to the teacher for further learning and growth, but in preparation for that learning and as a part of it they must be healed; wounds received from previous attempts at learning hamper or block their further learning. We must remember that we are not referring here to advanced pathology but to the common problems of students who are involved in the everyday process of teaching and learning—my classroom and yours.

As the general processes of civilization become better (that is, more appropriate to the needs and potential of man) and as formal education is improved, doubtless the growing-up process will become less hazardous. People will come to each level of education with fewer wounds and scars and better prepared for the next levels of learning and growth. Such improvement, which is steadily taking place, is a matter of centuries or generations, so the thoughtful clear-seeing teacher must face life as it now is and as it is likely to be in the foreseeable future and learn to do his job within that framework.

A few illustrations may make the principle we are discussing more meaningful. Often students either from a home or school experience will feel seriously threatened by any person in what is or seems to be a position of authority. The reaction may be one of resentment or rebellion making simple cooperation nearly impossible, or an ardent "yes, yes" attitude, or an overtly quiet withdrawal reducing contact with the adult to a minimum. Each of these reactions has its special dangers. Then there are the ego-starved individuals who must have attention at almost any price—perhaps by noise or showing off in the lower grades, by interminable talking or arguing in graduate school.

Adler's emphasis upon the enormous power of inferiority feelings still has much validity.[7] Perhaps most of the foolish (inappropriate) things we do in classroom and out are basically reactions to a feeling of inferiority. Nearly all students beyond the third or fourth grade will carry wounds from former experiences with evaluation or testing. The hurt that seems most hampering at the graduate level (where I have taught in recent years) is the almost pathological fear in the students of their own ideas and particularly their imaginations. Apparently most students by this time have been by some process so beaten down that they do not dare present their own ideas. They must forever hide behind an "authority." Strangely enough oftentimes what are called the able learners are the worst hurt in this area. Finally, it is a little sad to note that very few people at any level above the very early grades can express their thoughts orally even in a classroom situation without all the signs of gross fear. What a history of previous wounds this would seem to suggest.

The point then is simple but far-reaching in its importance: students will come to teachers full of wounds and scars, sorely in need of a counselor and a confidant. Now we can consider briefly some of the problems that accompany this aspect of being a teacher.

Some students will have been so hurt by life that they will need special help beyond what the regular teacher can give. Balance is very difficult to achieve in this area. There is a danger that the teacher, keenly interested in being of the most possible help, may undertake to deal with advanced levels of pathology. In cases where the behavior is persistently bizarre the teacher should be quick to seek medical, and if need be, psychiatric care. However, there is an equal danger that the teacher will mistake the ordinary (and oftentimes not so ordinary) manifestations of growing up for serious pathologies. Fearful over-quick referral is often a more harmful attitude in the teacher than the opposite. In cases of doubt, it is wise to allow a little more time, with regular understanding and acceptance, and to provide the best possible conditions for normal growth. Frequently these procedures and changes that may be taking place will enable the learner to escape his special blind alley and move forward.

It is encouraging to remember that there is a strong inner— what might be called natural—tendency to healthy growth. Given even a minimum chance the strong forces for health and integration often will take over and do their healing and growth-producing work. If the pathology is not too deep and fixed, a reasonably good environment, a little success, a special interest on the part of an admired teacher, a reduction in pressure or demand, and a little common-sense guidance will solve the problem.[8] But the teacher, especially the less experienced, should note the qualification at the beginning of the preceding sentence. Beyond a certain point pathology seems to feed on itself and even on a good environment, and then special treatment is indicated, but these cases are relatively few and should not deter the teacher in his regular work of healing which is an important part of all teaching.

There are many times in the growth cycle when the learner feels strongly the need for a confidant outside the family. This fact is not a criticism of the family. The need for an outside confidant may be as great in a "good" family as in one that seems less desirable. The need is an aspect of finding oneself in the world and is a reflection of the natural limitations of the family. The teacher is in an excellent position to fulfill this need. Here is the most natural opportunity for the establishment of a psychological relationship that will extend the growing self. Of course, care must be taken by the teacher not to take advantage of this need and undermine the student's respect for members of his family. Naturally there is some danger of the development of emotional attachments that are damaging to growth. If the teacher himself is reasonably mature, this danger is relatively small.

The relation of confidence so important to this part of a teacher's work arises out of mutual respect. This means that the teacher respects the students as individuals who doubtless have many problems but who also have an all-important integrity and self-regard. Also, mutual respect means that the students respect the teacher. Now a teacher cannot expect or demand this relation simply because he is a teacher: respect must be won. And we must remember that these students have had much experience with adults and teachers. They have often been helped and guided and often been hurt by them. The teacher in a sense inherits all that has gone before. It has been my experience that in a college or university class it requires about half of a regular semester to establish a reasonable degree of mutual respect and confidence. The time needed would vary with the skill of the teacher, the level of the class, the previous experience of the class, and other factors.

Crucial to an atmosphere of confidence and mutual respect is the keeping of trust. There is always a serious danger that an

adult will underestimate the importance that a student puts on
a matter. Few things will destroy good relations between people
more quickly than the actual or apparent betrayal of trust. Some
of the severest hurts in the process of growing up (and even later)
are those when an adult, sometimes inadvertently, makes public a
confession or a thought a child believes he has given in confidence.
If it seems wise and necessary to speak with parents or another
teacher or a principal, it is of utmost importance that the person
involved understand and agree to this procedure. Otherwise, the
relation basic to confidence and counseling will be destroyed.

Counseling may be done in many ways and at many levels.
There are as many kinds of counsel and of counseling as there are
people and human problems. We should not be too technical
about counseling as we are conceiving it here, for it is a natural
part of every teacher's work. A simple piece of kindly advice about
manners or a basketball shot; a hint as to how to outline a talk;
listening to a student's concern; even an approving or disapproving look or gesture—all of these are counseling. Some, taken with
one theory, will almost never give a direct suggestion, however
evident the need may be for information or a little practical guidance; others are brusquely opinioned and directive in every situation. Indeed, there are a multitude of stances a teacher may take.
Common sense, experience, and the best theory would urge a
flexible attitude toward the counseling situation which encourages
the teacher to use the most appropriate approach for the particular case. It must be said, however, that teachers are inclined to
talk too much; they find it very hard to listen as much as they
should. Yet there is a time to talk.

In reality, the essence of this kind of counseling seems to be
simply giving a friend the benefit of one's experience. The teacher
has taken a number of boats down this river. True, the student
has to learn for himself but there are times when he can ask what
are the major hazards of the stream and how they have best been
dealt with; and he will profit greatly from a clear, sincere answer

from one who has special experience. He will profit, that is, provided the teacher has his confidence and is respected. Further, it will probably be better if the counsel is asked for. The wise teacher carefully resists the temptation to force either counsel or confidence.

One very interesting point, almost an aside, remains to be made. It is what might be called the psychology of "my last duchess." Some of you will remember the poem by Robert Browning with that title in which the Duke does away with his Duchess, not because she is unfaithful or otherwise bad but essentially because she expressed her charms to everybody equally. The Duke wanted to be special, and since he wasn't he "did her in." Here is a powerful psychology at work. Ashton-Warner in her book *Spinster* gives a charming description of her work with a little hurt Maori child who longed for their relation to be especially and uniquely their own.[9] I recall that again and again through the years in counseling people, the thing they fear and, I think, hate most is the thought of being merely one more patient or client.

Of course, the teacher is not a professional counselor, nor even a lover in the usual sense, but the principle holds nevertheless. Every individual longs in the very nature of his individuality to be and to be treated as special for deeply he is special. When the teacher is in the role of counselor and confidant every student is special and unique, and must feel so. No pretense will do: the special nature of the relation must be genuine.

Many years ago when I was a graduate student I had an experience that I believe will stay with me always. It was late in the afternoon toward the end of a long and somewhat discouraging week. I was sitting in an old classroom at the university writing on a paper on personality health. The woman who did the cleaning of the rooms in those days came in to begin her work. We were friends and I asked her, "Mary, if you were in bad trouble or had a difficult decision to make, what would you do first?" She looked at me a moment and replied from her unschooled wisdom, "I'd

find someone I had confidence in and talk it over with 'em alone."
Every student has this need again and again along the journey of
learning.

E. V. P.

Questions and problems
for dialogue

1 What is the difference between the way the term "counselor" is
   used in this chapter and its use in the technical literature on counseling? Is there a serious conflict between the two uses?
2 Some teachers maintain that the classroom teacher should not undertake to "counsel" students—that to teach is enough. What is
   your view on this question?
3 Are the hazards of growing up greater in a modern urban society
   than they were in more rural times? Give reasons for your answer.
4 In your judgment, is the difference between animal behavior and
   human behavior a difference merely in degree of complexity or is
   the difference one of kind? Be able to support your response.
5 What is meant by the term "openness" as it is applied to human
   personality? What implications does this concept have for education?
6 What is the meaning of the term "wound" as it is used in this chapter? How do these psychological hurts relate to the educational
   process?
7 Why is the real or apparent breaking of trust such a serious blow
   to student-teacher relations?
8 Emerson once said in effect: two people are almost always sincere;
   upon the entrance of a third all three become hypocrites. To what
   extent is this true? How does the statement relate to counseling?
9 How can a teacher tell when a student merely wishes to have
   attention or "possess" the teacher and when he genuinely needs a
   confidant? Are the two needs related?
10 What are some of the dangers in the classroom teacher's being a
   confidant or counselor?

Exercises
for further learning

1 Interview three or four experienced teachers in an attempt to learn what proportion of their time over the years has been given to some kind of counseling. Also, strive to get their judgment as to the significance of this aspect of their work as teachers.

2 Make a list of the types of counseling problems that come to a classroom teacher in the course of one or two weeks of work.

3 Review your own life as a student. Recall the teachers you went to for counsel and those you seldom or never went to. Undertake to describe the differences between these teachers. Were the teachers in one group in general "better" teachers than those in the other group? If so, why?

4 Make a list of the "wounds," the psychological hurts, that seem to you to appear most frequently in the students you have known. Note the types of problems that recur most frequently.

5 Distinguish between the work of a trained or full-time counselor in school and that of a regular classroom teacher. What seem to be the basic differences in the work of the two groups?

6 Make a small study of your class or a group of fellow teachers to determine what training they have had in the area of mental hygiene. How much of such training would you recommend for the classroom teacher?

7 Interview a few people to discover when and under what circumstances they seem to go outside the family for special counsel or to share a confidence. How often did they turn to teachers? What types of problems were involved?

8 Develop a brief list of criteria that might guide a teacher in making the decision to refer a child for special counseling or medical help. Note especially the indications that a psychological problem is failing to heal, is beginning to feed on itself.

9 Examine and analyze the proposition that much of foolish or inappropriate behavior results from feelings of "inferiority." Observe yourself and others as you make your study.

10 Recall instances in your own growing up when confidence seems to have been broken. Were teachers often involved? Suggest ways of avoiding inadvertent breaking of confidence.

I too will something make
And joy in the making;
Altho' to-morrow it seem
Like the empty words of a dream
Remembered on waking.
—*Robert Bridges*

9

A teacher is

a creator: a stimulator of creativity

The teacher is a creator, one who demonstrates and releases the creative process. To understand this part of teaching our first task is to make clear what is meant by creativity. There is a strong tendency in man to limit and to draw circumscribing lines in terms of prejudices and preconceptions—in terms of ideas that reflect one's own smallness. Thus our conception of human talent and ability has been distorted by artificial distinctions sustained by class, privilege, and limited opportunity. Very often, perhaps usually, we have made God in our own image. The meaning of truth or love has been limited by what *we* can know or feel.

This limiting, distorting process has been at work on the concept of creativity. Much of the recent literature on creativity manifests this narrow conception of the process, placing a special and limiting emphasis on unusual instances of creativity. We have made almost a fetish of the creative process, putting fences around it, walling it in to satisfy our fears and protect our preconceptions. Creativity is one of the most universal processes we know. It is the characteristic aspect of the living world manifested around us; it is probably equally characteristic of the wider universe, material and spiritual, that we know so little about. All that exists seems to partake of two interrelated processes: that of life which is infinitely creative through new birth and growth, and that of death which disintegrates that which has been created. The evidence seems to suggest that the processes of death serve (make possible and enrich) the processes of life.

The creative process is persistently at work in the living world. These sentences are being written near Hemet, California, in February. This semi-desert country is teeming with the creativity of its life. Birds, animals, plants express in numerous ways their deep need to be a part of the creativity of the spring that approaches: swelling buds that will soon be flowers and leaves, the songs of birds that forerun the building of nests and the life drama that follows, the burrowing and play of animals, the ceaseless work of bees and other insects. Also, there is the creativity of inanimate things: wind and rain which carve the rocks and shape the hills; the slow but steady change of granite into gravel, and then to soil; the return of lifeless vegetation to its source in the earth. Only the deeply insensitive person would fail to perceive this abundance of natural creativity.

In addition to the natural or what might be called instinctive creativity, man partakes of other dimensions of the creative process. His making of physical things has been greatly extended beyond animal activity, as manifested in architecture, crafts, tools, games, roads, inventions. The creativity in the mental realm has been fabulous and perhaps is just in its beginning: literature, art, music, philosophy, law, science. These all depend on the greatest creation of all in the mental dimension: that of language. But there is still another dimension of creativity which goes beyond but perhaps envelops all the rest, the dimension of the spiritual. Here man partakes of that Ultimate Reality which searching men have called God. The deepest things by which men live seem to root here: love, faith, truth, beauty, goodness, imagination, purpose. The creativity that might flow from this dimension has been barely touched by man, only a few persons breaking through to its power.

There is no implication intended that the three dimensions or levels of creativity mentioned are separate or in any sense stand alone. They are intimately interrelated in ways that the mind of man has not yet fathomed. The terms physical, mental, and spiritual do seem to describe three levels of complexity and it may be of meaning, but probably they are a unity. Each reflects a type of creativity, and all together they form a field for creativeness that is awe-inspiring.

A modern scientist puts the thought in this way:

It seems likely that we human beings have unique mental and spiritual qualifications and that the theology and philosophy upon which we have been raised are correct in indicating the uniqueness of man on earth. . . . But until we understand more about the theoretical limits that intelligent human beings can develop or until we know enough to understand the functioning of our brains, it will be difficult to set any limit on the capabilities of living matter in the direction of intelligence, either the capabilities that lie ahead of us or the capabilities elsewhere in the universe.[1]

A teacher's classroom is a miniature of that creative universe. The teacher as creator senses this fact and all his activities are sustained, guided, and inspired by this realization. He is himself a creator; he is in the midst of stored creativity in the process of being released; as creator and stimulator of creativeness he is at the center of the educative process.

I can hear a teacher saying, "What romance! That does not

sound like a description of either me or my classroom." Perhaps true. But we are envisioning what the optimum educative process could be or should be. Might it not be that we are imprisoned by our own lack of imaginative perception? Should we not examine anew, unfettered by custom and fear, the material with which we work? Could we not seek and perhaps find a process of education—a way of learning—more in keeping with the nature and potential of that material? The teacher as creator will be moving in that direction.

Our notion of creativity and creating should be extended until it includes all the forms of making things of which people are so capable. Then we might be able to find joy and satisfaction in the process and not be so concerned about the end product. Creative action and thought would thus become an intimate part of life and growth. We might even escape some of the destructive competition and odious comparison that erode much of the joy of modern life.

There are standards by which to measure what we make: the external standards established by the experiences of man, and the internal standards of satisfaction with a job well accomplished that seems to accompany the release of talent. This kind of balanced pressure, external and internal, might move us steadily toward the best achievement of which we are capable, and at the same time safeguard the freedom and spontaneity so vital to all creativity.

There is a danger that the teacher will become enthralled with the extent or degree of originality in either himself or his students. In one sense, anything that is sincere, genuinely of the self, is for that reason original. In another sense, almost nothing is original as anyone who has tried to find the source of an idea or even a quotation will know. The degree of originality and the significance of the thing created will vary in terms of the talent of people. There will be, now and then, a Plato, a Shakespeare, a Beethoven, or an Einstein, and frankly we know little or nothing about the nature or origin or cause of their appearance. The teacher's greater concern is the release and cultivation of the varied creativity in all normal individuals. It is here that his chief contribution and main satisfaction lie.

The teacher as creator will likely have some special skill in which his creative energy will most effectively express itself. It probably does not matter too much what the "making" ability is so long as it has been brought to a reasonably high and satisfying standard. Now and then as a co-worker with the students he will bring to class a product recently made or one in the process of being made: in the early grades, it might be music or a story or a toy; in the college or university, a paper recently written or being written or research in process. Beyond these specific products it is well to remember that all the teacher's work from day to day in teaching is significantly creative.

The teacher develops a special sense as to how this more advanced creativity can be displayed so as to encourage and free the less mature to try their hands at making. Improperly presented, advanced accomplishment (or what seems advanced to the student) may frighten and inhibit the novice. Doubtless the key is in the attitude of the teacher and the relation that has been established between the teacher and the students. The genuine teacher interested not so much in himself as in the thing created and keenly interested in the process of creating will find in most cases that his very best accomplishment is accepted in such a way as to release and stimulate creative energy in his students.

A related principle should be stated in this connection. The classroom presents excellent opportunity for developing the deeply rewarding ability to find satisfaction in the creative work of one's associates. If the atmosphere is right, just as the students find a vicarious joy in the special creativity of the teacher, they may learn to find a like satisfaction in the creative work of fellow students and of the group working together on a meaningful project.

Such mutuality is more likely to arise if the teacher is sensitive to the areas in which various students may be particularly creative. Perhaps almost more than anything a learning situation is a relaxed search for and opening of avenues of creativity for the varied learners. We can assume that every person (young or old, bright or not so bright as we often see brightness) has a need to create, to make. The teacher's task is to help the student to find a constructive outlet for that need. The evidence is strong that a failure to widen that "creative vent" may be the chief cause for the distorted expressions in the various kinds of destruction and violence. Sir Herbert Read put the thought this way in his Preface to *Teacher* by Sylvia Ashton-Warner: "Destructiveness and creativity are opposed forces in the life of the mind. To create is to construct, and to construct cooperatively is to lay the foundations of a peaceful community." Miss Ashton-Warner states the principle in one place: "I see the mind of a five-year-old as a volcano with two vents; destructiveness and creativeness. And I see that to the extent that we widen the creative channel, we atrophy the destructive one."[2]

The fragmented and hurried nature of much of learning in school is a great hindrance to creativity. Often in our frantic attempt to cover everything and to get on to what is coming next, we do not give the student time to master anything well. Genuine creativity arises out of a foundation of familiarity or mastery that allows the mind to move out to unfamiliar or creative ground from an area of safety and confidence. An illustration will help to make this point clear. A young student had a special taste for and ability in mathematics. He liked algebra, but just as he was getting a feel for algebraic processes and was beginning to explore the theory of the study he was pushed on by the customs of the curriculum to unfamiliar ground. Even more he felt an affinity for the calculus and could feel his mind beginning to move out from the basic processes to ideas and processes which he longed to explore, again to be pressed on to new areas. Eventually by this progression it seemed that his creative interest in the subject waned. It may be that an important principle is demonstrated here: creativity

begins to take place chiefly when the learner has achieved sufficient mastery that the major portion of his energy is not used in
meeting new externally imposed demands.

If one would grow toward increasingly effective creativity
(whether in shoeing a horse, giving and receiving love, playing a
game, or writing sonnets), he must discipline and refine the creative energy. Spontaneous outflow of energy whether in dance,
speech, writing, or building rarely results in significant creation.
Surely in the early stages the spontaneous outflow should be
encouraged, but if excellence is desired, and the human potential
for skilled accomplishment is to be realized, then disciplined
work is necessary. Probably this kind of control and discipline
cannot be imposed from the outside. In some way it must be one's
own discipline. This means that the only meaningful discipline as
it relates to creativity is that which arises out of keen interest and
sustained purpose. Such inner discipline becomes essentially unconscious and almost as routine as the bodily processes. Further,
in contrast to imposed discipline it stimulates and sustains the
creative activity.

Over many years, I have asked a variety of people to tell me
about their best teacher. As a rule, their eyes light up and they
say, "Oh yes, I remember her." Then they say in effect: she wasn't
afraid to be different; she seemed to have fresh ideas; she would
bring strange things to class, animals or things she had found;
she told us special stories; she encouraged us to have ideas and
was interested in them. She had by some means escaped the
teacher stereotype, the deadening rut of expected behavior. This
is a rough description of the teacher as creator.

One additional thought about the teacher as creator must suffice for now. A perceptive woman many years ago told me she
had noticed an interesting and strange thing about children. She
lived in a rural community where there was a wide variety of
people, including many who were very poor and what we now
call culturally deprived. She noted that small children were much

alike whatever the circumstances into which they were born and were being reared. They were alert, curious, interested, vibrant: expressing man's magnificent promise. Then, as a rule, in a dull, constricting, narrow, sometimes fear-filled environment they lost much of this special spark and gradually took on the drabness of their surroundings. She thought this was very sad. It is sadder still to remember that this process has been going on throughout the long history of man, and still almost everywhere on the earth man's promise is thwarted by this stunting. And there is a deeper tragedy: often formal education contributes to this dwarfing of human possibility.

Most of us who have worked closely with children, personally or professionally, have observed that in most cases imagination, creativity, and even curiosity tend to wane with increasing years. Three boys will serve as examples. One was very creative mechanically. He was the kind of boy who could do wonders with wheels and cogs and chains and a plank or two. He was only average or so in some kinds of abstractions. Steadily, after the third grade when he began to get D's in school, he grew duller and rebellious; finally he became delinquent.

The other two boys (the three were playmates) took a somewhat different road. They were better in books, but particularly they were creative in language, making up vivid terms, having fun creating stories, playing with mathematical processes and with elementary philosophical ideas. Slowly under the pressure of life and of formal school this vibrant imaginative creative quality of mind faded out "into the light of common day," or perhaps one should change Wordsworth's phrase to the light of *uncommon* day, for this common day is really a distortion, a dwarfing of life as it naturally is.

The fact must be faced that this progression away from creativeness toward dullness may be a part of the nature of things: that it may be inevitable and cannot be remedied. Since we do not know, one may prefer another belief or hypothesis: that man does not need to travel this fateful road to dullness and the death of that which is best in him; that, on the contrary, through proper experience—education—he can enrich, deepen, refine, intensify, and release the qualities so characteristic of early childhood. One might be permitted a dream that a great corps of teachers working as creators in the classrooms of the world are the principal hope for the new world this kind of education would make possible. True, it is a dream, a vision, but a dream not to be relinquished until it has been carefully tested against reality.

E. V. P.

Questions and problems for dialogue

1   How would you define the term "to create" or "creativity"? When does making cease to be merely making and become what might be called creative?
2   How does one determine whether or not or to what extent a piece of work is original? What does the term "original" mean to you?
3   Why do we tend to limit "create" or "creative" to special instances of creativeness?
4   If it is true that children seem to become steadily less creative and spontaneous as they grow older, what would be some of the causes?
5   Does increase in experience, especially vicarious experience as through reading, tend to reduce or to increase creativity?
6   Of the three levels of creativity of men mentioned in this chapter, which one seems to you to be the least well developed so far in man's history? Give evidence for your answer.
7   What do you feel is the relation between the creative expression of energy and the elimination of violence in human life? Search for an underlying principle.
8   In your own case, what seem to have been the special conditions that stimulated creativity in you? Think of your best work, when and where and why it occurred.

9 Is creativeness an advantage or a disadvantage in the general day-to-day work of life? Why do you think so?

10 What as you see it is the relation (a) between discipline and creativeness and (b) freedom and creativeness?

Exercises
for further learning

1 Prepare a brief report on some of the more recent evidence on human ability, especially creativity. Make a few generalizations on the basis of your study. (For sources see William B. Michael, ed., *Teaching for Creative Endeavor: Bold New Venture* [Bloomington: Indiana University Press, 1968].)

2 Recall the three most creative teachers that you had in your educational experience (any level). Attempt to list the reasons why you considered them especially creative. Be as specific as possible.

3 Out of all the people you have known in school (either as fellow-students or as students in your classes) select three to five that seem to you to have been the most creative in adult life. Try to recall if they showed some of this creativeness as children.

4 Have a teacher suggest to you the three or four children in a grade in the elementary school that she considers to be particularly creative. Interview the children in an attempt to determine what is special about them.

5 Locate in the same way or by other avenues children that seem to be non-creative. See if you can find areas in which they are creative.

6 Explore the relation between fear and the expression of new or creative ideas. Interview a few advanced students. Ask for their views or hypotheses on two or three clear issues. If their answers seem to be stereotyped or unimaginative, try to probe for the reasons for the inhibition.

7 Set as a task for yourself the finding of the original author of an idea or a quotation. Keep careful notes on your experience. What do your findings suggest about the nature of originality?

8 Ask each of ten of your acquaintances to mention the most original or creative thing they ever did. Note carefully the reactions of your informants as they report on the specific things they mention.

9 From your own experience and that of others which you have

gained through association or reading, describe (a) the factors that seem most likely to stimulate creativity and (b) those most likely to stifle creative action or thought.

10 Evaluate the evidence for the proposition that creativeness is widespread in man. Also, evaluate the evidence for the hypothesis that most people are dull and uncreative.

He who knows, and knows that he knows, is wise—
follow him.
—*Persian Proverb*

10

A teacher is

an authority: one
who knows

The teacher is an authority: one who knows and knows that he knows. He must know; not everything of course, not anything completely for that is impossible, but he must know much. Tradition of a thousand years and more expects it; the very term demands it, for does not teaching imply knowing something to teach? True, the teacher cannot know much in comparison with what is to be known, but he knows more than those who are with him on a particular learning journey.

Illustrations rush to mind: Teacher, what is the great commandment in the law? Teacher, why have you brought us into the wilderness to perish? Teacher, is there life on other planets? Teacher, what is the nature of the world? Teacher, what did I do wrong in this arithmetic problem? Teacher, how do you pronounce this word? Teacher, why is there so much suffering in the world? Teacher . . . . Teacher . . . . Teacher . . . . That cry will never cease as long as the young must learn; as long as man at any age longs to know, and there are those who would teach.

There is a deep paradox here. By some means not easy to find, the teacher must be as humble and searching as Socrates and as confident and courageous as a Hebrew prophet fresh from hearing the voice of God. He must be one who knows and is confident of that knowledge, and at the same time one who is aware of the limitations of all human knowledge and is forever learning. The proper balance between these attitudes tends to produce a special quality in the personality that is designated by many terms: *charisma, wakan,*[1] *mana.* This quality, although extremely difficult to describe, is relatively easy to perceive or sense when it is present. It creates a special relationship between the person who has it and those who are associated with him which seems to be fundamental to all leadership and even influence.[2] Doubtless this quality exists in people in varying degrees, but probably without a minimum of it, the teacher rapidly becomes a cipher or even a minus. It may be that a failure to achieve this quality in the teaching situation, where the power is expected and greatly needed, makes teaching a burden and accounts for its negative effect on personality.[3] To be under the demands of teaching without a measure of *mana* is perhaps to be in a destructive position.

The teacher must be willing and able to say, "I do not know," for this will often be true and for the teacher truth is very precious. But it must not be necessary for him to say, "I do not know" too often or in too many areas or he will not be able to be a teacher. The wise teacher does not deny or downgrade what he knows; nor does he pretend and bluff when he does not know. The key to effective balance here, as so often, is sincerity or integrity.

Further, what the teacher is as a person is expressed not only in his special knowledge and skills, but also in his attitudes and thought. The kind of person he is speaks in all his behavior, from simple human relations to major decisions. Whether he is inquiring about a student's tennis score or discussing the causes of war and peace his *being*, the kind of person he is, reflects itself.

The teacher cannot be too faulty too often in his personal and professional behavior. Now and then a teacher can lose his self-control, can come to class depleted or unprepared, can be sloppy or inaccurate in statement or thought, but if often repeated these actions will destroy him. True, even Homer nods, but nodding too often he ceases to be Homer.

Adequate knowledge and skill are fundamental for the teacher. A guide in the weird wastes of the arctic north must know much of snow and ice; a guide in the Swiss Alps must know the mountains; a guide on the wide seas must know his instruments and the stars; a teacher of arithmetic must know mathematical principles and processes.

The qualities of personality are more difficult to illustrate but surely the effectiveness of a teacher or guide is greatly influenced by his personal qualities as reflected in attitudes toward himself, toward his students, and toward learning.

Surely the teacher is not perfect, but as authority he *knows* more and *is* more than those he teaches. Still the paradox is apparent: there is much he knows, there is more he does not know; there is much that he is as a person, there is more he is not. Continuous growth in knowledge and being seems to be the key.

Superior knowledge (relative to those with whom one regularly works) has its dangers. Like power, superior knowledge corrupts, and habitually used and unchallenged, it is the soil out of which some of the worst personality traits can grow. In the very nature of his work, as we have tried to show, the teacher knows more than his students, whether he teaches in the kindergarten or the university. Accustomed to this situation, he tends to speak, if he is not very careful, in the "teacher's tone." He speaks with authority not only with his students but with other associates. He may form the habit and tone of pontificating in class and out. It is good, no doubt, to know how to spell *cat* (if a child asks and wishes to learn) and there seems to be nothing wrong about a certain confidence in one's knowledge of that spelling, but to come to answer in a tone of certainty and finality all questions that arise can become almost a disease. The teacher seeks a creative balance on this point all through his professional life.

There is another subtle danger in being an authority. The teacher tends to conclude that because he knows a subject well, his mere telling or speaking about that subject is good teaching. He may come to believe even that such thorough knowledge concisely presented is the best teaching. Serious consideration of the nature of teaching and learning reveals that much more is involved in teaching.

Also, the teacher may fall into the trap of believing his judgment is infallible or very nearly so. It seems that this danger increases as we go up what has been called the educational ladder. There are offenders in the undergraduate college and university, and doubtless at all other levels of education, but probably the worst offenders appear in the graduate school. A distinguished authority in an area of knowledge (or one who is considered so by his students and perhaps by his colleagues) may be arbitrary and ruthless in his judgments. At times this distorted sense of authority may be used to destroy able and sincere graduate students. However, the temptation to misuse real or imagined superiority is in no sense limited to the graduate professor.

But there are positive aspects to the teacher's being one who knows—significant advantages for the teacher and teaching. Let us think about the values to both teacher and taught of the teacher's being an authority. Perhaps it would help to have a particular classroom in mind as we examine these advantages.

1. There is strength and comfort in being in the company of a veteran when one makes a hazardous journey. The teacher as a veteran is one who has been along this way, or one very much like it, and he is here to show that he has not only survived the trip

but also that he has used it as a means of growth and that the journey can be a joyous adventure.

The teacher is thus an example of the keen, perhaps incomparable, satisfaction of knowing something well. The inevitable uncertainty and faltering steps of the early learner give way to the smooth movement and thought of the expert. As examples, one thinks of the exhilaration of skiing, when after long and often painful practice, there is the full run, the long leap, the flying snow that lift the performer out of himself; or of the thrill of managing a team of spirited horses or of flying an airplane; or of the deep satisfaction that comes from playing a musical instrument, or using mathematical symbols, or speaking a foreign language. Slowly, slowly up the hill of learning and then over the hump and there is the full joy of knowing and understanding. The pieces now fit nicely together and the whole, whether as a skill or a thought process, is deeply satisfying.

This does not mean that the learning process—the practice—cannot be an interesting adventure, but that there is a special quality that arises out of the accomplished skill. Nor should one think that the satisfaction comes from the fact that one can do this better than others; rather the chief joy comes from the skill itself.

The teacher knows something (more than the learner) of the pitfalls on the learning journey, of the hills, valleys, and dangerous places; some things to do and some to avoid. Or to change the analogy, he knows something of ships and the seas and the winds. In my childhood I knew intimately an expert seaman, from a long line of seamen. He had survived and learned from a dozen wrecks. His experience had spanned the transition from sails to steam. He knew ships, the sea, and sailors. Had I wished to learn the ancient art of seamanship his knowledge and authority would have been strengthening and inspiring.

2. Expert knowledge beyond that of the student not only sustains and steadies the student but also lures him on to learning and the experience that is crucial to learning. The teacher knows

characteristics of places distant in time, space, and thought; he knows legends of heroes and villains from the experience of the race; he knows ways of learning, understanding, and being that are new to the learner; he may have attained a small measure of wisdom, of insight, that enables him to know something of what may happen and of what is unlikely.

Thus he opens doors for the growing, searching mind. He points to paths that lead to faraway and intriguing places. He is an example to the student that the journey is not impossible. He steadies the younger learner for the task before him and gives him confidence. And all of this the learner needs, for human life is a constant illustration of how often man gets lost or takes the wrong roads.

3. The teacher as one who knows exemplifies the fruits of knowing and learning: its uses, its joys, its responsibilities, its limits. The teacher at his best shows that a man can know and know that he knows, and still know that he does not know fully, and respect and be interested in those who know relatively less. Thus he bridges the often ugly and frightening gap between the known and the unknown. For the awkward and beginning learner he makes the difficult and almost impossible seem possible and even easy.

The petty, uneasy, insecure "authority" whose little treasure of knowing is his all to be hoarded and displayed to support a wobbly ego is not at all like the expert who has the unassuming confidence and unconscious sureness of the "one who knows" and whose genuine accomplishment is put in proper perspective, is taken in stride, is a part of a larger whole. The former tends to be pompous, quick to talk about or display his knowledge and skill, or coy, wishing to be wooed into its use. When around such a person, a student feels a rasping difference between the one who knows and the one who doesn't know.

The genuine expert, in contrast, tends to wear his accomplishment lightly and naturally. Lord Chesterfield put the principle

in this quaint way: "Wear your learning, like your watch, in a
private pocket; and do not merely pull it out and strike it merely
to show you have one. If you are asked what o'clock it is, tell it;
but do not proclaim it hourly and unasked like the watchman."[4]
Since the satisfaction is in the accomplishment itself, he is not likely
to be petty either in the display or the withholding of his skill.
Most important for the teacher as one who knows, this attitude
enables the authority to meet the learner naturally as man to man
in mutual respect. Such a teacher neither looks up to the one who
knows more nor down upon the one who knows less, but eye to
eye, on the level. The following account is a classical example of
this attitude: "Emerson knew everything, had read everything.
Moreover, when you asked Emerson a question he looked you
straight in the eye with neither amusement nor condescension, and
answered you as man to man."[5]

Such a teacher builds respect for knowledge, its power, its
limitations, and its relation to human growth. He helps the learner
to appreciate the three great ways of knowing: science, philosophy, inspiration. And perhaps he can show him how these three
ways of learning can and should be partners in man's lifelong and
agelong search to know and to understand.

The teacher's special knowledge and the authority it gives him
are worn lightly like appropriate clothes, or courteous manners,
or words fitly spoken. Empty pride and its ugly child arrogance are
always near at hand. Probably the best safeguard against this
danger is growth in self-understanding and a gradual wholesome
escape from self. Knowledge and its corresponding authority that
have come to serve ego-inflation needs, that have been attained
principally as a defense against deep feelings of inferiority, will
likely be used badly in one's dealing with all associates and especially with students.

Perhaps most important, the learning atmosphere or climate is
characterized by mutual respect and concern. Then the senior
partner in the learning endeavor, the teacher, will not be resented

and feared because of his skill, superior knowledge, and experience but will be loved, honored, and respected. Such an atmosphere in an ego-dominated world is not easy to build and maintain but it can be done.

E. V. P.

Questions and problems for dialogue

1 Does the notion of the teacher as a special authority, as "one who knows," still have real meaning in modern life? Is his knowledge so partial and tentative that he no longer can hope to be considered as "special"?

2 In the best teacher, which should be dominant, which should characterize the personality, the confidence of "knowing" or the humility of "not knowing"?

3 Do you believe the concept of *charisma* or *mana* has real meaning or is it just another myth? Have you had direct experience with this quality?

4 What do you consider the chief dangers of being an expert or of being considered one? Give illustrations.

5 What is your view on the continuing controversy as to whether one who knows his subject well can teach it well?

6 Is the teacher's personality inevitably adversely affected by the fact that he is continuously in the position of knowing more than his students? In your experience, at what levels of education is the effect likely to be more pronounced? Why do you think this is true?

7 Do you feel that you know any one thing (knowledge or a skill) quite well? Analyze your experience in this area and its meaning to you.

8 What do you believe are the distinguishing marks of the genuine expert or authority as compared with the "phony" authority? Give examples.

9 What term would express the central idea of this chapter more adequately than the term "authority"? Why?

10 What is the meaning of the term "being" as used in this chapter? What does this concept have to do with authority?

Exercises
for further learning

1 State the central thesis or thought of this chapter in a paragraph or two. State clearly the main idea.

2 List the *five* best teachers you have had. Try to remember how you felt about them when they were your teachers. Analyze the extent to which they seemed as special authorities to you.

3 Give some concentrated attention to the concept of *charisma, mana,* or *wakan.* Recall the people you have known who seemed to have this quality in considerable degree. Describe your experiences with these persons.

4 Make a list of historical figures that seemed to have *mana* in marked degree.

5 Make a list of cases in which you lost confidence in teachers. Analyze the loss of this confidence. What appeared to be the principal cause?

6 Develop a series of examples of the "corrupting" power of knowledge. Strive to understand what caused the special knowledge to spoil the teacher's personality.

7 Bring to mind the area in your experience where you have had the most confidence, where you have felt most nearly an expert. Describe the specific circumstances in some detail and the influence of this confidence on your behavior.

8 List cases of the times when you have worked with or been on an assignment or task with a "veteran"—one who was experienced and expert. Analyze this experience. Show how it affected your behavior.

9 Make a list of teachers that seemed to you to take a special joy in both knowing and learning. Describe them briefly for yourself and for others.

10 Make the opportunity to observe persons who know something very well, who are recognized as very good in their fields. Study their attitude toward their skills or knowledge. Do they seem humble or arrogant?

Moral education is impossible apart from the habitual vision of greatness. . . . The sense of greatness is the groundwork of morals. We are at the threshold of a democratic age, and it remains to be determined whether the equality of man is to be realized on a high level or a low level.
—*Alfred North Whitehead*

11

A teacher is

an inspirer of vision

The teacher provides a vision of greatness for his students. He perceives their varied and abundant potential as human beings. He believes in the rich possibilities of this human material with which he works. He is inspired by the thought that teaching at its best has always been in essence the educing, releasing, and development of that which is in the learner.

The teacher as a provider of a vision of greatness becomes skillful in communicating to students of all ages this conception of the worth and significance of each individual. Every phase of the educative process comes to contribute to this vision of the greatness of man. Even the routine skills, and the drills that may be necessary to refine them, if properly related to the vision, achieve purpose and meaning and cease to be drudgery. Reading, number, composition, philosophy, literature, science are the living means and the alluring goals that both express and release man's potential.

Perceiving themselves in terms of the varied qualities of their full nature, students rapidly grow toward that perception. Imprisoned by age-old distortions of what they are and what they can be, students perform in terms of those distortions. Hence, perhaps the teacher's most significant function is to provide a vision of greatness.

This conception of the rich potential of man as man is extremely difficult to make clear, meaningful, and convincing. All of us are a part of the history of man. In spite of our best efforts to spring free, we embody in our ways of thinking and even in our deepest assumptions the results of that history, including its major misconceptions. Teachers have not escaped from these historical preconceptions; indeed, they bring them into the classrooms of the world.

Until relatively recent times the whole framework of civilized society rested upon the institution of human slavery.[1] Even where the system of slavery was not so evident and gross, as it was in ancient Rome or the pre-Civil War South, the conceptions of the nature of man were equally degrading and the exploitation almost as gross. By a long process, societies had come to accept and live with a view of man that only a small minority were of worth beyond the worth of other chattels or other things to be used and discarded at will. In general, this notion remained unchallenged in theory until the Renaissance and in practice until the American and French revolutions.

Of course, the seeds from which the change in conception finally came had been sown in the form of ideas and ideals since ancient times. The Hebrew conception of man made in the image of God and some of the teachings of the Hebrew prophets had in them the power to unhinge the conception on which human slavery and exploitation depended. The best thought of classical Greece, the teachings of Jesus and the early Christians, the ideas of the Stoic lawyers of Rome, and many other thinkers expressed attitudes and beliefs that could not be harmonized in the long run with a concept of man that made slavery or its equivalent acceptable. But the change in general thought and in institutions came extremely slowly.

Evidently, we who are teachers cannot become acquainted in great detail or depth with the history of man's thought and institutions.[2] Such understanding would require time, but perhaps more inhibiting is the fact that we are afraid of and tend to be repelled by what that study reveals—especially as it becomes clear that we have not freed ourselves from many crippling misconceptions. Yet it seems to me that honestly facing the facts of where we have been and where we are is necessary to an understanding of many current attitudes that profoundly influence the teacher and teaching.

The point is that to the extent that the teacher at any level brings to the classroom and the educative process the deeply embedded conceptions of man that sustained rigid class distinctions and that have made slavery and gross exploitation possible, to that extent he cannot be a modern teacher; he is still bound by the mentality of slavery. It would be valuable to know how typical teachers from the elementary grades through graduate and professional school conceive the human material with which they work. Eventually research may provide the answer. Perhaps most of us are always looking for the small per cent that we conceive as worthy and able. We find it very difficult to rise to the conception that every individual is and ought to be free and equal, and is capable and worthy of receiving an education that will give that freedom its full meaning. We simply have not in reality escaped the slave mentality, although we may be in the process of freeing ourselves from it. Perhaps a wise man will not be irritably impatient in the face of these conditions: it may be that he should accept the fact that another thousand or two thousand years (assuming that we are moving in that direction) will be required to clean our minds and our institutions of prejudices and misconceptions inherited from the slave- and class-burdened past.

Yet the clear-eyed, deeply seeing teacher cannot be so patient, for he longs to be free of those things that hinder his work. He knows he cannot provide a vision of greatness to his students if he himself does not have that vision. Failing to see what is in man, he tends to perpetuate the slave conception: that a few are capable and worthy of full education; that it is in the nature of things that the worthy few at the apex of the societal structure will always hold their place sustained by the unworthy many. And it should be said, in passing, that an acceptance, also prevalent in our time, of the attitude or mentality of "merit," or meritocracy, in the place of class, or aristocracy, may prove to be more brutal, shortsighted, and conducive to exploitation than the older system. This substitute is probably an attempt, perhaps unconscious, to avoid the change and movement that a basically different conception demands.

Now we must face a fundamental question: What in reality is the nature and potential of the human species—not of a few special individuals but of that huge body of people who made up the slave base of the Roman Empire, who compose the bulk of the population of the present world, who fill the classrooms of the schools? Although the evidence has been accumulating on this all-important question since the beginning of history, and particularly since what is called the rise of the common man in the eighteenth, nineteenth, and twentieth centuries, that evidence is still quite incomplete.

We cannot even begin to review here available general or research evidence. Our limited purpose is to stimulate teachers to open up this intriguing question and to examine it with objective care. What really are the possibilities of this human material in our classrooms? Can we as teachers in honesty give these students a vision of their greatness? Are they really, in the main, fit only for slavery or some modern substitute? Or are they something infinitely more and, if so, what? There are few questions more important for teachers and for the progress of man.

It would be pleasant and profitable to survey the evidence about the nature and potential of man: the evidence from history, philosophy, religion, literature, and particularly from recent research in psychology, anthropology, sociology, and related studies. But it must suffice to present a quotation from an insightful philosopher and psychologist, who was acquainted with much of that evidence, that captures better than any brief statement I know the variety and richness of man's abilities:

The talent for ideas and abstractions, essential for high scholarship, is but one of many lines of mental power. Vigor of imagination, depth of feeling, of sympathy and love for men, sagacity in judging character, intuitive perception of the controlling factors of complex situations (a quality I do not find singled out by psychologists, but central in the genius of leadership), planning ability, eloquence itself as skilled communication of emotion, powers of loyalty and endurance—all of these and various other unmeasurable and unexaminable dimensions of the self go to make up human magnitude.[3]

This then is something of the amount and variety of ability in the classrooms of the world's schools.

Such a conception of man's potential does not imply any sentimental refusal to face the facts. Of course, human beings vary greatly in all of the various abilities and talents. The voice of Marian Anderson, the insight and sagacity of Lincoln, the brilliant talent of Mozart, the intellectual grasp of Plato or Aristotle, the perception and skill of Shakespeare, the mammoth scope of Einstein—these will appear only rarely and for reasons not clear. They are peaks in the range of human ability that do that range honor. We are justly proud of their achievement.

In addition to these special peaks human ability varies greatly. Some learn more quickly than others. Some learn one thing easily and some another. And others for various reasons learn little or almost not at all. Some doubtless have hereditary or prenatal defects; many more probably are hampered by cultural and psychological wounds. All of this and more, we as teachers know.

Yet our central question remains, What is the potential of man as man? Aside from the interesting peaks mentioned above, what is the level of the general range of the mountain?[4] We are urging that it is remarkably high—much higher than our outmoded conceptions of man and his abilities will allow us to believe. The potential seems especially rich in areas not so dependent upon intellectual power as it is usually conceived, such as those emphasized in the quotation from Professor Hocking.

Our point then is that every human being not seriously and fatally damaged has latent within him this great wealth of ability and talent. When we speak of a vision of greatness we mean the awareness of this ability and talent and the sharing of that awareness with students. This sharing does not imply preaching about what children or young people can learn and do, as tempted as we may be to such preaching. It implies rather a deep respect for the latent ability and a humble search for the means of its release and full development.

It is encouraging that the objective awareness of the presence of such ability creates an expectancy that tends to bring it forth. The point is stated beautifully by Cox in speaking of that creative teacher and poet, Robert Frost:

Robert saw through him all right. And he didn't see anything that wasn't there; he was too genuine and clear-seeing to be fooled. But his seeing what was there made it swell like a sun-stirred seed.[5]

When Jesus of Nazareth issued his universal invitation to become a part of the kingdom of God the implication was that all men could rise toward its great requirements, and millions have been stirred by that vision. In another way, the father of the American public schools, Horace Mann, perceived the children of a new nation as being capable and worthy of a common school education, and they and their teachers and the nation rose toward the vision.

There is a considerable literature on the training of animals which depicts the relation of the trainer and the animals. This relation is often almost mystical. In essence, the relation seems to rest upon a keen perception of and a profound respect for the animal's abilities from which arises an atmosphere of mutual respect and confidence that brings remarkable practical results. The same principle applies to a great coach who is able to bring high skill, energy, and concentration from his players. The examples could be multiplied. The point is: the vision (perceiving what is latent and possible) creates the expectancy and growing confidence so fundamental to achievement.

The teacher who respects and loves his material, and perhaps only that teacher, can most effectively bring out or educe its potential. Recently I have been reading of the modern English poet, Robert Graves, and his love of words, their meaning and music.[6] We cannot know for sure but certainly Shakespeare must have loved words, the material of his great art. Accounts of Michelangelo emphasize his almost physical love for the stone in which he worked. A carpenter friend who likes to do significant things with wood told me recently that he felt sure that wood responded better when he respected its special qualities and felt deeply its particular potential. Be that as it may, we can be sure that the teacher who provides a vision of greatness sensitively respects his human material, and that such respect is a great stimulant to growth.

When people are asked to describe the teacher that did the most for them, again and again they mention a teacher, often the only one in their experience, who believed in them, who saw their special talents, not only what they were but even more what they wanted to be and could be. And they began to learn not only in the area of their special interest but in many others.

One of the most interesting and dramatic instances of the significance of a vision of greatness for optimum development is the life of Helen Keller. Her great teacher, Anne Sullivan Macy, did many things for Helen, but perhaps the one crucial to all others was the opening up for this apparently fatally handicapped child vistas of what she could be. At best, in those days, a seriously handicapped girl in a well-to-do home would be cared for in her father's house, perhaps learning through careful tutoring to care somewhat for her personal needs. Anne Sullivan saw the matter differently and Helen came to see herself differently. To the question, "Must this girl remain a pitied invalid in her father's home?" Miss Sullivan answered "No."

From the stirring occasion when the blind and deaf child by the means of running water and matchless teaching perceived that things in the environment had names and she could learn them, through reading for her degree at Radcliffe on to great books and lecture tours, her teacher sustained and enriched that vision. Helen Keller grew steadily in terms of the vision and toward its realization.

Miss Keller is a world-famous case, perhaps with special natural endowments in ability and talent. Instances of "ordinary" relatively unknown people are, in a sense, even more convincing evidence of the relation of development to vision or clear perception of possibilities. Careful study might reveal that the real difference between those individuals who surmount very difficult conditions to realize a good measure of their potential and those who are bogged down in and destroyed by those conditions lies here: the former by one means or another are given a vision of what they might be; the latter flounder without hope.

Many other specific cases from my personal experience come to mind. Often, it seems, perhaps most often, the vision or ideal is given by a mother, but frequently also by relatives, friends, and especially by teachers. Recently a Negro student talked to me of his case. He was reared in the slums of a huge city, supported by his abandoned mother and a little aid from the government. He has a Master's degree from a distinguished university, has a very responsible position, and is presently working successfully toward his doctorate. We were wondering how and why he had achieved so well under such circumstances when so many in like circumstances are destroyed. The early years in school through the first attempts at college had been largely floundering, semi-failure, and close flirting with delinquency. Then there was an awakening, best described as a clear vision of what he could do, and after that there was steady and sometimes remarkable progress. Of course, there is great danger of oversimplifying the factors in a case of this kind.

The cases from among persecuted minorities are most evident because they are so dramatic. It should be said that there is danger in providing a vision of greatness, for a dream unrealized can be deeply frustrating and even embittering. But the point is that there seems to be a close relation between vision and sustained progress toward a goal.

This seeing of human potential does not mean a blindness to limitations. The teacher should see clearly and should report truthfully. Failure to see and to deal with reality is always dangerous. However, most of us perhaps have learned to be less dogmatic about the limitations of people when their purpose is clear, vision is high, and motivation is intense. We are more hesitant to say you cannot run, or play the piano, or be a doctor when we have so often found ourselves dramatically wrong. Nevertheless, there are limitations and the teacher helps the student to examine them and to face them when necessary. Doubtless some of these are simply a lack of what we call ability or talent, but probably more are a failure in concentration and motivation. Our knowledge is so thin in this area that it is unwise even to speculate.

A part of the complication arises from the complex nature of ability and its manifestation. A national amateur tennis champion will serve as an illustration. His interest in the game and the prodigious amount of practice he did from childhood were astounding. Did his talent stimulate and sustain the interest and practice? Or did the interest and practice bring out the ability? Really we do not know, but we do know that a clear vision of greatness and a strong persistent determination to achieve will often produce what seem to be miracles in achievement.[7] Surely vision—a perception of high achievement in an area—is closely related to the concentrated work so necessary to the release and development of potential abilities.

In the day-to-day routine of teaching, especially as it is organized and stereotyped in the formal schools, the teacher is in great danger of losing his own vision. Pushed by arbitrary, seemingly meaningless demands, surrounded by noise and clutter, frustrated by the problems of discipline which reflect the phoniness of much of formal education and the stresses of a confused urban civilization, urged to play a role that destroys the optimum learning situation, beset by vexing personal problems—under these rather "normal" conditions the teacher may be hard pressed to keep his vision of the central meaning of teaching and of the potential greatness of the material with which he works. This is a great danger, for the teacher will not be able to provide a vision which he himself has lost; he cannot do this job from a base of cynicism.

There are numerous sources of the vision of greatness to which the beleaguered teacher may turn. Only a few can be mentioned as examples. Perhaps the most potent source for many of us is the literature of the world, including legend and mythology and especially poetry.[8]

It is interesting to note that much of modern literature, apparently disenchanted by man's recent tragedies and reacting against a soft romanticism, often fails to perceive or present a vision of the potential of man.[9] The following statement of William Faulkner, the Nobel prize-winning modern American novelist, is almost typical of the attitude toward man of current distinguished writers: ". . . life is a phenomenon but not a novelty, the same frantic steeplechase toward nothing everywhere and man stinks the same stink no matter where in time. . . ."[10] Many observers of the current scene feel that may be an ominous sign for modern man for, in the main, man's vision has been sustained by the perception of his creative artists. Sir Arthur Quiller-Couch expressed this concern in this way:

. . . I am at a loss what to do with a fashion of morose disparagement; of sneering at things long by catholic consent accounted beautiful; of scorning at "Man's unconquerable mind" and hanging up (without benefit of laundry) our common humanity as a rag on a clothes-line. Be it allowed that these present times are dark. Yet what are our poets of use—what are they *for*—if they cannot hearten the crew with auspices of daylight?[11]

History is a useful and inspiring source. Often the account is uncomplimentary of man, but seen with perspective the story gives an inspiriting picture. For example, Sir Winston Churchill's *History of the English-Speaking People* provides perspective and lifts one out of the disconcerting morass depicted by the morning newspapers. Then there is religion, perhaps the chief source of a vision of greatness; and there are science, art, music, and much more.[12]

The teacher who would be skillful and balanced in his vision of man will find the sources, not least those inside his own personal experience, that most effectively renew and sustain his vision. It must be said that this implies no sentimental blindness to the dark realities of current life or the history of man's actions and ideas. The best can be fully perceived only when the worst has been squarely seen. This renewal of vision implies a steady, balanced view that reveals the full truth about man: his past, his present, his possible future; his strange weaknesses and distortions, his abilities and special talents; his cooperation and love at their best and his sordid hatred and blind cruelties. This renewal will be honest, genuine, and will have integrity. And from it will arise in a steady progression of new births a clearer and clearer perception of the nature and potential of this strange creature made in the image of God.

Our discussion has been limited to the nature and potential of man. The temptation is great to extend the consideration to the animal and plant world. A balanced perception of the potential of man does not bring arrogance, but deep humility in the presence of the rich powers of the whole expanse of the living world, not to speak of the wider universe. I am moved by the intelligence, style, grace, and apparent joy of two house wrens building their nest near my study. Are their abilities really so inferior to those of the builder of a skyscraper or a freeway? Perhaps. Man with his remarkable potential is a small and humble part of a larger whole. He is thus a brother to all that lives, each of the varied manifestations of life expressing an aspect of that larger whole in which our vision of greatness is rooted. Doubtless the perception of this larger truth caused Albert Schweitzer to emphasize so greatly his notion of "reverence for life."[13] Thus the sensitive teacher may extend his thought about the nature and abilities of man far beyond individual and historical man.

One final thought remains. To be best understood, a vision of greatness must be related to the concept of tragedy. Human life is in essence, and perhaps in its very nature will always be, a tragedy. That is, the dream or vision will always outrun the achievement. This yawning, painful gap between what we see we could be and should be and what we are will remain as long as we are man. For as accomplishment approaches vision it is the nature of man to extend and broaden the vision. Probably no amount of muckraking and cynicism in any generation will alter substantially this quality in man. He is a dreamer, a seer of visions, and the most powerful of those visions is that of his own potential and its full realization. This painful tragic gap between dream and achievement does not discourage or dismay the teacher. Rather he is encouraged and sustained by the fact that the tension created by this gap is probably the mainspring of all growth.

E. V. P.

Questions and problems for dialogue

1 What is the meaning of the term "greatness" as used in this chapter? Can you think of other terms that might be better?

2   Is the mentality of slavery still dominant in the world? In our nation? If you think so, why? If not, why?

3   Have you encountered any new evidence about the nature and variety of human ability?

4   As you see it, what are the chief dangers of giving ordinary students "a vision of greatness"?

5   On the basis of such evidence as you have, what is essentially your theory or view of human abilities?

6   If there are only a relatively few peaks in human ability (giants in the race of men), in what sense can a vision of greatness be honestly provided for the mass of men and women?

7   In your judgment, is ability changed by high expectancy on the part of teachers or does the person under such expectancy simply manifest more fully the ability he has?

8   Is it true that teachers tend to develop a cynical attitude toward the ability of students with whom they work? If so, why? What do you think is the difference between a sculptor's attitude toward stone or a carpenter's toward wood and a teacher's attitude toward people?

9   How much of what Helen Keller became do you believe was due to "Teacher's" vision for her? What do you think would have happened if Miss Sullivan had not come to the Keller home?

10 What do you think of the theory of tragedy stated in the last paragraph of this chapter? Is life in this sense a tragedy?

Exercises
for further learning

1   State in general in a paragraph or two your conception of a "great" man or woman. Share your statement with others in and out of the profession of teaching.

2   Interview five to ten people who have or do not have very much formal education in an attempt to learn their conceptions of human potential. Watch for evidence of what has been called a "slave mentality." Keep a careful record of your findings.

3   State briefly your theory as to who should have a "full" education in a modern industrial democracy. Defend your theory.

4   Study with care the quotation from Professor Hocking. Evaluate the statement (how much truth is in it) and indicate some of its implications for modern education.

5 It has been suggested that the learning of a language (English or Chinese) requires an ability equal to that needed to learn advanced mathematics. Evaluate this proposition and indicate some of its implications for learning and for human ability.

6 Interview a few people who have distinguished themselves in some area (athletics, music, acting, politics, etc.). Try to learn when and how they got the notion that they could distinguish themselves.

7 Develop a list of examples of people who it seems to you have been hurt or damaged by unrealistic goals for themselves.

8 Think back over your life and try to determine when and how you settled on the idea that you could finish college and be a teacher.

9 List five to ten best-selling books with which you are familiar. What conception do they give of man? Do the same for examples of modern art. What thoughts do these observations suggest to you?

10 Make a list of ten teachers you know very well. Try to put them on a scale indicating the extent to which routine demands seem to have damaged or destroyed their "vision."

Unless society is permeated, through and through, with
routine, civilization vanishes.
—*Alfred North Whitehead*

12

A teacher is

a doer of routine

The teacher does with some skill and a degree of
abandon a multitude of recurring and sometimes burdensome routines. If these activities are poorly done or neglected, they can
seriously harm the teacher's effectiveness in all of his other roles.
Further, if these routines become a distasteful and resented part
of the teacher's work, they may undermine and distort his general
attitude toward teaching. For example, in formal education relatively complex records are kept. If the teacher resents or neglects
this chore, his general effectiveness will be damaged.

The principle we are considering here is applicable to every aspect of life. A large portion of any person's activities in a complex society is made up of routines. This is necessarily so for the intricately interrelating activities of any civilization require a large groundwork of dependable order which is possible only because of the network of routine. Many people, both adults and children, seem to resent these routines. They long for unrestricted freedom, and may fail to perceive that such freedom and spontaneity are rapidly destroyed unless there is a measure of routine and a corresponding restraint.

Every profession and even the more personal aspects of individual life have their body of routine skills which must be mastered and done with regularity. As illustrations of professions let us look at two of the oldest. Young persons interested in the practice of medicine may be inclined to take a romantic attitude toward the healing art. They may wish to overlook the prolonged training needed to get the information and the beginning skills fundamental to diagnosis and treatment of disease. The foundation work in the sciences (chemistry, biology, physics, anatomy, etc.) and the varied clinical skills all require demanding routine learning. And the situation does not change after one enters practice. A large portion of the doctor's work is composed of careful attention to detail which basically is recurring and relatively routine. The moving, inspiring aspects of healing, the large events in practice certainly come, but in the main they arise out of a huge plateau of demanding, day-to-day routine.

The same is true of the ministry: prolonged study needed to master the necessary background material; extended practice to refine the skills and knowledge, and work them into the mature, apparently effortless performance of the master workman. Even the fuller development of the rich inner life so basic to the minister's effectiveness is not the easy routine-free accomplishment it may appear to be. That poise, that inner peace, that serenity— these powerful and appealing qualities are likely the result of hours of meditation, prayer, listening, and painful inner probing. The point is even clearer in the case of the polished, informed, interesting sermon. The structure, the meaning, the illustrative matter seem to appear almost without effort as a beautiful whole. But all rests upon and arises out of a large body of knowledge and skill, as well as from the deep inner qualities of the man.

Perhaps the point is clear, but it is so important for the teacher that two other very commonplace illustrations must be given. First, that of a home. Few things are more satisfying and appealing than a home properly maintained. There are the beautiful, relaxed, healing, and growth-producing moments or even hours in a good home. But every experienced person knows that such a home is possible only because someone is able and willing to do the mountain of routine work that makes the home situation possible. The house must be kept clean and in some order, clothes and dishes washed, meals planned and prepared, buying done, and on and on and on. And this leaves unmentioned the work needed to bring in the absolutely necessary income.

The other illustration is that of an advanced student. Again and again, very fine prospective advanced students will come to an office for counseling, discouraged and perhaps disgusted. They are losing their way in the flood of routine that stands between them and the degree they want. They often say that they like great ideas, and are eager to learn them and to apply them to life's problems. But all this information, these hurdles of languages and examinations, these endless papers, this review of lifeless research frustrate and threaten to destroy them. Whether or not some of this routine could be reduced or eliminated in advanced study is a problem we cannot pursue here; our point is that advanced scholarly study and research are and seem always to have been in great part routine, often amounting almost to drudgery.

These illustrations are given to drive home the understanding that a large proportion of human activity, especially professional activity, is and perhaps must be routine—recurring, relatively uninteresting, often highly fatiguing work. The teacher faces this basic fact and strives toward the attitudes and skills that enable him to do these routines with style—in such a way that they become a means of growth and effectiveness rather than a burden and frustration. The first step toward this goal is to accept the fact that apparently in the very nature of things a large proportion of every part of life will be of this routine type; and that such inspiring, "sacred" peaks as may appear will arise out of, and perhaps only out of, a plateau of routine, "profane" activities well done. Only then can one cease to waste his energy scratching irritably against the proportion of the routine to the creative so characteristic of life; and perhaps he can learn to refrain from whining about what great things he would do were he free from endless routine.

Anything like a full list of the routines a teacher does would be discouraging to the student in training for teaching or to the new teacher. There is danger that the routine demands will seem overwhelming and will blur and distort the vision of the more generally appealing aspects of the teacher's work. Yet it is important that the young teacher bring these routines to conscious focus and that the more experienced teacher keep them in proper perspective. Developing skill in them will probably best be achieved in actual practice on the job, beginning with student teaching and continuing through in-service training during the early years of teaching.

Here is a partial, randomly selected, illustrative list of the more common routines important for all levels of teaching: (1) Being prompt at beginning and ending of periods, for appointments, etc. (2) Keeping records and reports that meet standards of care, accuracy, and time deadlines. (3) Reading, evaluating, and returning student work. (4) Regular responsible class attendance. (5) Organization of class periods, days, semesters. (6) Setting deadlines for student work. (7) Establishing rules and procedures of group activity, including group discussion. (8) Holding parent and/or student conferences. (9) Arranging classroom seating. (10) Taking records of student attendance. (11) Becoming acquainted with students. (12) Preparation of learning materials—outlines, charts, bibliographies, audiovisual materials, etc. (13) Attendance at meetings—faculty, committee, parent, alumni, etc. (14) Providing optimum room condition and appearance. (15) Administering necessary learning drill to refine skills. (16) Planning of special programs in class, field trips, etc. (17) Care in personal grooming.

The climate of learning so vital to the most productive and creative teaching situation depends in considerable degree upon the finesse, the style, with which these routines are done. Carried on with a light touch, they are almost unnoticed. Yet they produce the order and general confidence fundamental to maximum freedom and spontaneity. Clumsily or poorly done, they become a deadening end in themselves, absorbing the major effort of the teacher and killing the interest of students. Neglected, such a spirit of disorder and lack of general respect may arise as to make "discipline" the chief concern and burden of the teacher.

There is an important relation between careful organization and routine and freedom, understanding and creativeness. The relation is complex, difficult to understand and to describe. In general, it may be said that a floor of order based upon accepted routine is a necessary condition of freedom, understanding, and creativity. If the basic order is not routinely provided there is no energy or opportunity for the trying of alternatives—the essence of freedom, of deeper understanding, and of creativity.[1]

Illustrations come to mind. One evidently has the greatest freedom in traffic when the rules are specific, clear and generally observed; accepted and widely observed law is the necessary condition for the optimum degree of freedom for the citizen; rules make a game possible and of interest and meaning to players and spectators. The principle then is that a certain degree of order is necessary to optimum freedom.

But the apparent simplicity of this principle is dangerously deceptive. The balance between order and freedom that is optimum for learning is extremely difficult to know in a particular case and even more difficult to achieve. The teacher because of temperament and background or training will be tempted to go to extremes: he will be in danger of taking a doctrinaire position for "freedom" at any cost or for "order" whatever the price. There seems to be no easy once-and-for-all solution to this conflict. In each class period, in each course, for each group of students, in the institution where he works, the teacher seeks throughout his professional career for that balance which provides a core of order around which a maximum freedom and the resulting thought and creativity can flourish. The teacher will never be satisfied and certainly not smug in this area. At best, he will be working toward the desired balance.

To praise the value of desirable routine is not to overlook its dangers. Organizations, especially large ones, are dependent upon effective routine. The unexpected or variation from the regular path disturbs or threatens smooth operation. It is natural therefore that administrators tend to overvalue routine at the expense of the flexible, fluid atmosphere so necessary to the best teaching. As school organizations grow in size and complexity there is a danger that more and more time-consuming routine tasks will be imposed from above until the teacher has neither the time nor the energy to do well his central tasks. Records, reports, meetings —all the varied machinery of an organization—can become burdensome.

The goals of the teacher and of the administrator are (1) to keep the routines to a minimum, (2) to see that they contribute to the large educational goals—that they serve and release rather than enslave and confine, (3) to put necessary routines in proper perspective by understanding their vital relation to the purposes and processes of teaching. If these goals in respect to routine can be achieved to a reasonable degree, then the smooth routinization of that which should be routine will free the teacher for thought and creativity where these are possible and important. If a person had to give thought to or make a decision about every step as he walked, each breath, and each heartbeat, he would not be free to ramble with abandon nor see much on his walk. The fact that these bodily processes are automatic is the foundation of his freedom to see and feel.

A philosophy of life tends to serve the same purpose for the personality. Gradually the person develops a frame of reference, a set of standards or values, in terms of which he usually behaves. Thus the reasonably healthy person does not need to make an agonizing decision as to whether or not he will steal as he browses in a store, whether or not he will spit on the floor, whether or not he will be courteous in a traffic jam or in line at the supermarket—these and innumerable other decisions are made almost automatically in accordance with a basic philosophy. If each such decision had to be considered and thought through, ordinary living would become very nearly impossible, an exhausting burden. The personality has a desirable freedom simply because most decisions are routinely made.

There is, of course, great danger that the ways of the personality (or the activities of the teacher) will become fixed and rigid, and genuine growth will stop. A well-developed philosophy of life does make many decisions and actions relatively automatic, but a band of flexibility is kept and carefully protected. This is the growing edge where careful thought is given and decisions are made after consideration of many alternatives. Effectiveness and health of personality are perhaps more dependent upon the proper balance between a stable core of principle and a flexible area of growth than upon any other single factor.

It becomes clear then that the teacher who is able to understand the significance of routine in teaching, who comes to accept the large place it has in all activity, who is able to relate it properly to large, meaningful goals, and who can use it with style and grace is in position to demonstrate one of life's most useful principles. The learning situation produced and guided by such a teacher comes to have a quality of ease and freedom which arises from relaxed order. In such a learning environment there is a minimum of whining, of complaining against the routines, even the drudgery, necessary to the larger goals. To live in such an environment during the school years is to have the opportunity to learn by example one of life's most valuable lessons: to achieve the proper balance between the "profane" (the exacting routine demands) and the "sacred" (the deeper, larger, more meaningful activities) in life.

E. V. P.

Questions and problems for dialogue

1 Is it really necessary that a large proportion of one's time and energy be given to routine? Could not the amount of recurring routine be greatly reduced in most aspects of living?

2 Does not the burden of the routine demands undermine one's ability to do the creative meaningful aspects of one's work?

3 Does teaching seem to involve more or less burdensome routine than other professions? Why would this be true?

4 Why, in your judgment, do people so often resent recurring, routine responsibilities? What makes them so distasteful?

5 Is it possible for routine chores to become meaningful and interesting through their relation to more meaningful tasks? If so, give some thought to specific suggestions as to how this may be achieved.

6 Are routines and order so closely related and interdependent as seems to be suggested in this chapter? Can there be order without routine?

7 How dependent is a complex organization such as a school system upon efficiently done routine?

8 In your experience have school administrators seemed to overemphasize the importance of routine?

9 What is the relation between smooth-running routine and effective morale or discipline in a classroom?

10 What are the advantages and the dangers in a person's making a large proportion of the decisions of daily living in terms of a relatively fixed set of principles or standards?

Exercises for further learning

1 Make a relatively full list of the areas of normal living that involve the relation between what might be called the routine (the "profane") and the creative or thoughtful (the "sacred"). Give thought to this relation, beginning with those areas mentioned as examples in the text.

2 Examine your own attitude toward a variety of the routines you must do regularly, beginning perhaps with simple routines of personal grooming. How do you approach them? Do they relate consciously to the "larger" goals they support?

3 Interview a doctor, a lawyer, a minister or priest that you respect for the quality of his work. Strive to determine the proportion of his life that is taken up with recurring routine tasks. Undertake to learn how he handles routine.

4 Make a list of the most thoughtful, creative people, other than teachers, you have known. Study with care the way they seem to deal with the routines involved in their work.

5 Do the same as in No. 4 with teachers you have known.

6 Recall the instances in your educational experiences where morale broke down and disturbance was destructive. Try to determine if the skills of the teacher in doing routine seemed to be involved.

7 The ancient Greeks were fond of saying that freedom could be achieved and maintained only if it were self-limited. What do you think of this idea? What is its meaning for education? You might try your hand at writing a brief paper on this theme.

8 Study carefully the illustrative list given in the text of the routines done by a teacher. Divide them into those that could be done by an assistant or clerk and those that must be done by the classroom teacher.

9 Interview an administrator: principal, superintendent, assistant superintendent, etc. Study this individual's attitude toward routines and their relation to the work of the school.

10 Organize a dialogue or a forum with some of your friends to explore the relation between law or order and freedom. When does law threaten freedom and when does it protect and promote it?

For everything there is a season, and a time for every matter under heaven: a time to be born and a time to die; a time to plant, and a time to pluck up what is planted; a time to kill and a time to heal; a time to break down and a time to build up.
—*Ecclesiastes 3:1-2*

13

A teacher is

a breaker of camp

The teacher is a breaker of camp, a mover-on. He helps the learners to leave the old that the new may be experienced. The teacher as a breaker of camp strives to know in the case of each learner what beliefs and habits he clings to that now obstruct progress, and he helps the student to remove them or leave them for more appropriate ways. To carry out this function the teacher must perceive what is useless and perhaps harmful at a particular stage of development, and also what might be useful and beneficial.

Teacher and students working together learn the priceless art

of relieving the personality of that which has served its purpose
and of replacing it with what the present demands. This process
becomes a way of life for both teacher and taught. Steadily they
learn to practice with balance and wisdom the ancient philosophy
from the Sanskrit:

> Listen to the Exhortation of the Dawn!
>   Look to this Day!
> For it is Life, the very Life of Life.
> In its brief course lie all the Verities
>   and Realities of your Existence:
>   The Bliss of Growth,
>   The Glory of Action,
>   The Splendor of Beauty.
> For Yesterday is but a Dream,
> And To-morrow is only a Vision;
> But To-day well-lived makes every
>   Yesterday a Dream of Happiness,
> And every To-morrow a Vision of Hope.
> Look well therefore to this Day!
> Such is the Salutation of the Dawn.

One can "look well to this Day" only if he has dealt effectively
with the idols of his past—if he has transmuted them into that
which enriches the present and prepares for the future.

As the personality grows from birth to maturity, it develops certain fixed points around which growth takes place. Doubtless one
of the earliest of these is the mother or the mother-substitute. In a
sense, after birth she takes the place physically and psychologically
of the stable condition for growth—the womb—which provides for
the prenatal child.

In the prenatal life of the child perhaps we have the epitome of
the principle we wish to understand in this chapter. For this stage
of development the mother's body is the optimum place for the
growing child. If he is pushed from this "home" too soon, he will
be hurt; if he lingers there too long, he will be damaged or destroyed. Probably we can say that the developing child "wants"
or needs to be born and at the same time he does not wish to

leave the safety, the simplicity, and the comfort of the prenatal
state for a new and danger-ridden experience. This kind of conflict is characteristic of every stage and every aspect of life. There
is the longing to stay with the familiar old, and the even more
urgent and persistent longing to move toward the new and unknown.

The principle holds equally for the infant becoming a more
independent child, the child on the verge of adolescence, the
adolescent becoming an adult, the young adult taking up the
demands of maturity, the man of late maturity entering old age,
the old facing death. The same is true of nations, churches, business organizations, educational institutions, and probably even
civilizations.[1] Enthralled and enslaved at a point in development
and unable to experience the new birth required by the new
demands of changed conditions, individuals or institutions may
destroy themselves or be destroyed. As is the case with the unborn
child, in each phase of life the need to stay is strong; the need to
go on is usually stronger.

The personality in each aspect of development has its special
ways of dealing with the demands of reality that are more or less
effective in their time and place. When because of the changing
demands of growth they no longer serve well the new needs of the
person they become what we may call idols; they are remnants
or remains of that which was once an important aspect of truth,
believed or embodied, but which now has lost its significance and
meaning.

Every learner at every stage of his education, perhaps even of
his whole life, is in this deep conflict. He wishes to go out to the
world of new experience which requires new ideas, habits, and
skills. At the same time he wishes to hedge himself around with
the ways that have served him so well in the past. These old ways
(beliefs and behavior) were once alive, satisfying, and appropriate. It seems so foolishly wasteful to leave them for the untried
new. Often when the forward movement is made, the past or a
part of it is kept as a symbol of safety just as one preserves

ribbons from childhood parties, pennants from college, or trophies from one's special achievements. A few of these as remembrances have a place but too many can clutter the whole house and give it the tone of a graveyard.

Yet this process of leaving the old and taking up the new is subtle and complex. It is not that these idols were bad; rather they were the very essence of life in their time and place. Indeed, they may have been very good, serving well an important need. Because the child cannot now linger fondly at his mother's breast does not mean surely that this nursing was bad; because the mature man does not now engage in defensive rebellion does not mean that this behavior at adolescence may not have played an important part in the establishment of wholesome independence.

The personality is formed essentially in this way: (1) ways of behaving which are the organism's best possible response in terms of its needs and the prevailing environment are developed; (2) gradually, and sometimes not so gradually, both the needs and the demands of the environment change; (3) the responses previously developed that were reasonably effective become less effective and even harmful; (4) the personality continues to embody all the ways that have been used in the past; (5) yet all these modes of behavior are constantly reworked to meet evolving needs and demands; (6) under this constant pressure the evolving personality develops what one psychologist called "a style of life"—a characteristic way of dealing with all of life's problems, including himself;[2] (7) this style of life tends to become more fixed or crystallized as time passes, and thus the personality becomes more rigid or inflexible.

This picture of the nature and development of human personality would be extremely dark and discouraging except for two powerful facts: (1) the innate need to grow and (2) the powerful hunger for experience that is the means of this growth toward the fulfillment of the self. Except in the case of serious pathology these two forces are sufficiently strong to keep the personality moving and to some extent flexible, at least up to what may be called physiological and psychological maturity. Indeed, there is considerable evidence that under optimum conditions the human personality might remain flexible, alive, and growing, through to the deteriorations of senility; but this eventuality would require a special quality of education and of society.

One other psychological process must be mentioned. Anywhere along the journey of personality development, the organism may lose its confidence and refuse to move forward. This process is most evident in advanced pathology because in this advanced stage the major outlines of the condition become clear. For example, a pathetic pathology frequently appears in late adolescence. For reasons not yet clear the personality cannot make the rather drastic step from childhood to adulthood, and in response to inner and outer demands to make this move it retreats into earlier ways of behaving and develops bizarre symptoms that seem to defend the personality against the new unmanageable demands. In our present state of knowledge, this condition may develop into a relatively chronic pathology that is extremely difficult to heal.

This type of pathology illustrates and makes clear a highly significant principle in all development, namely, that there is a strong tendency for the personality to fix upon a belief or a mode of behavior which hinders wholesome growth rather than opening the way and contributing to it. Thus a major function of the teacher at all levels is to keep the process of development going forward. Very nearly the essence of the best education is that which enables the learner to so deal with the all-important present that he can handle effectively the immediate future that is forever becoming that present. There are essentially two choices here: (1) life and growth; (2) attempted crystallization, death, and deterioration.

In a deep and important sense, death is an aspect of life. Unless the old form disintegrates and disappears the new cannot arise. This principle is illustrated in every manifestation of life. The seed must fall into the ground and give up itself (die) before the life within it can take new form; the old leaves must drop off before the new ones of spring come; animals must die or the old ones would literally cover the earth. Even in the individual organism there is a continuous decay and renewal. Hence it is not death that is bad; what is harmful is the refusal to accept the verdict that the old has served its purpose and must give way to or be transformed into the new.

Good education and effective teachers are, or strive to be, on the side of growth and life. But teachers are themselves personalities and hence a part of the process we have been describing; they are "a part of all that they have met" and in various ways drag remnants of a no longer appropriate past into the living present. Education as an institution is even more subject to stultifying crystallizations which are defenses of its procedures; it drags with it also innumerable ways of doing things that were once appropriate and effective (the best available at that time) but have become a hindrance to its chief purposes. It follows therefore that teachers and organized education oftentimes find themselves on the side of crystallization rather than life and growth. We believe it need not be so.

The teacher in his natural eagerness to be on the side of life may be tempted to seek oversimplified, all-or-none, drastic, too-easy solutions to this very complex part of his work. Evidently this kindergarten child needs to leave the warm nest of his home and the steadying presence of his mother and to quit these baby ways, so the teacher may feel he should do it and be done with it and no nonsense. Or the idealistic early adolescent girl needs to know more of the selfishness and ugliness so common in the world; she has dozens of idols that must be broken, or remade, and the sooner she gets on with the process the better. Perhaps the worst offenders in this area are college and university teachers. Young people often come to college with beliefs and modes of behavior that have taken shape in a provincial and perhaps over-protected environment and hence have not been carefully examined. Many college teachers make almost a profession of crudely and irresponsibly crushing these idols. Strangely enough they often do not seem to feel any responsibility for helping the students in the vital transitions involved in this phase of growth.

At every stage of development the stability of the personality is dependent upon a core of belief and behavior that is relatively fixed and dependable. This stable core or center is surrounded by a flexible periphery or growing edge that is in immediate contact with the environment. In the best growth this flexible band is the trying ground for the new which is being steadily assimilated into the core, and thus remaking it to meet inner and outer demands. The sudden shattering of this center or foundation from which wholesome growth and change can proceed endangers the health and effectiveness of the personality. The inevitable result is the development of some kind of defense for the integrity of the individual. In general, these defenses (these coping efforts) may be of a retreating or an attacking type, but in actual life they take an almost infinite variety of forms. The important point is that when the demands on the organism or personality are drastically and persistently more than he can handle with his present behavior equipment, his efforts to find answers will be desperate and often compulsive. That is, the methods of behavior are likely to be ineffective for the present and harmful to future growth.

The thoughtful teacher aware of this danger takes great care as to how idols are broken and new or wider truths presented. The kindergartner must make his transition, but the important professional question is how it can be most wisely made. The provincial over-protected college freshman surely must examine his narrowly based beliefs and habits, but again the question is how can it be done so as not seriously to disturb the stable center of the personality that is crucial to further growth.

A corresponding and equally serious evil is the allowing of the learner to stay too long in the nest—encouraging and protecting him too long in one stage of his development. Not wishing to risk the pain and possible damage of too sudden breaking of idols, the teacher may go to the other extreme and refuse to assist the students to break them. He may rationalize by saying that "life will take care of this problem" or "disillusionment will come soon enough without my aiding it."

Here, as almost always, there is no easy solution for the teacher. He seeks a precarious balance between too soon and too late, between too much and too little. In truth the greatness of his profession arises from the baffling complexity of his tasks. So the teacher in the case of every student (and in the case of himself) searches for the optimum use of the old and the optimum acceptance of the new: that which is best for this person at this time.

The figure of "the idol" we have been using in this discussion is actually not very good. For the best development of the personality, the old ways are not in a meaningful sense "broken" or discarded but are assimilated into the growing whole. The old is in reality not repudiated nor destroyed but fulfilled. There is then a wholesome continuity in growth rather than drastic, jerky breaks. For example, the developing boy begins to perceive that his father is not the paragon of perfection the small child perceived him to be. This broadened perception need not mean that the boy no longer believes in fathers or in the ideal of manhood; rather he develops a view of the father that retains the truth of the earlier perception but is enriched by wider truth. Another example is the child's assimilation of various myths, such as Santa Claus. He does not as a rule awake suddenly to the stark fact that "there is no Santa Claus," but begins to see that the concept that this myth represents is broader and deeper and richer than his childish conception. The growing child need not be embittered by this transition, nor discard the imaginative quality of his earlier perceptions.

One other illustration must suffice, i.e., that of religious faith. The beliefs and practices of religion are extremely complex. They embody deep insights and profound truths, but often these insights and truths are propagated through and are intricately interrelated with relatively faulty and perhaps outmoded organizations.[3] Also, they may be couched in language that no longer expresses their essence. The student who needs to move from a conception of God made in the small image of man to a conception more nearly appropriate to the nature of Ultimate Reality does not need to suddenly throw overboard his earlier beliefs and all that accompanied them. Instead, he may build his new beliefs on the foundation of the older ones.

Such, in my judgment, is the nature of wholesome growth. Of course, this growth will not be always smooth and peaceful. Even with the best guidance it will be painful and often stormy. Not a few of us and of our students will lose the way, fall far short of potential, or even be destroyed. One thinks of mental sickness, delinquency, crime, alcoholism, and other ways men take in their attempt to deal with life's demands. But one thinks too of the better roads men take, and we can be inspired by a few who find ways that befit the best in man.

There are many important things the teacher can do to keep the process of growth moving, but let us examine four as illustrations. First, he can be understandingly available. As the conflict between staying and moving on becomes acute the student will both consciously and unconsciously wish for and seek someone with whom to share his problem. This twelve-year-old girl likes her pets, her play clothes, her free ways, but she begins to sense, probably within herself and certainly from without, that she will soon be in a different world with different demands. If there is a fine relationship of mutual respect between her and her teacher, she may be able to talk the problem over with him on a person-to-person level. By this means she may get some of the perspective and strength she needs for the move. This point is very well made in the great book, *Islandia*, in these words:

> But we in Islandia believe in a friend's making himself manifest, even though he says nothing. So friends have a way of suddenly appearing. I have appeared.[4]

Secondly, the teacher strives to provide a breadth of experience that will enable the student to evaluate where he is and what he is in terms of where he has been and what he has been and what he is about to be. In other words, breadth of experience is probably the surest means towards the self-understanding and increased perspective necessary to a going out to the new. Evidently this experience must be wisely suited to the maturity level and special needs of the student, else it may confuse and baffle, making the desired progress even more difficult. As a rule, if the growing personality can be given through reading and direct activity a variety of appropriate experiences, the natural tendency toward growth will do the rest. There are times, of course, when the student will resist the needed extension of his experience, and then the teacher seeks wise, appropriate means to lead him out.

Also, the teacher is a "swinger." The term is taken from that excellent little book by Sidney Cox about Robert Frost.[5] Among other things, a swinger is one who moves from one position to another, especially in the area of ideas. If an idea is in vogue he is inclined to examine it and call it in question. If after his questioning and counter-arguments the students move to his position, he moves over to another and looks at the problem from another point of view. Thus students accustom themselves to the process of looking at things freely and frankly from many angles.

This swinging does not mean that the teacher has no position of his own or that he is hesitant to present it. Rather it means that he as teacher is always ready to present the other side of the question. Or to put the matter another way, the teacher is an ever-present and effective ingredient in the eternal dialogue, the on-going exchange of ideas. This process of free and ardent interchange of ideas and points of view is perhaps man's most effective means of refining his ideas and of safeguarding against false notions. The classroom from the earliest grades through the graduate school is an arena for such dialogue. The teacher is an expert in this process believing earnestly with one of his fellow teachers that "the unexamined life is not worth living." Yet the teacher is eager to adjust the level and quality of the dialogue to the growth needs of his students. His questions and presentation of the "opposite" or other positions must not be such as to undermine confidence and drive the student member of the dialogue from the field. This continuous dialogue is beautifully designed to keep the student on the move in his development.

Finally, the teacher is a constant student of the drama of human development. Through wide reading, observation, and his own personal experience he achieves a growing understanding of the cycle of human life. He tries to see the relation among all its stages and phases from birth to old age and death. As a professional in the matchless art of the education of man he comes increasingly to know and to sense the trajectory a human life tends to make. Not that he overlooks or refuses to see its variety and even its mystery, but he is more and more one in Arnold's phrase "who saw life steadily and saw it whole." Such a teacher is less inclined to be disturbed by his students' getting stuck at some point of growth or their tendency to rush compulsively and rebelliously forward. All this in his long view is an expected part of the process.

This role or task of the teacher provides an opportunity to live and to teach one of life's deepest truths: the journey is more important than the destination; the process is more significant than the end. The desire in man is almost overwhelming to pitch tent here and settle down; to stop the ceaseless flow of life at a given point and pronounce it finished. Thus in art, in literature, in language, in government, in law, in religion, he strives to embalm and preserve the "truth" as he perceives it in his generation. But whatever ceases to grow dies and withers in his hand.

At a deeper level, man knows this principle and his tendency to break camp is even greater than to stay at this safe, known spot. The teacher above all feels and lives this principle with his students. With him they learn that the very best goals that can be envisioned will, when reached, be merely a point of departure for the next leg of the journey.

And slowly answer'd Arthur from the barge:
"The old order changeth, yielding place to new,
And God fulfills Himself in many ways,
Lest one good custom should corrupt the world."[6]

E. V. P.

Questions and problems
for dialogue

1 Does the phrase "breaker of camp" or "breaker of idols" catch better the central thought of this chapter? Why do you think so?

2 In what sense is it possible or wise to live principally in the present? What is your criticism of the philosophy of the "exhortation of the dawn"?

3 In your own life have you found the need to "stay" or to "move on" to be stronger, in general? Has the pull been different at different ages? Why, in your judgment, is this true, if it is?

4 What does the term "style of life" mean to you? Do you feel you have a characteristic style of life? If so, what seem to be its central reference points—its chief priorities?

5 How can a teacher best decide when a student needs to break camp and move to the next phase of development?

6 What seem to you to be the chief symptoms of life and growth as contrasted with crystallization and death? In one's self? In students?

7 In your experience has formal education usually been on the side of life and growth? Give illustrations and reasons for your response.

8 What do you think of the concept of a stable core of belief and behavior in the personality surrounded by a flexible growing band? Does this concept fit your experience? Illustrate.

9 Of the three things mentioned that the teacher can do to help the growing student move forward wisely, which have you found to be most helpful in your growth? Which of these activities have you found to be most helpful to your students or others you may have helped?

10 To what extent and in what ways do former "idols" influence the personality after they are broken?

Exercises
for further learning

1 Make a list of some of the things you once believed strongly but no longer believe. Explore the ways in which the change took place and look for what seem to be good and bad ways of making the shift.
2 Recall instances when you or a friend of yours seemed to halt too long at some phase of growth. Try to determine the principal causes for the delay and study the moving-forward process as it occurred.
3 Read with care the poem "Renascence" by Edna St. Vincent Millay. Show how the poem relates to the problems of this chapter.
4 Show the relation between experience (type, amount, etc.) and staying too long at a given stage, moving appropriately forward, or moving too fast.
5 Interview a few of your acquaintances as to how they adapted to shifts or changes in belief. Explore minor myths such as Santa Claus or fairies and other more far-reaching beliefs.
6 Recall those individuals who gave you the most help in the growing-up process. Analyze what seemed to make them helpful to you. Are many of them teachers?
7 Study cases where youth at various levels of development appear to be rebelliously driving forward in their growth. Give some possible causes of this process in college youth or in early adolescents.
8 Evaluate the concept that the process is more important than the goal, the journey than the destination. In what senses, in your judgment, is this principle true? In what senses, false?
9 Give specific examples of educational practice that seem to you to be on the side of life or on the side of crystallization.
10 Give some thought to the major institutions of our culture: education, family, government, religion, law, business. Look for examples of lingering "idols" that seem no longer appropriate or useful.

The one thing to be said for encouraging the
frightened reader is that if he perseveres,
if he lends his mind attentively to whoever
it may be—Goethe or Descartes—it will be
returned to him, not as good as, but better
than new. . . .
—*Jacques Barzun*

I could a tale unfold whose lightest word
Would harrow up thy soul, freeze thy young blood,
Make thy two eyes, like stars, start from their spheres,
Thy knotty and combined locks to part
And each particular hair to stand on end,
Like quills upon the fretful porpentine. . . .
—*William Shakespeare*

14

A teacher is

a storyteller

It is the very nature of man to be preoccupied with
himself—and to ask questions about existence and how he relates
to it. It would be impossible for him just to appear in his environment and to know how to relate to it appropriately. He is curious
about his beginnings and although an explanation may not change
the fact that he *is*, he is sufficiently curious to want to know when
and how and why he happens to be a creature of the earth.

The stories which have been handed down through the centuries by word of mouth until they reached the era and the crystal-
lizing effects of the written word have provided successions of

new generations with many answers about the immediately passing generation and their forebears and have thus provided man
with a record of his heritage.

Great libraries have become magnificent monuments to all the
significant thinking of mankind. The wealth that man has left to
the world lies entombed within the books, pages, and lines which
hold the written word. It is man's pleasure and duty to breathe
the breath of life back into those ideas and to let them live again,
even as the flowers of the desert, dormant for a season, come to
life anew when blessed by rain and snow and sunshine. These
are exterior forces which urge life for a time and provide food so
they can flower and be fragrant, and then again become dormant
until another season of life disturbs them to waking and useful-
ness. A delicate balance is essential. As the young plant, awakened
by the season, stirs and begins to grow, it can be withered by a
desert wind, drowned by an excess of water, destroyed by any
number of diseases and pests which may attack it.

Plant life thrives on disturbance. So, with the written word:
when it is disturbed and set in motion at varying speeds by human
speech sounds, vocal shadings, and appropriate silences and is
cast on the sound waves between the lips of one person and the
ears of others, if the lips of the speaker and the ears of the hearer
have a common understanding of the word configurations and the
vocal intonations, it breathes again in the hearts of men with *new*
vigor, power, significance, purpose and promise.

The teacher, by the use of human sound, restores life to the
minstrel, long dead, who once bore tales of wars; of kings and
distant civilizations; of the hopes and dreams of mankind; of the
tragedies and failures of man as he was—and is; of the earth and
all that's in it.

The teacher is not afraid to become the means by which the stories can be told for he knows full well that stories have a unifying
effect on a civilization. He is willing, therefore, to give himself to
the demands of good storytelling.

The human being is arrested by anything that reminds him of himself. When a human being, even as a baby, sees himself in a mirror, he becomes totally preoccupied with what he sees. He becomes quiet. He moves this way and that, experimenting, seeking to know and to understand what he sees. As the maturing human being looks in the mirror (hopefully unobserved) and makes faces, moves his head, winks, purses his lips, and so on, he wants to be sure he approves of what he sees, and he hopes his view is accurate. Alas! however, he can be no more objective about what he sees than he can be about what he hears. Few people recognize their own voices—or even admit they're theirs when they hear them on the tape recorder.

A greater fascination and a greater objectivity come when the child sees another and as they begin to find a common ground, watching each other and acting in accordance with what they see. They are able to measure what they do, each against the actions of the other and this shapes their ultimate attitudes and performance. When each is again alone, he tries to get to the mirror again to test the way he looks against the way he felt he looked when he was in the company of another human being.

The story is a marvelous mirror or measuring stick. In it, people can experience how others have solved problems similar to their own, discover ideals and standards of living found to be desirable in others, which they can incorporate into their own living, learn to appreciate their own lives as they compare with what they read about others, sometimes feel inferior, sometimes feel superior, be repelled or be inspired. The story gives one a sense of place and of identity in history and the teacher looks for and reads or tells those stories which will provide some idea of "Whence we came," "Where we are on the continuum called history," and "What the possibilities are for our future as a race."

As listeners we are able to identify with the characters in the stories. We can objectively view, analyze, and evaluate people and events and ideas. We can fall in love and test our ability to love; we can hate and without having to bear the pain, we can come to know the destructive power of hating; we can dream and know the joy of hope and the pangs of disappointment; we can be purged in the intensity of great tragedy and in a sense experience life before we have to live it. We can also experience life we never have to live ourselves, but the vicarious experience deepens our humility and intensifies our compassion for our fellow man.

In Lillian Smith's book, *The Journey*, she tells of a teacher who never left the state of Georgia but who, because of her own imagination, her intense love for the children, her sensitivity to work, could transport those children far beyond the dismal setting of the one-room school.[1] The children in her little room were transported by her enthusiasm, her voice, her speech to the Washington monument and to the Empire State building, to the Statue of Liberty, to canyons, to mountains, and to wildernesses of her own land; to the Taj Mahal, to Egypt and the Pyramids, to the Orient, to Africa, and among all the other peoples of the world. All this was done when the children trooped each day to their "education capsule" and, almost as if they were being launched into outer space, for to them it was beyond their own confined existence, set forth through the magic of imagination powered and guided by a master storyteller on many adventures beyond the walls of their little room.

Certainly one of the master storytellers of all time, Jesus of Nazareth, knew that He must explain the questions asked by His followers in terms of what they knew rather than in terms of what He knew. His answers were never direct, but as He pondered the questions of His disciples, He studied the kind of person and the reasons for his question as well as his backgrounds, before formulating the answers. His answers were given in the form of a story or an analogy which could be understood and correctly interpreted by His questioners. He made no attempt to impose His thinking on His listeners. He simply illustrated what He wanted them to see by taking pieces of their experiences and putting them together with comparable experiences of people in comparable situations, in new and specific ways so that they could gain fresh points of view and clearer perspective.

One of the attributes of the good storyteller is that he knows how to use the experiences and ideas of his listeners as a point of contact in leading them to a point of departure and beyond the immediacy of those experiences to their adventures into the past, to new interpretations of the present, and to the flights of fancy which may become the future. He teases and awakens the dreams, longings, and deepest urgings of his listeners and guides them into thinking which they sometimes resist but which they must follow either to the point of acceptance and commitment or to the point of denial so that there is a rationale for their committing themselves to a point of view.

As a musical instrument is sensitive and responsive to the fingers and lips of the artist, so is the good storyteller sensitive to the many sounds of the earth. He remains in tune with the many moods and changes in his environment.

The good storyteller relies on his physical advantages and is aware of his physical limitations in order to achieve maximum effectiveness. He understands the range of his voice and knows how to depend on it; he develops the ability to vary the pitch and the volume; he gains a knowledge of the uses of speed variations which will allow him either to skip along or to linger over an idea that needs more time; he uses clear diction and is able to enunciate clearly and to pronounce words accurately.

Besides his own performance, the good storyteller makes eye contact with his audience. He does more than look up, or look toward the audience. He looks at their eyes. Eye contact has a steadying effect on an audience by offering them recognition; it identifies people and helps to counteract indifference; it enables people to become better acquainted with themselves and with the speaker who comes to realize by watching individual responses that the world is not after all composed of a mass of earth-worms that want to look alike, but is individual response in the presence of many.

Looking directly at an audience has a steadying effect on them and an enlightening one on the storyteller. The audience is com-plimented to realize that the storyteller is aware of them. There are few, if any, who do not wish to be recognized. This awareness makes the good storyteller know, if he becomes sensitively attuned to facial expressions and responses from his audience, that they accept, reject, understand, misunderstand, or just tolerate. One of the biggest problems a storyteller can have in developing sensi-tivity to others is his reluctance to look—and if he does not look, he will not know their responses.

The storyteller is aware of the need for visual design to sup-port what he is telling his audience. When he is talking in abstrac-tions of love, war, God or any concept for which his listeners have no reference point of actual experience, the storyteller must rely on the appropriate lift of the eyebrow, the tilt of the head, the slight smile or frown, the flick of the wrist, the raising of the arm or some other gesture either in isolation or in combination with others to give specific meaning to the concepts he is handling. The use of these visual designs, whether gross or minute, must be deliberate. There is nothing more useless or confusing than the unrelated or unmotivated gesture. The storyteller is deliberate in his choice of visual designs which give definition to what he is saying.

Nora Waln tells of an old Chinese storyteller in the little village of Noonday Rest, where she lived as the adopted daughter of an ancient family.[2] The old man was blind, but he had traveled far and wide with great freedom among the widely scattered provinces of China. The landowners of Noonday Rest looked forward to his return at harvest time because he was hired to sing or tell his tales in the great sheds where the harvesters were win-nowing the grain and in the great barns when the villagers gath-ered for weaving. He was particularly desired by the landowners because when he told his stories and sang his songs, production among the workers rose often more than double what it was without him. The old singer discovered through years of experimentation that his greatest power lay in the restraint used in his work.

In his youth when he was becoming a storyteller, he used too much gesture and put on too much of a show. People often became interested in him as a performer and missed the essence of the stories he told. When he began to realize that he must use only enough visual designs to hold the interest of the audience, he learned that he could move them great distances by what they heard in his voice and that they went then far beyond him as a person or storyteller and in their flights of imagination, set in motion and unrestricted by what they saw, they could travel the vastnesses of China, discover people like themselves who inhabited that enormous country, and feel that they were not alone upon the earth. They heard of rulers, people like themselves, wars, peace, ideas, exploitation, gentleness, gods, and devils. The storyteller released their imaginations. He freed the minds of human beings who were held captive by flesh and circumstance.

The old storyteller used fewer and fewer gestures as he perfected his art. He deliberately developed "non-gesture," the deliberate omission of a visual symbol which may be expected but which, because of its very absence, is powerful. If it were present it would go unnoticed. The gesture and the non-gesture have equal power and value because the individual responds to design in space and visualizes or anticipates design. If what he anticipates is absent, he reacts perhaps more strongly than he would if it were present.

An artist is one who not only works with the materials at hand, but who, more importantly perhaps, has the courage to omit what is available to him. This deliberate use or non-use of materials gives the artist, teacher, or storyteller, control in his art.

It might be well for us to examine more specifically a few of the categories into which stories may fall so we can be sure the teacher will be aware that they exist and can make an effort to bring many kinds of stories to the classroom. No doubt many stories will fit more than one category so there will be no attempt to be too rigid in the definitions nor too exhaustive in the references.

The curious will want to go on many adventures. Perhaps all stories could be classified as adventure of some form but for the sake of discussion, adventure here will refer to those stories which lead the reader or listener into danger, excitement, discovery, new experiences, and even fantasy. A person is never more secure or more brave than when he can scale a precarious peak, fight with dragons, become lost in a wilderness, travel into the Congo—and all within the safety of a comfortable classroom, together with his friends but alone in his fears.

Historical fiction will take the reader to an actual time and place in history and will allow the storyteller to people that time and place with fictitious characters. This allows great freedom to let the storyteller examine what the effects of a moment in history could have on those who may have peopled it.

Biography allows for the examination of real people and not only their responses to the world in which they lived, but also the effects they had and the changes they brought to the place and the era in which they lived. This provides a fascinating and valuable reference point to children, many of whom may come to realize that they do not have to accept life as it is. Great models may provide them with inspiration and hope and with the idea that they can achieve levels beyond those in which they find themselves.

There are many other kinds of books available in the schools and libraries and it is the duty of the storyteller to stimulate the desire to seek and find these books. He cannot tell or read all of them to his classes but he can deliver the key to the treasures that lie there. When treasures are available but unused, we must agree with Ruth Sawyer, who said in her *The Enchanted Schoolhouse*, " 'Tis a strange sort of poverty to be finding in a rich country."[3]

J. D. Y.

Questions for discussion

1 Discuss, "Mankind, as a rule, likes to hear stories about himself."
2 Are storytellers born with the talent for storytelling or can they develop the art? What is your reasoning?
3 Discuss: "The individual measures himself against the various stories he reads."
4 How is it possible to "experience life which we never have to live?" Is this to be desired?
5 Recall two or three of your teachers who used storytelling as a classroom technique. What do you remember most vividly about their performances?
6 How can a storyteller bridge the distance between a student and "reality"?
7 Discuss the techniques which every good storyteller should possess.
8 Define and discuss "non-gesture."
9 Mention five types of stories and list a specific book illustrating each type. Annotate briefly.
10 Should any or all elementary school teachers, secondary school teachers, college teachers be required to study storytelling? Why?

All the world's a stage,
And all the men and women merely players.
They have their exits and their entrances,
And one man in his time plays many parts,
His acts being seven ages. . . .
—*William Shakespeare*

15

A teacher is

an actor

Thomas Mann describes the disappointment experienced by a child who accompanied his grandfather to the theatre
and witnessed there the exciting performance of a brilliant actor.[1]
When the show was over, he insisted that his grandfather take
him backstage to see the man who could captivate and move to
such excitement the great audience. The grandfather was reluc-
tant but finally agreed. The disappointment began as the young
lad and his grandfather made their way onto the almost darkened
stage, moved down a long and dusty corridor illuminated by two
naked light bulbs, and finally stopped at the dressing room door of

the handsome young actor. His disappointment became revulsion as they entered a smelly, untidy dressing room when invited in by the tired and rasping voice that answered the grandfather's knock at the door. Among the reeking costumes, on a wooden stool in front of the makeup mirror, which was lighted by a bulb at the end of a cord hanging directly above it, sat a baldheaded old man, stripped to the waist, his wig on the floor, removing the last vestiges of greasepaint from the wrinkles in his face. His body was pockmarked, his shoulders stooped, and his attempted smile revealed he was very tired and perhaps not well. The boy was moved almost to tears as he realized that this was the young man who, a few moments before, was singing, dancing, smiling, and throwing kisses to an audience that had come to shed its frustrations, to laugh, to escape for a short time the many oppressions of life.

Why was it necessary for this actor to perform for the audience? Why couldn't they have read the lines and sung the songs themselves? After all, they left the theatre laughing, jostling one another, humming the songs and repeating the lines from various portions of the performance, discussing the techniques of staging. Obviously, it took one who had the talents, the determination, the enthusiasm, the willingness to forgo other aspects of living in order to give himself to a life in the theatre. He first had to have an instrument or body which could respond to the demands made of it just as a piano responds to the touch of a person who plays on it. He had to train that body and keep it in tune so that it would respond appropriately to the demands made on it—to sing or dance, to say lines, or to move appropriately. He had to see the possibilities in the script he was performing and then be willing to make himself available to the demands of the script personally. He may have liked the script extremely well, or he may have disliked it at first. In either case, however, after his initial response to it, he had to develop an objectivity. He had to move to a neutral point of view and consider the script in terms of audience and how they might react to it; neither liking nor disliking it himself. His personal attitude either way could have caused distortions in audience response.

He had to consider what he could do for the script that the audience could not do. In making himself available to the demands of the script, he had to analyze and review his own abilities, his preparation, and he had to strengthen his weaknesses, perfect new aspects of performance, wear the costumes and makeup demanded, and condition himself to take the night-after-night strain on his emotions and his physical mechanism. He also had to prepare himself to receive the approval or disapproval of his audiences and of the newspaper critics. Emotional involvement does away with objectivity at the moment. When a person loves or hates, he is not objective and his behavior is likely to be distorted and uncontrolled.

Somewhere in his preparation for performance, the actor had to so strongly empathize with the character he was portraying that he became emotionally involved to the extent of either liking or disliking that character very much, and perhaps to the extent of losing emotional control. Uncontrollable laughter or tears are evidences of lack of control. An individual who is experiencing a strong emotion for which there is no other language, will resort to laughter or to tears as a kind of expression which has very little form or shape but which at least provides an outlet for that strong emotion. The actor, having experienced deep emotional involvement once, had to return to the work of rehearsal and preparation. He had to develop the realization that at the time of the performance itself he had no right to response and involvement himself. He could not let his enthusiasm for the script distort his presentation of it to the audience. At this point it was necessary for him to be able to deliberately manipulate the lines and scenes in such a way that the audience could become involved and could laugh or cry appropriately, according to the demands of the play. The audience has no need for the kind of control which the actor must have at the time of performance. In fact, the actor attempts to get the audience to lose control and to become involved. It is then the problem and responsibility of the audience to regain and restore its own control.

In the development of a play, a director adds new elements at each rehearsal. Often by the third or fourth rehearsal, the actors are required to have memorized their lines. As the director adds the blocking to the show, telling the actors where they should stand and when and where to sit, and how to turn toward one another or to the audience, and when and how to cross the stage, lines are forgotten momentarily because the new elements create new situations for the performers. They become self-conscious. They are aware of themselves in new and changing and unfamiliar situations although they have memorized the lines. The new elements, however, make new situations and even give new meanings to the lines. The level of involvement changes from rehearsal to rehearsal until, finally, all the elements are present and the director has the play ready for performance. He tests it about three times with dress rehearsals in which all the elements are present: costume, makeup, lighting, choreography, lines, scenery, sound effects, and others.

During this time, the actors are capable of going through the routine of performance very objectively, using proper diction, vocal inflection, gesture, and all, to give the audience a sense of reality. The play appears to be a replaying of real situations. The performers have become objective and are able to say all the lines without becoming involved emotionally either in the dramatic or humorous aspects of the performance. Their timing is perfected, the lighting is meaningful, the hand props and scenery contribute to the total show, and the performers use excellent diction and good voice control very selectively to give the audience the chance to become involved and to laugh or to weep as they are moved to do.

On opening night the final element or ingredient—an audience—is added and the actor, in this new relationship, is again spontaneous in performance, subject to forgetting his lines or using the wrong lines or stage movement. In describing their feelings on opening night, many have indicated that their own ears are buzzing, that so many things are happening that they are not too sure of all that went on. Often the actor gains new insights concerning the meanings of the lines he is saying and comes close to losing objectivity and control in the role he is playing when he becomes involved personally in the audience response and tends to join them in laughter or in tears. However, the routine and discipline of rehearsal carries him through to a successful performance and he remembers the responses of the audience and their applause at the end of the show.

The succeeding nights make it possible for the performer almost to detach himself from the play, to become even more objective about the performance, and as the play continues for a long "run," the performer is more and more able to react to the changes in the audience and to make adjustments according to their needs. As a "run" continues for weeks and even for months, it is possible that the actor will even lose his enthusiasm for the play. The routine will become dull and he will have to work even harder to create the "illusion of the first time." He must plan for the long run beyond spontaneity. He manipulates and contrives in such a way that each audience feels that the performance is fresh, live, and only for them.

As he continues the long run beyond spontaneity, the actor must rely on his ability to control the physical mechanism in such a way that he will seem to be involved. He seems to laugh or seems to weep over situations which he has created and which he now presents again and again night after night after night. This, of course, becomes an artificial situation because he is contriving to give the "illusion of the first time." He seems happy. He seems sad. He seems angry. He relies on the vocal inflection, the volume control, the position of the body to convey the meaning of what he is saying and this becomes so routine that he can think of other things during the actual performance.

It is wrong to think that the performer has become insincere as he relies on technique to sustain him in performance. Actually, the reverse is true. He becomes less self-centered, less self-conscious, and more audience-conscious as he gains objectivity and control in his performance. It is when boredom with repetition becomes so strong that he is not willing to hide it, or exhibition of his personal talent becomes too strong a need, or his lack of concern for the audience involvement develops that he becomes selfish and artificial to his audience.

The only other time he becomes insincere is at the time he develops the role. If his motive is, and continues to be a desire to show his personal abilities, he will so distort the performance that he will never have known real involvement with the role and it can only follow that his approach will be artificial and contrived from the very beginning. It will indicate his desire to demonstrate himself.

This has happened to so many people of the theatre and such people receive so much publicity, that the general public tends to feel that all actors and actresses are frauds and artificial persons in the least desirable sense of those terms.

One of the major attributes for which the actor strives is "selflessness." For the sake of his audience, he will submerge his ego needs and his exhibitionistic tendencies and will maintain a genuine concern for his audience even though his own familiarity with his role and the many repetitions required by performance may subject him to utter boredom.

Every individual plays many roles in a day but many, particularly teachers, reject the idea that a teacher is an actor. It would be an interesting parallel to compare the student's experience of seeing his teacher in a habitat other than his stage—the classroom —with the experience, as told by Thomas Mann, of the young lad witnessing the unadorned and unpretending actor backstage when the show was over. It could be very disillusioning for the student if he could hear some of the remarks the teachers make about the classroom and their students when the day is over. It could be very disillusioning for the student to hear what the teachers say about hard work and boredom in the classroom. It must be granted, however, that the teacher has gone through the preparation for the "long run beyond spontaneity" and though he is now "pretending" to be interested in the same things he has been saying for many years, he makes the same kind of sacrifices other actors make for the sake of their audiences.

To desire to teach, a person must have been enthralled by an idea or an experience of some kind himself and must desire that others have the opportunity to know about and be inspired by that same event or material in some way. To be able to transfer ideas, he must develop, in addition to the knowledge he accumulates, the ability to communicate that knowledge. This ability to communicate is an art or skill also known as teaching.

He makes a deliberate study, not only of the material that is to be transferred, but also of the human personality so that he can understand responses of classes or audiences and preplan his work so that he can *control* them. To do this, he learns all he can about his own talent and physical mechanism and he learns to control that mechanism, by his voice, gestures, diction, pace, so that he can use his own self most effectively.

He begins with a sense of deep dedication and inspiration which will give purpose to his basic driving force. As the years go by, he has to become an actor, willing to overlay his boredom with excitement and a contrived interest in the classroom for the benefit of the students or audiences that come to him year after year. In their development, new classes and new audiences are at about the same level as the preceding ones were but he makes each class, and each student in each class, feel that there is no place he would rather be than in that classroom at that moment talking about that specific subject. If the truth were known, he may be beset by boredom, personal problems, a physical ailment, the longing for a vacation, the desire to be engaged in research which can lead him to the outer edges of the existing knowledge in his field, the desire to be teaching advanced students and to be guiding their research projects, or any other problem, many of them totally unrelated to that classroom.

A look at the teacher on his first day in his own classroom—alone—an authority responsible for his class and responsible to higher authority for what takes place in that room, will reveal that he is perhaps as near as he will ever get to spontaneity in teaching. He has real dedication, concern for his pupils, and is in absolute command over the knowledge he will present to his charges. No doubt within himself many prayers are offered, insights are gained, fears are stifled. But no doubt there is also the exhilarating, rewarding, exciting, and exacting experience of watching knowledge take root in the minds of students, causing them to react. He may have some stage fright and fear that he is not fully prepared or that what he has prepared is not what his students can learn, or that he has prepared either too much or too little. When they enter the room, his students add another factor, a new one, to the teaching situation with problems and situations for which the teacher had not prepared. He somehow gets through that hour and gains new insights as he sees his students respond positively, negatively, overtly, or otherwise and realizes that their responses are rarely the ones for which he had planned. This can be compared with the opening night in the theatre when the prepared but uncertain actor—replete with costume, voice, literary line, and stage setting—first experiences audience response to and interaction with the deep and moving ideas supplied by the playwright, and all the aspects of the performance which are new and which an audience necessarily supplies.

By its very nature, the teaching experience is artificial in the best sense of artificiality. The teacher-to-be spends money, time, and energy in preparing for the role of "teacher." He masters subject matter, improves his personal skills, and develops his own ability to transfer that subject matter. He studies his potential audience, the student, and he devises means by which he can capture the attention of that audience at a given time on a given day and hold it to a piece of learning which he, the teacher, has determined shall be the center of attention for his audience at that moment.

In a sense, as the school bell rings, the student moves from a natural environment into a carefully designed, well-lighted, scientifically ventilated room. The color schemes have been chosen with much deliberation. The seating has been adapted to the needs of the student; in fact, in many schools today provisions are made for the left-handed child. The clothing the child wears is not the same he wears on "stay-home" days and weekends. Under these conditions, he moves into the "theatre of learning" and takes his place.

The subject matter he is to learn has been selected as a part of a pattern of knowledge called "curriculum," and he is to learn it within the framework of a predetermined time span. The time of day for learning the specific part of the curriculum is established to be sure that it will be related to the other parts of the pattern and so that there will be no wasted motion. To further limit and control the imagination of the child and to focus his attention on a specific phase of the curriculum, careful attention is given to the visual "staging" of the learning moment, such as bulletin boards, paintings, dimensional designs, motion pictures, filmstrips, the color of the walls and the ceiling, and the lighting.

Onto this stage moves the teacher. Whatever may be his emotional state, his desire to be in the classroom or elsewhere, his personal desires, wishes, or turmoil, he too is costumed in keeping with his theatre of operation. He is well-groomed and appropriately dressed. He puts from him any personal problems and assumes the "role" of teacher—an image he carries throughout the day when he is on stage before his students.

To reassure all those who feel that the teacher is not an actor, or should not be an actor, let us review the process of his becoming a real teacher. He chooses teaching as a career. He becomes dedicated to a particular major or discipline. He spends time, money, and energy, mastering his field and learning how to teach it to others. He experiences the first years of spontaneity in the classroom and develops routines that are successful for him. He moves into the era of boredom where he develops real "selflessness" by carrying out the "act" of teaching and keeping the "image" of the teacher alive for his students. He survives the long run beyond spontaneity.

J. D. Y.

Questions for discussion

1 What various acting tasks does the teacher perform in the classroom?
2 Should the teacher feel that acting is dishonest? Discuss.
3 Is it possible for the teacher to be vitally interested in his students at all times? Why?
4 What does the teacher bring to the learning situation that the student cannot produce himself?
5 How can the teacher's enthusiasm for his subject matter distort his presentation to the class?
6 Why does the beginning teacher have doubts in his first year of teaching?
7 The singer sings old songs that the audience knows and loves. The actor presents the same play and plays the same role over and again. Compare this with the teacher teaching in the same class level every year and teaching the same subjects. How much should the teacher revise his approach? Why?
8 Can a person who wants to demonstrate his personal abilities be a good teacher?
9 Discuss the artificiality of the classroom situation.
10 Do the students lose confidence in the teacher when they know he is acting?

The world is too much with us; late and soon
Getting and spending, we lay waste our powers:
Little we see in Nature that is ours;
We have given our hearts away, a sordid boon!
This Sea that bares her bosom to the moon;
The winds that will be howling at all hours,
And are up-gathered now like sleeping flowers;
For this, for everything, we are out of tune;
It moves us not. . . .
—*William Wordsworth*

16

A teacher is

a scene designer

The teacher is a scene designer. He moves into a vacant room and it becomes his stage. There he creates a setting and a mood, which is sufficiently evident to cause the students to respond but not enough to overwhelm them. The designs must stimulate and support student responses. They should never overpower nor arrest the student's attention in the dynamic processes of his learning.

Either visually or verbally, or both, the teacher establishes a place, a time, a color scheme, a design, which will provide appropriate support to the material being taught. He may use vocal coloring as a background to fear, joy, excitement, love, hate, and other moods. He may vary the speed of his presentation for emphasis, a casual air, or haste. By using this kind of punctuation, he sorts important ideas for the students. He may use gestures to provide additional visual evidence of mood or attitude, and these designs are not by chance. They are deliberate.

He may use color schemes to arrest the imagination and to hold it to a period and place. In discussions of Shakespeare's *The Merchant of Venice,* I have placed swatches of cloth side by side and hanging off the edge of a lectern so the audience can see them. Then, as I have read and discussed the play, I have pointed to greens for Nerissa and Gratiano, blues for Bassanio and Portia, yellow for Shylock, etc. This helps to identify the many characters and character traits. During the reading, I have moved the swatches of cloth and rearranged them according to the relationship of the characters as revealed in the script. Thus, Portia (blue cloth) is at one time next to Bassanio (blue cloth) and, later, next to Nerissa (green), and then the succession of kings (gold, silver, and blue), and so on. Not only does this keep the characters clear in the minds of the audience and focus their attention, but it helps them to understand the many intricacies and relationships in the structure of this complex play.

Sometimes the teacher changes emphasis in control by adding minute details so that there is little for the imagination of the student to do and, at other times, by omitting detail so that the mind and imagination of the student must supply what is only implied. Of course, an artist, whether teacher, director, or painter, develops the skill to so control the responses of his audience that they, the audience, are unaware of the technique.

Let us examine a scene from *A Midsummer Night's Dream* by Shakespeare to see how these principles apply in drama. The designer has had to be careful, of course, to avoid creating scenery that would draw attention to itself instead of blending in as a part of a total scene. He also has had to deliberately withhold design in order to force the audience back on its own resources, and later to include detail and remove doubt. Where the audience does not have sufficient experience or imagination to be able to supply the information, more is required of the scene designer. It is vital that the scenery not be so overpowering that the actors and the ideas become only incidentals.

A high-pitched sustained sound comes from somewhere above the heads of the audience. A faint green begins to glow in the center of the stage, highlighting irregular strips of pastel chiffons hanging from the ceiling. There is a flutter and a sudden silhouette of something flitting through the light. Another flutter and another and another following in rapid succession; without knowing when the changes began, the audience senses the emerging of new colors, fuschias, steel blues, pinks, and greens making their way through shafts of light into a dawning chiffon forest. There is a sudden move of the trunk of one of the trees holding the filmy leaves of the forest, and a voice arresting the frolic of the fairies proves to be that of Puck, chief of Oberon's fairy band. Act II of *A Midsummer Night's Dream* begins to spin magic in the eyes and ears of the audience, forming a web of suspended belief. Memory, woven by the shapes, colors, and sounds, in later years will be vibrated again and again, as all those designs stir the deep impressions of imagination and remembrance.

The imagination of the audience is controlled by the designer who in effect says: "Here is the place. This is the time. These are the people. These are their problems." The audience is willing to believe whatever "conventions" are established by the director and designer so long as they do not break their own laws.

In the theatre there are two basic purposes of scene design: to aid the audience's understanding, and to express the play's qualities. As an aid to understanding, the stage setting may define the time and place of the action, clarify the relationship of the offstage and onstage space, and assist in establishing characterization. The designer is aware that the physical arrangement of the setting, the nature of offstage space as revealed by what the audience sees onstage, the onstage space and its use for the studied grouping of actors, the stage setting and its style will give an indication of the style, the type, and the theme of the play. He knows that a good setting is a visual statement of the values of the script. In fact, when deliberately contrived, the stage setting can either limit and control the imagination or free it, releasing it from limitation and control.

An emotion or mood can also be heightened by the proper uses of sound and color. Changes in the intensity of lighting hold the attention of an audience. All the aspects of staging are important tools for handling the emotional involvement of an audience.

Based on the premise that most of mankind, equipped with sensory organs, is at least capable of responsiveness, the teacher deliberately stages an atmosphere which will limit the attention of the students to a space within the confines of the room, then gives that attention some direction, sets it in motion, and releases or even boosts the student's imagination, causing it to move beyond the limits of physical environment and into the realm of the fanciful, the idealistic, the philosophical.

One of the greatest challenges facing the teacher is to create and develop an "experiencing nature" in his students. The person who is capable of the greatest sensitivity and "experiencing" is the one in whom all the senses are functioning. If he has stored memories of the different elements in the total experience, it will be possible for a designer to use any abstraction of that experience to call up the total experience again.

A person who lacks any of the sensory responses, who cannot see or smell or taste, will not experience to the fullest, and if the element to which his senses are deadened is used as the abstraction to stimulate a response to that experience again, he will not be able to respond. Another element will be needed in order for him to be able to react. For example, if the individual is blind, he may hold an apple, taste it, and smell it, and if he is told it is red, he must interpret "red" in terms of his active senses. These may not always be accurate because the next time he eats an apple he will know that it has certain qualities which are the same as those of the apple he ate before, but instead of its being red, it may be yellow or green. If he says it is red, he is in need of more specific information, which he may be able to get when he has had more experience in eating apples and has refined his tasting of apples to the point that he has learned which color accompanies the texture, taste, and smell of specific types of apples.

So much of life is meaningless because people merely react, let us say, to hunger pangs and, seeing an apple, will pick it up and eat it. The other senses have not been brought into "experiencing" and are so dulled that nothing is stored in the memory that can be stirred again. The color, the shape, the texture, the aroma of the apple, when experienced again, will not awaken an emotional response or feeling about apples.

Experiences are complex and consist of many dimensions. The person who experiences fully is able to respond again when stimulated by any abstraction of an experience, so much so that he can recreate his original responses instantaneously—and expand those responses to new and more complex levels. He becomes more and more capable of working in abstractions, because his strong responses to the total experience make it possible for him to recall that experience in its entirety when he is stimulated by any portion or symbol of it.

So much of mankind is insensitive to and untouched by the meanings of existence. There is a general acceptance and perhaps even some appreciation for a landscape or a balmy summer evening; but when man contemplates the Creator of the universe, he is overcome with wonder as to how the blackness, the void, the formlessness, the disorganization could be *spoken* into an existence of order and form, color and beauty, music and sensitivity, and motion and design—a superlative poetic drama authored by God and played on a multidimensional stage hung with sun, moon, planets, and stars for lighting. The scenery is a symphony of brilliant colors, changing seasons, heat and cold, light and dark, sweet and sour, harmony and dissonance, motion and sounds and silence.

In the midst of this scenery, the actors are allowed to observe, to experience, to commingle, to rearrange, to design and put together in multitudinous combinations, to star in their own "scenes from life." Each plays it his own way, but the show is in the same classroom. Each chooses the materials for his own uses and according to the sensitivity he has developed through experience. Each reacts differently to the stimulus of the supplies around him and each achieves at his own rate. Some are deeply sensitive and moved; others seem to be almost untouched by the great drama. Whether his scene is comic or tragic, it has in some variation been played before. But because this is his moment, it glows for a time for him and then fades as the curtain falls. As the scene ends and the lights go down on each one's moment in time, he makes a brief curtain call and then leaves the stage and takes his place in the offstage space, but he also becomes a very important part of the memory of those who knew him, either as a fellow-actor or as audience. New actors take the stage to play that scene or variations of it again in an attempt to improve on some aspect of the show.

So many go to the theatre and laugh or cry or even sleep for a brief period and then get up and walk away. Only a few really contemplate the magnitude of the task which made the show possible. Those who have some knowledge and have reacted more totally to their previous experiences marvel at the ability of the designer to pinpoint a moment in time; to push time back two or three centuries or to reach far into the future; to deliberately evoke moods of joy, or sorrow, comedy or tragedy; to make an orderly statement out of chaos: and to be able to do it with a few strokes of the paint brush, with the increasing or decreasing of the intensity of the lighting, with a simple design or setting, a few props, and a few costumes.

To be able to control the imagination of the audience and to set it in motion, he must be aware of the materials available to him and he must know how people generally will react to these materials in isolation and in combination. He must know how the audience might remember the materials he will use, and that he will need enough to tap the sensitivity of the audience in many ways since there will be some who perhaps do not react to color or to sound or motion or design.

He begins, of course, with his initial stimulation and motivation received from the playwright; he coordinates his responses with those of the director who wishes to evoke those same responses from the audience.

He is deliberate in his plan to bring dimension from formlessness; light from darkness; statement from confusion and disorganization. He uses lines and partial lines, shapes, color, space, lighting, sound, and other properties in various combinations to help evoke the specific responses he wishes from the audience. Though the audience may not know why they react either positively or negatively to a scene, the designer will have made an effort to control their responses with his work so that he can predict and achieve specific reactions from them.

The designer-teacher seeks to elicit appropriate responses. He uses color schemes appropriate to the seasons during the school year and appropriate to the grade level. In the autumn, he does not use the same shades of red and orange and green that he uses in the spring. He works for a related setting which is artificially contrived and abstracted from a total experience: a picture of a bare tree, red and white streamers, a few colored leaves. He is aware that some of the students may never have had the total experience; therefore, he uses abstractions to reconstruct enough of an experience to reach as many as possible. In many instances, he will be providing the total experience as well as the abstractions. This he does by taking the students on field trips to dairies, harbors, airports, theatres, political conventions, concerts, and museums.

The teacher "stages" learning in the classroom. It may be too large or too small or, in rare instances, ideal in size. It may have no windows or too many windows, and no chalk boards. The desks may be immovable, or there may be tables and chairs or other types of furniture. The lighting may be adequate, excellent, or poor. The walls may be pale green, pale yellow, pale pink, or white. They may be dirty or clean. There may be charts and maps above the chalk boards. The floor may be vinyl or carpeted, or even just a wooden floor and the color may blend with the walls, and it may not.

Whatever the materials he has at his command, the teacher designs a setting from them. He selects those that will provide order and form and discipline, as well as design and sensitivity, for the student, so that each will react to and be affected by the deliberate design and be stimulated to build a system of responses that will be valuable in developing his creativity. So, in a small way, but like all of humanity, the student is moving on a stage— the classroom—that will make it possible for him to emerge to larger and more complex stages where he can apply and rely on the "experiencing nature" he has developed in the safer, more contrived arena.

As each moves into the reality of life, he will attempt to improve on the scenes that were played before. The maturity and success of his performance will be determined by his experiences and the freedom with which he was allowed to "practice for living" by moving the scenery, commingling, and designing in multitudinous ways the materials provided for him in the classroom.

In Thornton Wilder's *Our Town*, the author supplies the language, and dictates a "lack of scenery" to those who direct the play. Experimenters have demonstrated, by providing unnecessary pieces of scenery, that *Our Town* then becomes cluttered and distorted. Therefore, the designer must know when and for whom to include details and when to omit them. When he includes them, he must use care in deciding how much is needed.

Certain visual details are important if the designer wishes to elicit responses. Bright colors and color combinations, curved lines, and a general decor of lightness establish a mood and tell an audience it should prepare to react to a romantic or comic scene. Surprise combinations generally cause an audience to react overtly as they do in comedy. Whatever materials are used, however, they should not be so prominent or overpowering that they arrest or hold the attention of the audience. They should merely give the clues so that the audience, because of previous experience, will be able to know how to prepare for what is to follow and will then concentrate on the show and react appropriately.

It was stated earlier that "The audience is willing to believe whatever 'conventions' are established by the director and designer so long as they do not break their own laws"; this same principle is true in the classroom. A convention is determined by the rules agreed upon by the designer and the audience. If the designer says, "This is a Victorian living room," and uses Victorian furniture, Victorian staircases, and the clutter and detail of furnishings, the audience will believe him until he breaks his own rules by including a lamp, or a color scheme, or some other item that is not in the period. If he says, however, "This is the *essence* of a Victorian room," and uses—in combination with any other nondescript furniture or setting he wishes—a chair, or a lamp or two, or a scarf, something to which the audience can anchor its imagination, they will often believe him more readily than they would if he purported to create the complete setting for them. When he claims to do that, they may become suspicious and look for places where they can prove him to be inaccurate.

Theseus in Act V of *A Midsummer Night's Dream* says, "As imagination bodies forth the forms of things unknown, the poet's pen turns them to shapes and gives to airy nothing a local habitation and a name." The scene designer, then, relies on elements that the author did not supply to give dimension and form to the "local habitation." He is wise if he creates the essence of time and place instead of striving for accuracy of detail.

Perhaps the ultimate of human achievement is the ability to make instantaneous decisions, to sum up beliefs, to communicate feeling, emotion, attitude, mood, and to predict. To do this, the student must learn to react to cues rather than to total experiences. As he achieves higher levels of education, the designer-teacher therefore provides less and less of the total experience for him in the interest of moving more rapidly. Sounds and silences (language) in the forms of lecture, poetry, novels, discussions suffice, and if visual symbols are needed, they are ordinarily provided by gestures. The general atmosphere of the room is contrived to provide a comfortable place conducive to learning. From a minimum setting—room, seating arrangement, color of walls, lighting—the teacher "speaks" into existence mature concepts for his students.

J. D. Y.

Questions for discussion

1 Is it possible for a person who "has all of his senses" to be able to react to an abstraction of an experience to which he once responded? Discuss.

2 Discuss: "The person who 'experiences' fully, will be able to respond again when stimulated by any abstraction of an experience, so much so that he can recreate his original responses instantaneously—and expand those responses to new and more complex levels."

3 Compare the ideas: As God spoke the universe into existence, so the teacher can speak "universes" into existence in the students' minds.

4 In order to use his materials effectively, how much does a scene designer need to know about his audience?

5 Is it possible that scene designers sometimes use too much scenery and thereby damage the responses of the audience?

6 Discuss "convention" in the theatre, and the importance of the scene designer's being sure not to break his own rules.
7 Are audiences overtly aware of *why* they react to certain visual stimuli? Discuss.
8 Should the designer strive for accuracy of detail or should he attempt to design "essence"?
9 How much of the design should the students be allowed to provide?
10 Compare the design of language with the visual designs in a classroom or stage setting.

Professor Holcombe's great impact was not in his erudition
but in his personality and character.
Dispassionate, reserved, self-restrained,
without illusions yet persistently idealistic,
he was extraordinarily well equipped with qualities
and principles to meet his responsibilities as a
teacher and as a citizen.
—*John F. Kennedy*

17

A teacher is

a builder of community

There are those who seem to feel that the teacher should
be set apart from the community: a kind of "knowledge island"
to which children go each day for a time to learn what the community feels they need to know and from which they return to
their "real" worlds of home and family and church and daily problems which make up all the other elements of "real living"; a kind
of "knowledge island" to which adults go on "information hunts"
and from which they return, laden with bits of information which
will be of identifiable use to them for specific tasks but for no
other use.

It is often a surprise to a child to see his teacher in the super-market or at the beach in swimming attire or shopping with her own children. The setting in which he knows the teacher is at the school in the classroom and on the playground and he seems to assume that the teacher lives at the school and somehow emerges from the walls when it is time to teach.

Even adults at the college level are often surprised to know that the teacher is a citizen of the community whose voice is heard in current affairs. They are more likely to share the feelings of John Dos Passos toward Dean Briggs of Harvard, "I thought of him as a museum piece, quaint, the way in these latter years we have come to admire American primitives; provincial. I was among his irreverent students who spoke of him as Aunt Betsy."[1]

It must be recognized that a teacher is a member of a com-munity, and has the same rights as do all other members of the community, and is responsible, even more so than others, as a builder of the community. This is not simple. The voice of the teacher should be influential in the very best way possible on the community.

In the interest of clarification and accuracy, it seems wise here to examine some of the meanings of the word "community." Web-ster says that "A community is a social group whose members re-side in a specific locality, share government and have a cultural and historical heritage." As is true with most definitions, this one is considerably oversimplified. It is, of course, impossible to state all the possible meanings of words because the meanings vary according to the context in which they are used. The meaning as stated in the dictionary cannot include the many complex com-munity groupings which are the result of overlapping interests. Briefly examined, the community may include some people who may live in a specific locality with others but who do not have a common cultural and historical heritage; or it may include people who share a common cultural and historical heritage but who do not share government; or it could be that a group of people who share government have neither cultural and historical heritage nor reside in a specific locality.

An individual can belong to a community, "whose members reside in a specific locality." The size of the locality is not defined and it is presumed that it can range in size all the way from a small plot of ground to that of an entire nation. The members of the community, whatever its size, share government, and to maintain citizenship under that government must comply with the rules which both govern and protect them. Perhaps the smallest community unit is that of the family. The individual is born into this unit. As he grows and takes his place in that community, he does so according to the established government and traditions of that family. When he breaks the rules imposed on him by the government which he shares, he becomes subject to the penalties which are due all who break those rules, even though he had no part in making them. In Virginia Sorensen's *Plain Girl*, Dan, the son of an Amish father, was so curious about the "ways of people outside the Amish community," that he started driving automobiles and dating girls who were not Amish.[2] His actions caused him to be disinherited by his father who had no alternative but to abide by the established rules of his religious community. Dan had shown earlier signs of rebellion by having the audacity to ask a question, "What's wrong with a button?" Such a question was unheard of. In fact, his father had never asked it because it had never occurred to him to ask. Indeed, few people ask why rules exist; they merely learn either to abide by them or to forfeit their rights to membership in the community which is governed by such rules.

As the family unit takes its place in an expanded community formed by the grouping of several families, it becomes necessary for the members of the families to agree upon rules under which all members can live. These are ordinarily general standards which do not conflict with the beliefs and standards of the individual family unit. The general standards are more permissive than are the standards of the smaller community unit and this often poses a threat to the survival of the smaller unit.

The individuals who are born into the small specific community groups will have access to and be influenced by those born into other small specific groups because of the common codes of conduct and government under which they can communicate. As they live in the specific locality and develop an awareness of and an acceptance of one another's specific traditions and customs, they begin to find ways to blend ideas, customs, and traditions; and as new generations emerge, they take on characteristics of all the cultures that have existed in that locality and become one community with an identity of its own.

The teacher actively engages in the process of building the community. He remains neutral as far as the specific community groups are concerned and works to help develop standards under which all members of a community can live. He also helps the members of the smaller community units to understand each other. In the classroom he works to break down the suspicions and the need for defense that develops between units of people, he strives to build pride, and he tries to provide understanding between groups who have different backgrounds and customs. He tries to provide avenues of understanding and respect between people so that they can communicate freely and respect one another's individual standards, at the same time cooperating and building a better large community in which they can all live.

As the social group, "whose members reside in a specific locality, share government and have a cultural and historical heritage" continues to expand in size and numbers, it clearly becomes more complex. The small narrow-based groups will always be the elements of the larger community. These groups are often committed to preserving a way of life which they have inherited. Thus, a democracy or a republic has within it people of opposing views who, for the sake of process and progress, will work together even under protest when a majority in the community votes the direction which should be taken; or when there is danger from outside forces which cannot be tolerated or incorporated into the large community. Though the two major political parties in the United States may appear to be at extreme distances from one another in points of view, they become one in the face of threats from the Communists. Until very recently at least, though the various splinter groups in Protestantism are frequently at odds, they become one in the face of encroachment by Catholicism or other world religions. The recent ecumenical movement is an attempt to unite all Christian religious groups under a great general standard of agreement, but small groups within this community will preserve their individual rites and denominational beliefs.

Perhaps one of the most difficult areas of expansion into the larger community is that of blending cultural backgrounds and historical heritage. It is difficult for a person from one cultural and historical background to deny all loyalties to family tradition, religious tradition, and political tradition and to develop loyalties to the heritage of other groups. It is difficult even for a high school student to be transferred from one high school to another in a city. He finds the adjustment difficult as he takes up the school colors, the yells, the traditions of his new community and tries to become loyal. One of the most difficult problems for the teacher is to help such a person find a place in his new community. Not only is it hard for him to develop new loyalty, but the new-to-him community is established and finds it difficult to accept foreign matter in the form of a new student who brings ideas and loyalties and tradition from another community. Especially where there are rivalries, the teacher works to structure a community which will negate their effectiveness and which will blend the new student into the established community.

People tend to group themselves according to racial backgrounds, professional interests, religious beliefs, social aspirations, financial standing and, of course, on many, many other bases. If it were of any value to know the many combinations upon which special community groups could be formed and identified, it would be necessary to rely on the latest in computer technology to supply the information.

Just to mention a few, notice the possible community groups which could be formed by the following components: Caucasian, Negro, Republican, Democrat, Protestant, Catholic, poor, wealthy. In some instances the individual must accept the heritage imposed on him by birth; in other instances he must choose the group to which he will belong; and in still other instances he will have grown into what he believes. Thus, some of the following combinations are possible:

> Negro, Catholic, wealthy, Republican
> Negro, Protestant, wealthy, Republican
> Negro, Protestant, poor, Republican
> Negro, Catholic, poor, Republican
> Negro, Catholic, wealthy, Democrat
> Negro, Catholic, poor, Democrat

Obviously, we have only begun to list all the possible combinations, but surely the point is made. Clearly, too, it is possible for the individual to participate in any one of the above-named communities as long as the other attributes do not preclude him. Therefore, whatever other characteristics he may possess, it is possible for the Protestant to belong to the Protestant community, whether he is Negro or Caucasian, wealthy or poor, Republican or Democrat. His community becomes smaller and more restricted as he acquires more and more of the identifying characteristics of those who belong to his community.

It is possible for some groups, wishing to perpetuate themselves, to build their own schools and to hire their own well-screened teachers, to insure that the students will learn a point of view and build strong defenses against other points of view. In such instances, the teacher may become a tool of the organization and what he teaches is dictated by the community to preserve it.

Although the teacher's membership is in one community—religious, political, or otherwise—in his relationship with students, he is objective and helps them to see across the often artificial lines which separate people. Help is given to the students to at least understand other points of view, whether they subscribe to them or not. The teacher does not allow antagonisms to develop because of racial differences. Nor is he the tool or slave of any one idea or belief. His is the difficult problem of hearing and presenting all points of view objectively, at the same time maintaining his own personal beliefs which may be in conflict with other points of view.

In order to teach most effectively, the teacher must command the respect of those who are his students. If their minds are closed to him because of his beliefs, or for any other reason, he cannot teach. Therefore, his role as a member of a community is complex and often difficult. Though he is entitled to the same freedoms as are other citizens, if he talks on a political platform or engages actively in a partisan political campaign, he is in danger of antagonizing those whose views do not coincide with his and of losing contact with those whom he would teach. People tend to resist learning from those with whom they differ sharply even when the views obviously are not related to the subject matter being taught.

Though others may speak freely of religion and religious viewpoints, teachers must deal with problems of religion with restraint and responsibility and thus avoid unnecessary and destructive conflicts with ideas which have been imposed on the minds of the students in their previous relationships.

Education tends to provide great distances between social groupings and between generations. Antagonism has always existed between generations but education can create even wider gulfs. Many children of parents from foreign countries have told of the difficulties they have at home with parents who do not speak English. These people become afraid of the distances that develop between them and their children who are growing up in a culture different from the one their parents knew. New methods of teach-

ing reading and mathematics in the public schools make it difficult for parents to help their children or to understand their
ways of working. Curricula are changing in the schools. Many of
the literary contributions that have been studied for generations
are being replaced by contemporary contributions. Where generations of people were once united by a common literary bond,
they are now isolated from others, unless they work to maintain a
contact by reading the same things. The teacher, while helping
the student to prepare for the world in which he will live, helps
to provide stability and continuity of the community by being
sure the student learns at least a portion of the heritage of his
forebears.

While maintaining an identity of himself for himself, the teacher
works to develop a personal understanding of the people among
whom he lives and with whom he works. He moves freely among
communities not as a judge but as a teacher who attempts to get
people of differing backgrounds and beliefs to cooperate and to
build together. The teacher belongs to everyone and to no one.
He is free and works to keep a clear perspective. In a sense, he
provides the link between and among often opposing groupings
whether they are religious, racial, social, or the younger and older
generations. He tries to see all points of view—and they exist. He
sets an example, and strives to live up to the expectations of the
community.

Teachers are sometimes forced to refrain from participating
fully in community life and have to remain unidentified as leaders
and builders. Some are not allowed to play the roles of leadership of which they are capable. They are told what is expected
of them and they become "trainers" who do as they are told.
Society dictates to them, either directly or subtly, their codes of
conduct both while at school and at home. They are used as
tools—as program chairmen for community events and to lend
dignity to public events. They are expected to enforce the social
standards dictated by the community. They sometimes become
the objects of political maneuverings. They are sometimes looked

upon as if they were slaves to the whim of that community. Instead of being supported and allowed to build, they sometimes become the scapegoat of the parents or a community that has failed the children. Before they have a chance to structure and build in a community, it is sometimes too far gone and the teacher arrives in time to be accused of the destruction.

The teacher works to educate the community to recognize and to understand the place he fills as a leader and as a builder in that community. He has the courage to handle material that is controversial. He helps to break down the artificial walls that divide communities and he strives to get people at least to look over those walls, whether they ever go over them or not, so there will be understanding. He maintains his freedom as a teacher who is trying to bring objectivity into the minds of the people of the community. He never becomes a tool for the perpetuation of any point of view. He interprets groups to each other and thus breaks down walls of suspicion. He strives to get people to actively work together to build a community which will protect and exist for the good of all.

J. D. Y.

Questions for discussion

1 Why do communities tend to dictate the codes of behavior for teachers?
2 Do you feel that teachers should attempt to become leaders in communities? If so, to what extent? If not, what would be your reasons?
3 Name four or five teachers you have had who were active community leaders. Do you feel that their participation in community affairs affected their teaching in any way? How?
4 Do you feel that a teacher should strive to create an image in the community that would mark him as a special kind of person?

5 Should a teacher be responsible for deepening the faith of the students in an ideal or a way of life which the parents wish him to follow?

6 What special problems do teachers have in maintaining their own personal religious beliefs in a classroom where many faiths are represented?

7 What is the responsibility of the teacher in getting people of different beliefs to tolerate one another?

8 Do you believe that a person who agrees to help perpetuate the specific beliefs of a certain group is really a teacher? Discuss and explain.

9 How can a person of any particular persuasion teach ideas from the opposing point of view?

10 Discuss "Antagonism has always existed between generations but the power of education creates even wider gulfs."

. . . and I saw in the turning so clearly,
a child's forgotten mornings when he walked with
his mother through the parables of sun light . . .
his tears burned my cheeks and his heart
moved in mine.
—*Dylan Thomas*

18

A teacher is

a learner

What can a teacher learn when he is teaching? In the teacher-learner relationship, it is generally assumed that the teacher is one who instructs, enlightens, trains, indoctrinates, educates, gives instruction. Although the casual observer may be aware that some learning by the teacher must attend the teacher-learner relationship, it is the purpose of this chapter to examine the active and purposeful learning in which the teacher engages as he is teaching.

It is the total individual, not just his mind, that comes to the learning experience. This is true, not only of the student but also of the teacher. In *Heaven in My Hand*, Alice Lee Humphreys clearly demonstrates that the teacher, in order to be able to transmit knowledge, learns from the child. The child teaches him that he must know about the heart and makeup of individual children. He must know where they are in their thinking and feeling in order to be able to contact them and lead them out of themselves.

I call to thy remembrance the little Fire-brand Ginnie, and the flower of forgiveness which blossomed in her heart. How in her ignorance she would have given unto me back-talk. And I, in greater ignorance, being young, thought that to flourish before her eyes my small measuring rod would establish discipline. And lo, as I reached in rising irritation, mine own hand struck a table's edge, hurting it mightily. And Ginnie was sore distressed. And forgetting mine harsh intentions she essayed to ease the pain by holding my offending member against her own soft cheek, saying in compassionate tones, Thy poor, poor hand! Yes, and when it was better, she rejoiced as one healed of her own hurt.

Then was my Lesser Self silenced. And it descended to a Prompter's place near mine elbow.

And I pressed mine advantage, saying, Henceforth, shall I follow Ginnie and mine other little animated signposts to the Kingdom of Heaven. And perhaps if I learn from them, then will mine own passport be paid for and ready at hand.[1]

As the teacher works in the classroom, on any level from the kindergarten room to the college seminar, he is engaged in communicating. In order to communicate, he must know as much as he can about his subject matter, new contributions to his own particular field, his students, and how the students react and relate to the subject matter.

As a learner with other learners in the classroom, what are the sources of knowledge for the teacher? It has been said that to really learn a subject you should teach it. After all, knowledge has little value unless it is related to people or to other knowledge. The sources of knowledge for the teacher include reference books, textbooks, other teachers, original research. As he teaches, however, knowledge begins to emerge for both the teacher and the student.

During the flow of knowledge, the student learns new information and the teacher gains new insights as he realizes that learning is easy for some and difficult for others. He becomes more keenly aware of the need to find the paths along which he can communicate to others, and he learns that the paths differ for each individual. Some will be hungry to learn, some will not want to learn, and there will be degrees of desire and ability between these two extremes. As he learns the means necessary to communicate what he knows, he develops a more thorough understanding of his subject matter and begins to see even more possibilities for further research and learning in his subject.

Unless he learns to communicate, it is possible for a teacher to be lost in his own classroom. There are persons who hunger and thirst after knowledge: They delight in the pursuit of a thought, in the discovery of more information, in the realization of relationships between various aspects of learning. They often become smitten with learning for its own sake. The little prince would say, "Grownups are like that."² Like children who pursue an object into a wilderness, or chase a ball into a busy street, some seekers after knowledge will lose all sense of how and what they are learning relates to the people among whom they are living. A person who went out to teach came to this realization much too late and wrote the following account:

I TAUGHT THEM ALL

I have taught in high school for ten years. During that time I have given assignments, among others, to a murderer, a pugilist, an evangelist, a thief, and an imbecile.

The murderer was a quiet little boy who sat on the front seat and regarded me with pale blue eyes; the evangelist, easily the most popular boy in school, had the lead in the junior play; the pugilist lounged by the window and let loose at intervals a raucous laugh that startled even the geraniums; the thief was a gay-hearted Lothario with a song on his lips; and the imbecile, a soft-eyed little animal seeking the shadows.

The murderer awaits death in the state penitentiary; the evangelist

has lain a year now in the village churchyard; the pugilist lost an eye
in a brawl in Hong Kong; the thief, by standing on tiptoe, can see the
windows of my room from the county jail; and the once gentle-eyed
little imbecile beats his head against a padded wall in the state
asylum.

All of these pupils once sat in my room and looked at me gravely
across worn brown desks. I must have been a great help to those
pupils—I taught them the rhyming scheme of the Elizabethan sonnet
and how to diagram a complex sentence.

—Author Unknown

Knowledge can create gulfs between members of a community,
between cultures, between generations, between members of the
same family, and between teachers and their students. It is possible to hoard knowledge, just as it is possible to hoard money.
There are those who cannot evaluate knowledge in meaningful
and useful relationships. They may be compared to misers who
do not know the value of money because they do not see it used
in meaningful and useful ways.

As the teacher delights in the pursuit of knowledge and revels
in discoveries, he is like anyone who has good news to share and
looks for understanding and communication from those among
whom he is living. If he has not maintained communication, however, he may realize too late that he has run deep into the wilderness, losing all sense of relationship and direction. He may realize
too late that he has run into the busy street of a society that does
not understand him. Many teachers—Socrates, Jesus Christ, Gali-
leo, and hosts of others—have been crushed in the busy streets of
satisfied social and political groups who were not prepared for
their wisdom and advanced knowledge.

The wise teacher learns from his students and learns with his
students. In *Teacher*, Sylvia Ashton-Warner has written about
human relations between children and adults and between differing cultures.[3] She is realistic as she states, "the method of teaching
any subject in a Maori infant room may be seen as a plank in a
bridge from one culture to another, and to the extent that this
bridge is strengthened may a Maori in later life succeed." She is

aware, too, that at a tender age a wrench occurs from one culture to another, from which, either overtly or subconsciously, not all recover. She reveals that her Maori children taught her that they could read their own words. In conversation, she discovered their key words, and wrote them down for the children to keep. In this way, they learned to recognize their own words at a glance, to print them, and thus to begin the nucleus of individual reading vocabularies. Her own knowledge had come from experimenting with "first words" from imported readers which the children had not been able to respond to because they in no way suggested their way of life. She had, first of all, to learn from the children before she could teach them.

As a teacher finds, here and there, people who respond to him, who want to understand and to pursue the knowledge he has mastered, he delights in allowing them to wander through his thinking. As they pick and select from his mind, it helps him to organize and bring more order and logic to the knowledge he possesses. It helps him to understand these students as they use what he knows to give them stability. Then, instead of trying to force learning, he continues his pursuit of new information and relationships, while providing guided tours through his mind by way of lectures and discussions.

Teaching is a demanding and exciting venture. The person who has learned much and who learns how to impart what he knows avoids becoming a lonely creature in pursuit of knowledge and lost from society in a maze of knowledge and discovery. Instead, he becomes a leader who creates a following that learns and explores what he has discovered while they point out to him areas he has not explored. He blazes trails for them to follow and he observes, as they move into areas of thinking where he has been and he encourages them to go, that he must respect their efforts and give them time to bridge the distance between their and his scholarly achievements.

The teacher gains much from this relationship as his students ask questions and explore what he has learned. Sometimes they provide answers to questions he has wished to pursue further. When he observes the enthusiasm and delight of his students' learning, he is encouraged to move with more vigor and care into frontier and wilderness areas of knowledge seeking information, truth, and beauty.

No matter how much he learns, nor how wide the gulfs between him and others, the scholar, or teacher, can only claim to "know in part." He is never sure of what he really knows until he tests that knowledge and examines the fragments in the light of other responses to it. In the act of communicating, or teaching, he often discovers new insights as he learns from the many points of view in the classroom and the students' reactions to that knowledge, and these responses give dimension and meaning beyond his own interpretations. He approaches the classroom with deep humility and a sincere desire to follow the paths of truth wherever they may lead. In so doing, he connects what he "knows in part" with the reactions he gets from the students, looks for meaningful patterns and relationships, tests old and new evidence, and with what he has learned, he advances into further frontiers of knowledge and seeks other students to teach him.

It is very important for the teacher to have the confidence of those whom he would teach. If his record of education, research, experience, and study creates for them an image in which they can have confidence, they will accept what he has to say. His own achievements can work two ways, however, either to inspire his students or to alienate them. If the distances between him and his students are too great, he will be unable to achieve the esteem in the minds and hearts of his students that he must have to be effective with them. He then must defend the distance he has traveled and can no longer continue his own travels into enlightenment. His research is stymied and his own progress is arrested.

The effect a teacher has on a student can also be in jeopardy when there is alienation because of the image, in the mind of the student, of what a teacher should be. There are those who feel that his presuming to teach in a classroom means that a teacher has all the answers. The teacher who wishes to learn at the same time he teaches may thus be forced by his students to seem to know all.

Any "truth" becomes many truths as it is seen with different eyes, seen from many points of view, measured by different standards, placed in different relationships. The enlarging concept, for teacher and student, of any truth should be encouraged. If a teacher is placed in the position of committing himself to a point of view so that he is not allowed by his students to change his mind, or even seem to change it, he will find himself in a defensive position, unable to learn and to grow.

But the teacher who is able to learn and grow is fortunate. As he perceives a larger truth, as it is reflected in the minds of his students at their own level of development, it will enlarge his own. For example, as the teacher describes an object or a concept to the students and is as specific as he can possibly be, he will know by the students' reactions when they are thinking with him. When they begin to describe what they understand, however, the teacher will realize that there is more than his own point of view to be considered. When he begins to understand what the students know about the objects and concepts and realizes how they differ in understanding, his own concepts will be enlarged with ideas he had not thought of before.

There will be moments of enlightenment for the teacher in the classroom which will help him spontaneously to summarize that which he has not specifically prepared. One of the real secrets of teaching will then reveal itself to him, "To appear to have known all your life what you learned this afternoon."

In summary, then, the teacher is a learner with other learners. He realizes that what we know takes on different dimensions in context with other fragments of knowledge. If he ceases to grow as a learner, he is in danger of becoming just a trainer who is arrested in his own development. The teacher expands and learns as he tests ideas with learners who are in turn expanding under the influence of new knowledge. The teacher learns about himself

and his own inadequacies and develops humility in the presence of
a greater awareness of the far reaches of knowledge. Instead of
merely transmitting information, he gets a reflection of the meaning of knowledge and learns to teach with a purpose.

                                                                    J. D. Y.

Questions for discussion

1 Is there a time in his career when a teacher can feel that "because
   students can learn only so much anyhow," he will not need to
   add to his own knowledge in a specific field?
2 Are children pretty much alike or do they change much from generation to generation?
3 In addition to his responsibility to the furtherance of his own field
   of knowledge, what is the responsibility of the teacher to his students and their interest in his field?
4 Should a teacher feel the need of maintaining the confidence of
   the students by seeming to know all about his field?
5 Carl Sandburg, upon hearing a famous actress read one of his
   poems, jumped up from his rocking chair and said, "I wish I had
   meant that the way you read it." Discuss.
6 In what ways can a teacher gain and develop the confidence of
   those whom he would teach?
7 Should a teacher let a class know he has learned something from
   them?
8 How can the teacher's achievements alienate his students?
9 Discuss "Any truth becomes many truths when seen with different
   eyes."
10 Discuss the place of spontaneity in the teaching-learning process.

O wad some Pow'r the giftie gie us
To see oursels as ithers see us!
It wad frae mony a blunder free us,
    And foolish notion.
—*Robert Burns*

19

A teacher is

a facer of reality

Reality is not necessarily desirable; nor, however, is it undesirable. A bride marching down the aisle to the wedding altar is facing a reality. She may not have it fully defined, and the reality of marriage as she views it does not guarantee the reality of marriage as it is. To be more accurate, the condition of marriage is in a constant state of change and adjustment as two people become accustomed to one another's ways, likes, and dislikes. The condition of marriage changes more dramatically as children are born, financial situations change, social standing and economic demands change. There are innumerable influences that will cause the reality of marriage as faced by the bride or groom to change. Divorce and disintegration of the family unit will follow if either of the two parties to the marriage is unable to accept the realities that come to pass as a result of these many influences. There is a spine of truth that will cement the relationship and keep it firm and strong when it is threatened and buffeted by facts which are momentary and not necessarily true. Man is so often strongly in pursuit of facts that he sometimes fails to perceive the truth.

Roark Bradford in his *How Come Christmas* tells the beautiful story of a plain and uncomplex little Negro minister who gathered all the facts he could by standing outside the white folks' churches in the South and gleaning what bits of information he could overhear from the preachers who talked to the comfortable people in the comfortable interiors of those churches.[1] With joy in his heart, he went with the news he heard and gathered the little Negro children of his parish around the little potbellied stove in the one-room schoolhouse that served for their church house to tell them a story of hope. He told about a baby named "Po' Little Jesus" who was born at about the time Gawge Washington "put kaingin' out'n style" by "whuppin' all de kaings from Balmoral to Belial and den back again." At the same time "Old Sandy Claus went to visit the new baby at Mis' Mary's house," and as he was entertaining the baby with a big red apple he had brought as a cradle gift, the Lord stepped in and asked Old Santa Claus to make the children happy each year at Christmas time. The little preacher's final statement to the children is, "De Lawd made Jesus for the grown folks so when he grew up they could lean on him and moan dey sins away. But de Lawd knows the chilluns got to have some fun too, so dat's how come it's Christmas and all dat." We are amused that the little minister has incorrectly combined facts, but we are moved by his ability to preserve the spine of truth which is of greater value than are isolated facts.

Everyone must face up to many kinds of reality. Some he seeks with a purpose; others elude him as he is diverted in his search. As he finds fragmented evidences of fact, he sometimes summarizes and draws conclusions before he has enough evidence. He is also in danger of acting on the basis of that evidence, having lost touch with the central truth. One of his problems is that of recognizing reality when he is in direct contact with it.

What, then, is reality? What must the teacher face? What must the student face? Philosophers, teachers, scientists, poets and others have attempted to define reality and it is agreed by many that just as "beauty is in the eye of the beholder," so is reality determined relatively.

The teacher learns to identify reality in terms of himself and his students and he faces that reality and helps the student to discover interaction and purpose and to relate what he learns to reality as he comes to perceive it.

To be more specific, the teacher learns to face a concept of himself from the standpoint of the student who may see him as (1) a symbol of authority against whom there should be rebellion, (2) one who does not care about the student but who is imposing on him information or learning that is of interest and value only to the teacher, (3) an individual for whom there should be no respect because teaching is not a respectable profession, (4) an object of pity who cannot keep pace with social and financial achievements of the community, or (5) an obstacle in the path to adulthood and ultimate independence.

As suggested by Robert Burns, the teacher must try to see himself as others see him. His next task, then, is to seek an objective view of the students and to realize, among other things, that (1) some are not interested in learning, (2) their capacities for learning are varied, (3) few of them are objective about their talents, (4) the student's concept of the teacher is not objective—it is either totally positive or totally negative, (5) many students do not have goals and have no idea why they are in the learning situation.

The teacher makes an attempt to be objective about the students. He makes an effort to accept them as they are with no reservations. He faces the reality of the student as he is and tries to teach him to face the realities, many of them not desirable, about himself so that he can capitalize on his strengths and place his weaknesses in the right perspective.

In literature, there are many examples of people who cannot be objective about themselves. Bottom the weaver, a rustic and one of the funniest of all of William Shakespeare's contrivances, is largely funny because his concept of himself is so out of tune with what the audience sees. Though he is an unlikely looking creature with little talent, there is no doubt in his own mind that ladies are enthralled and overwhelmed by his handsomeness. It is no surprise to him then, when Titania, the Queen of the Fairies, having been fooled by the scoundrel fairy, Puck, who had slipped a love potion into her eyes while she slept, should, on waking, fall in love with him. He accepts her comments on his handsomeness with aplomb, unaware that Puck also has affixed the "asses nole" on his shoulders. Bottom is proud of his wit which, to his hearers, is witless, "nay, I can gleek upon occasion," and is not aware that his audience is laughing at him and not with him. The same is true of all the rustics who have banded together with excellent intentions to present a play in honor of the wedding of Theseus to Hippolyta. Several groups of players offered to present their plays in honor of the wedding, but the rustics were chosen—although not for the same reasons which the players had intended—by the King, to be used as entertainment for the wedding party. The rustics, their intentions good, had obviously attempted a project for which they were ill-equipped. They displayed a lack of knowledge and a lack of sensitivity to the skills required of good actors. As they reveled in their performance, their audience laughed at them for being goons.

In the tragedy of *Macbeth*, Shakespeare chronicles the life of a man who does not wish to face reality as it is. He is not content to progress in the normal processes, but desires to bypass certain steps in the process in order to achieve his goal. When he falters in his decision as he becomes more aware of the reality of his limitation, he is supported by an outside force, Lady Macbeth, who pushes him even beyond his own will to achieve heights which are not within his reach. Macbeth, as he is tormented in the dagger scene, wonders, "Is this a dagger which I see before me, the handle toward my hand? Come, let me clutch thee. I have thee not, and yet I see thee still. Art thou not, fatal vision, sensible to feeling as to sight? Or art thou but a dagger of the mind, a false creation, proceeding from the heat-oppressed brain?" In his desperation, Macbeth wishes a confrontation with reality although his vaulted ambition clouds his views. He is able even to suggest that the dagger he sees is but a figment of the imagination, and a warning. Even though his own "heat-oppressed brain" tries to give adequate warning, his best teacher, himself, cannot penetrate the strong desire for power that causes him to want to kill. When his desire for power wavers, his wife's desire for power and her inability to face the realities as they are, further distort Macbeth's reason.

There are many examples of problems teachers face in getting students to be objective about their abilities. Frequently students cannot face reality. Some years ago, I had a young man in my classes who was a severe spastic. His physical movements were grotesque and uncontrolled, and his speech was almost unintelligible. He wanted to major in Theatre Arts, and felt that he would be a good actor. More than anything else, he wanted to perform in the college plays. He could not "see" himself as he was. The reality of his condition was more than he could absorb or accept so it was up to the teacher to help him to realize that he should not continue reaching beyond his physical limitations, but that he should work within the framework of his confinement and try to achieve what would lie within his grasp and the realm of possibility.

Students who have never heard their own voices on a playback are seldom if ever convinced on first hearing that what they hear are their own voices. The perspective is different. We hear other voices, those we admire and respond to, and in our desire to make beautiful sounds, we may speak and sing with the feeling that we, too, are making beautiful sounds; not because we are making them but because we want to do so. The very objective tape recorder reveals to us that it is not so or that it is so. However, we are likely to destroy the tape recorder and face only what we wish were true about ourselves instead of either working to change what exists or merely accepting the fact.

The self-concept is perhaps the most complex and difficult aspect of the teaching process to be handled. Some years ago, when I was working in a speech correction clinic, an elementary school teacher presented a case to me saying, "Thith child lithpth and I don't underthtand why." The teacher was unaware that the child was reflecting or imitating her speech. It was not until we could record her speech on the tape recorder and play it back for her that the young teacher could believe that what we told her was true.

It is not a simple matter to cause one to take an objective look at himself. There are many dangers inherent in the process of facing reality. Every individual must have some sense of worth and adequacy to cling to and these must be preserved as the individual takes a more accurate look at himself that may not be altogether flattering. As the teacher points out inadequacy and limitation, he must also point out what avenues the student can follow toward enrichment and growth.

Ideally, the young teacher and all teachers for that matter approach their classrooms, their students, their colleagues, the subject matter, with enthusiasm and an air of excitement, not doubting that all within their hearing will be capable, motivated, responsive, and keenly interested in learning. Surely, teachers can recall more than one experience in which they did not achieve the desired responses by their classes to carefully planned lessons. It may be possible that they will discover, as they review the situations, that they planned the lessons in terms of themselves and that they needed more information about the class in order to be able to understand the responses.

Each student goes to school for a different purpose, just as each individual goes to the theatre for a different purpose. Not everyone goes to learn what the author intended. Some go simply for diversion, others go as critics for the local newspapers, or just as critics; some are interested in the content of the performance; some are interested in the techniques of staging; some are interested in costumes; some are interested in acting. In any case, the responses are individual and will be made on the basis of previous experience, knowledge, and interest. Responses will also be made in terms of the reality which the student or viewer wishes to find.

In the summer of 1966, seventy-two boys and girls from widely scattered sections of Orange County and all in the junior year of high school were part of an experiment called Upward Bound at California State College in Fullerton. The news media identified them as being potential college students from low economic backgrounds who were culturally deprived. An intensive program of classes and extracurricular activities was devised for the purpose of providing additional experiences of many kinds for them. They were introduced to art, drama, music and dance. Among the many extracurricular activities, they were taken to the theatre; all levels of the theatre. A local high school was performing *Carrousel,* the college theatre presented Maxwell Anderson's *Anne of the Thousand Days*, and the APA, one of the most successful and distinguished repertory companies in the United States, was presenting among others, *You Can't Take It With You* at the Huntington Hartford theatre in Hollywood. The students attended all these plays. It should be remembered that none of them had ever seen a stage play before. When they were asked, after having attended all three plays, which one they thought was the best from every standpoint, their unanimous agreement was that *Carrousel* performed by the high school students was by far the best. They liked the script, the staging, the music, and the acting. To those who may be disappointed in their responses, the reality must be faced, that the students were responding spontaneously in terms of their backgrounds and knowledge. They liked their peer group in a performance perhaps because it brought the possibility of success in this kind of work within their own range of possible attainment. It doesn't matter whether their choice at this level of their development was right or wrong. We merely face the reality of their being at this particular point in their growth so that the teacher can take them where they are and move them to where they ought to be.

Up to this point we have been thinking of reality only as it relates to the teacher and to the students and their concepts of each other. It is necessary, too, to realize the other aspects of reality as humanity perceives them.

In his play, *Our Town*, Thornton Wilder gives the line to Emily, a young girl who grew up in an average little town, "Does anyone ever really realize life while he's living it, every, every minute?" She says this line after she is dead and has requested the opportunity to relive the simplest and most uneventful day of the life she took for granted. Only when she takes the second look at her mother who has wrapped a little birthday gift and her father who remembered to get her a present while he was on a trip does she realize all that she let slip by her. Their simple expressions of love are much too overwhelming and she cannot look at their beauty and their love for her.

Many poets have been able to look at a sunset, or the opening of a flower, or the multitudinous aspects of beauty in the universe. They have been able to see what is beautiful there; they have been able to be hurt by it; they have been able to be healed; they have been able to crystallize it in words or in painting or in sculpture for others to see. There are so many who are unable to respond because they cannot face the fullness of reality and therefore look only with their eyes. They see only what they can stand to see and there are many who protect themselves from the powerful effects of facing reality because they are too sensitive and cannot cope with the price one must pay for tenderness. To face reality, one must see with the heart. The little prince in Antoine de Saint-

Exupéry's book, *The Little Prince,* looked at all the roses and said, "You are beautiful but you are empty . . . to be sure, an ordinary passerby would think my rose looked just like you—the rose that belongs to me. But . . . she is more important . . . because it is she I have watered . . . because she is *my* rose." The fox then said to the prince, ". . . here is my secret: It is only with the heart that one can see rightly; what is essential is invisible to the eye."[2] The teacher seeks to understand and to have faith in what is invisible to the eye. The teacher also seeks to understand himself as he faces reality in his relationships with the students who look to him, and believe in him as a confidant and guide.

Perhaps one of the most difficult realities for the teacher to face is that of planting the seed and setting growth in motion for the students, believing in the growth that will follow without ever being able to see it.

The teacher, then, is one who faces reality. He faces the facts that people are what they are at different levels and stages in process toward maturity. He accepts the students with their strengths and weaknesses and places their attributes in the proper perspective. He tries to gain a view of himself as seen by the students, and strives to be objective about what he discovers. He realizes that there are some students who wish to learn, and some who do not care. He is aware that capacities for learning vary, and helps the students to become aware of their own strengths and weaknesses. He realizes that every individual must have some sense of worth and adequacy to cling to and to build on, and that these must be preserved as the individual takes a more accurate look at himself; a look which may not be altogether flattering.

Whatever realities the student has to face, it is the responsibility of the teacher to help give him a sense of worth, perhaps best summed up in the following lines about "Rain Pools":

> I am so small
> That even the wind can't ruffle my surface . . .
> But I hold a star.
>
> J. D. Y.

Questions for discussion

1 Discuss: "Man is often so strongly in pursuit of facts that he fails to perceive the truth."
2 What are some student problems in facing reality?
3 What are some teacher problems in facing reality?
4 Why is teaching not a respectable profession in the eyes of some people?
5 Why is the student's concept of the teacher not objective?
6 Can a teacher be objective about students? What pitfalls must he avoid for the sake of objectivity?
7 What realities must an individual face in attempting to be objective about himself?
8 Name several reasons people may have for going to elementary and secondary levels. Compare these with reasons people have for taking certain courses at the college level.
9 Why would a group like a high school play better than a play given by a group of outstanding professional performers?
10 Discuss: "Some realities are much too grand for the human being to comprehend. Some realities are too beautiful for him to face."

Yet in these thoughts myself almost despising,
Haply I think on thee,—and then my state,
Like to the lark at break of day arising
From sullen earth, sings hymns at heaven's gate;
For thy sweet love remember'd such wealth brings
That then I scorn to change my state with kings.
—*William Shakespeare*

20

A teacher is

an emancipator

The teacher is a perceptive person who sees potential in the student. He respects the human being and is aware that many are slaves to cultural stagnation. When others wag their heads in disgust with some students, the teacher recognizes their need for experience, recognition, and encouragement. The teacher knows that these processes will often free the students from unfortunate self-images, from ignorance, and from feelings of rejection and inferiority. In this respect, the teacher is very like an artist who sees potential in bits of broken glass, or dried flowers and weeds, or stone, or bottle caps, or scraps of colored cloth or other materials that most people would throw away or at least disregard. The artist sees what is not visible to the average eye. He looks beyond what is obvious and sees possibility.

A nobleman once asked Michelangelo, "How did you come to make that astonishing figure of Night?" He replied, "I had a block of marble which was concealing that statue which you see there. The only effort involved is to take away the tiny pieces which surround it and prevent it from being seen. For anyone who knows how to do this, nothing could be easier."[1]

Although many others had perhaps passed by it, admired it in its rough-hewn beauty, and dismissed it from their minds, the artist was able to recognize in each block of marble with which he came in contact the potentials which lay within. He knew, too, how to carefully chip away the tiny pieces which surrounded the object of beauty and how to release it to the gaze of generations. Had he not lived, had he not developed skill as an artist, had he been unable to see the possibilities in a block of marble, had he not persevered, the mighty works of Michelangelo, "The Figure of Night," "David," "The Pieta," and all the rest would have been left as ineffective blocks of marble in a quarry. Of course, they could have been cut up in other ways to serve the utilitarian needs of mankind. But until the perceptive eye of the artist, having carefully developed his vision and his skill with his art, saw the main force within the stone and released from the great pieces of statuary "the tiny pieces which surround it and prevent it from being seen," those useless blocks could never command the respect and attention of the world, inspiring people as they have done and still do in all ages.

The teacher is aware that some information has already been absorbed by the students before they come into his classroom. He is aware, too, that what people know may be facts which they have not organized into meaningful relationships. The teacher sometimes has to "prime the pump" and get the ideas of the students to flow so they will have meaning for them. There is no need to pour more ideas in until the student is able to organize what he knows. Ideas and knowledge have meaning as they flow from the minds of people because when a person can say what he knows, it is more certain to have meaning for him and for those to whom he speaks.

In the ranch country in southeastern New Mexico, as in some other regions of the world, the people have to dig wells or cisterns, and every year during the rainy season, after the roof of the house is cleansed by the first showers, troughs are provided from the gutters on the roofs of each of the houses to the wells so the water can fill the cisterns. Hand pumps are placed in such a way that when the operator raises and lowers the handle, water will flow. When the rainy season is over and the dry season comes, the water level drops. It then becomes more and more difficult to get water from the wells, and it is necessary to prime the pump to get the water to flow. It is possible for people to die of thirst even with water so near if they do not know how to pour a cupful of water into the pump and, by gently pumping, make contact with the water that is so far below.

The steady hand chipping carefully on the marble, the rhythmic priming of the well accompanied by steady pumping, are very like the processes needed by the good teacher who must be able to prime the students, to chip away all that arrests and obscures them, and to keep producing a rhythmic flow of creativity from the students that will not cease. The statue lies within the block of marble. The water is in the cistern. A heavy blow to the marble without thought of the statue that lies within can cause the entire piece to lie shattered and useless. The sudden burst from restraint can cause severe damage; even total destruction. Even when the water is released from the well, there must be a steady rhythmic pumping to bring it from a cistern, so that the flow of water will be productive and not destructive. The even, gentle, exciting release from restraint will produce power that is deliberate and controlled. If the release is too sudden, there is danger that without control it will have no direction, will be unchanneled, and will result in severe destruction.

Humanity is not always aware of its bondage. Someone or some small group must see that there are those bound in ignorance or political slavery, or physical disease or spiritual sickness, or tradition or social position, or any number of other types of bondage. The masses tend to seethe in slavery until outlets are provided by philosophers, poets, artists, and teachers, who identify the kinds of bondage and communicate paths to freedom. Albert Schweitzer gave up his personal career to emancipate the peoples of Africa from disease and ignorance, from want and exploitation; Gandhi freed the Indian people from political bondage to the British; scientists have freed mankind generally from superstition and ignorance about the universe; the medical profession is dedicated to freeing the world from physical disease; great religious leaders of the world have given their lives to spiritual emancipation for those who follow them. And the teacher frees the student from cultural bondage, from ignorance about the material world, from social unawareness, from the lack of knowledge, and sets in him a rhythmic flow of growth that causes him to be able to absorb and to add to his knowledge, to organize and to produce meaningfully.

To many, the term "Emancipator" brings to mind the American Negro who has struggled for so long to understand the meaning of freedom and who has attempted to communicate to the other segments of the culture in which he finds himself that he can assume the responsibilities attendant to free men. The term "Emancipator" has been assigned to one man, Abraham Lincoln. It is understood, of course, that he was not the only representative of a movement, and could not have singlehandedly achieved emancipation for the Negro. In fact, subsequent history has demonstrated that in many ways the Negro is not yet free. There will be no attempt here to analyze the very complex problem of the Negro in America. The analogy is provided to show that each generation must work out its own freedom in terms of all the other conditions of change in living.

It is a truism that man inherits his life. He inherits a physical body to which many generations have contributed. He inherits social standing, his religion, his politics, his language, his moral standards, his intelligence capacity, and other attributes, some of them strengths and some of them weaknesses. As he grows and matures within the framework of all these influences, in a sense he becomes their prisoner. Without asking questions, and without exploring for himself, he simply accepts or assumes the role that is handed him. There is nothing that can be done about his inheriting either blue or brown eyes, the tendency to baldness, his stature and general strength, and other characteristics. This is all determined by genes. Although he may wear a wig, high heels, or any other artificial device, basically he will be physically the same individual who will pass on the genes of his inheritance to his succeeding generations.

Although he inherits the geographical setting, social standing, religion, politics, language, moral standards and although their influences are strong, it is possible for him to be emancipated from these bonds.

In her book, *Door in the Wall*, Marguerite de Angeli describes a young medieval lad who was crippled by the plague and was not allowed to be with his father, a knight, and his mother who attended the queen.[2] In his bondage which followed the sickness that had crippled him so that he would never walk again, he developed the ability to swim. When he was taught by an old friar, "be sure, lad, somewhere there's a door in every wall," he learned his lesson well. It was he who later saved the castle where both his mother and his father served, by finding the small door in the wall that surrounded the castle, making his way to the moat which lay below, swimming the treacherous waters of the moat, and hobbling as if he were mentally incompetent among those who laid siege to the castle. He carried word for help, and returned triumphantly with the forces which broke the siege. Later, he stood proudly with his father the knight to receive the blessing of the lord of the whole domain.

Virginia Sorensen in her book, *Plain Girl*, which gives an excel-

lent understanding of the Amish people, relates the concern of
an Amish father who, wanting to "will" his religion to his children,
warned his daughter Esther, as she was entering a public school
where the manners, mores, and customs were not compatible
with those of the Amish faith, never to take the first step away.[3]
Many generations had heeded that admonition and had not strayed.
The same is true in many religions. Subsequent generations seem
to have inherited the form and ritual and tradition of that religion
without understanding the purpose and meaning of it. Miss Sorensen writes of an emerging generation and its attempt to maintain
strong ties with its heritage while updating its existence to a new
century and generation, attempting to integrate their lives with a
religion they have inherited, at the same time attempting to understand that religion. Teachers often see the wells of potential where
the waters of creativity have seemed to run low. They see groups
who are isolated from the rhythm and flow of growth and they
prime those wells with ideas, knowledge, and hope. This helps the
individuals to achieve contact with culture and to live fuller, richer,
though often disturbed, lives.

A teacher is like the sculptor who sees potential in the materials
with which he works. He works to chip away confining shells without damaging the persons or the souls that reside within. He releases the individual to a realization of his abilities.

A teacher primes wells of creativity. He develops the skill to
generate a rhythmic flow from the student by providing enough
insights and focus and urging. He gently pumps from the deep
wells that reside within the student and brings him to the threshold of his own mind. He provides a path and is careful to guide
those who are emerging and growing to do so in a positive and
useful way, as long as he is able to help. He encourages students
to ask questions and to pursue them to conclusions in the free
atmosphere of truth and scientific evidence instead of bewildering
and arresting supposition and superstition.

Real freedom exists for the individual who understands why he
believes as he does, for the person who is not bound by fear or

guilt or superstition, for the person who learns and whose ideas flow freely, for the person who has the courage to free himself from confining bonds of religious ritual and superstition, for the person who does not need the protection of obscurity.

J. D. Y.

Questions for discussion

1 Discuss the kinds of bondage in which humanity finds itself. Give examples.
2 If an individual is pleased in his bondage should he be left there?
3 Discuss ways in which a teacher can prime the pump and get creativity to flow from the student.
4 How can the teacher do damage by chipping too hard or priming too fast?
5 Why should one person try to free or emancipate another?
6 How can a people be emancipated while individuals among them are still bound?
7 Discuss "Mankind often worships the symbol and the ritual instead of God."
8 How does a person grow into bondage?
9 Is it possible to emerge from a cultural and social way of life yet maintain strong ties with those who do not wish to do the same?
10 Discuss the attributes of real freedom.

Judge not, that ye be not judged.
For with what judgment ye judge, ye shall be judged:
and with what measure ye mete, it shall be measured
to you again.
—*Matthew 7:1-2*
To everything there is a season, and a time to
every purpose under the heaven.
—*Ecclesiastes 3:1*

21

A teacher is

an evaluator

Evaluation is perhaps the most complex aspect of the entire process of teaching, because it involves so many backgrounds and relationships and other variables which take on meaning only in context so that it is next to impossible to isolate any feature of evaluation. Even though he may not be aware of it and is making no specific record at the moment, a sensitive teacher is constantly evaluating, sizing up, summing up, and categorizing the students in terms of the evident responses they make to the learning situation. We must not overlook the possibility that the teacher may misjudge or miscalculate what the responses should be. Because evaluation usually involves evidences which are immediately tangible, it may not be possible to evaluate the subtle influences which bring change to a person's life even years after the actual classroom experience is long forgotten.

There will be no attempt to prove statistically the frequency with which teachers mention their dislike of testing and evaluation. However, anyone who has been around teachers when they have to make decisions about their students will recall that a common comment is, "Teaching would be fun if it weren't for grading." The grading problem has not yet been solved. Schools, school districts, and teachers have tried various methods including (a) no grades at all, (b) written evaluations of the individual as he seemed to relate to the learning process, (c) parent conferences in which the parents and teachers discuss the children, (d) simple pass or fail, (e) letter grades, (f) number grades, and of course many others.

It is clear that the student is anxious about how he is doing in a class. He wants to know what the teacher thinks of him and any response is better than none. A student who is ignored will do many things even to the point of distorted behavior to get a response—positive or negative. He may prefer approval but even disapproval is better for him than no response at all.

Let us look at a few of the many components of the evaluation process and later examine the interrelationships which specially involve the teacher. The following diagram is an attempt to show how, at the elementary school level and at the high school level, the various major components in the evaluation process relate to each other:

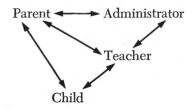

It is, of course, obvious that the child is the ultimate and central feature of this evaluation, although we are aware that the other participants are actively and strongly evaluating one another and their decisions affect the outcomes of the evaluations of the child. Pressures between the parents and the teacher are perhaps more intense than are the other relationships because these two are in direct contact with the administrator, with the child, and with each other. The administrator and the child have little direct contact with each other.

At the college level, the parent is not as closely involved in the evaluation process and neither is the administrator. It is true that the administrator must evaluate a faculty member before hiring him and it is true that for reappointment, promotion, and tenure purposes the administrator evaluates the teacher. In fact, the teaching ability and performance is so important that the direct evaluation by the student of the faculty member becomes significant. However, the place of the teacher as evaluator is the central theme of this chapter.

In making an evaluation, the teacher needs to understand the student in terms of his environment and his place in the home situation, his place in the community, or his place in the college community. He needs to know what pressures are brought to bear. He sometimes discovers some important information as he talks either directly with the student, directly with the parent, or with the administrator who has talked to the parent. At the college level, of course, he finds out what he can from the student, from recommendations, and by observation of the student as a member of a community. In the respective chains of relationships, each of the participants will engage in evaluation of the others, and it stands to reason that the student, having either "mastered" or "succumbed" to the parental environment will be evaluating his new source of authority. The teacher, on the other hand, will be discovering where his new pupil is in his climb to maturity. In the precollege situation, the parent and teacher will be attempting to evaluate one another, not only in their direct relations with each other, but also by innuendos and information they can gather, both from the student and from mutual contact with the school administrator as he tries to interpret each to the other.

However, though the general evaluation is complex, the most meaningful and influential evaluation takes place as the teacher reacts directly to the student in terms of specific performance. The teacher must consider and feel responsible for what such an evaluation will do to a student and what it may do for him. Care must be taken that the evaluation will contribute to the growth of the student and that it in no way arrests or destroys him. It should encourage him and give him an idea of the progress he has made. This, of course, should be as objectively done as possible. It would be unfair to give him an unrealistic evaluation that may indicate success he has not achieved, or potential which he does not possess.

Because he is being evaluated by all with whom he comes in contact, the student has to learn which of the sources he can respect and this can become a difficult choice. An example of situations where confusions can occur within students is the review of a college play in a campus newspaper. It is true that those who mount the play have been involved in the design, construction, and painting of the scenery; the design, cutting, and fitting of costumes; lighting; directing; acting; house management and all the other aspects of the production. When opening night, or "exam time" arrives, and the play is given the final test by performance for an audience, there is generally a feeling of excitement and anticipation and each person who has had anything to do with the mounting of the play will carry the strong hope within him that the play will be considered a success.

Strangely, an article in the campus paper written by a person who is not sophisticated in drama and who has narrow biases, likes, and dislikes can, by severely criticizing the play, destroy the confidence the students have in their director and in his years of background and experience. The student should listen to his teacher or his director who will know what progress has been made in the process and who will make an evaluation accordingly. The student will be better able to understand that if he were more accomplished, he would be out of place in a learning situation where he has a right to make mistakes. It is important for the student to know which evaluations and judgments are right for him.

The process of learning and the work of the classroom teacher who is trying to build confidence in the pupil can be destroyed in one sentence. The parent—or any other evaluator or symbol of authority whom the student respects—who looks for the end prod-duct rather than the dynamic processes which will later have the potential of producing many excellent end products, can, by one disapproving sentence, destroy initiative, confidence, growth, and motivation.

A teacher is an evaluator who sees potential and who develops that potential at a rate at which the student can grow, while there are others who are critics (and sometimes parents fall into this category) who are looking at the end product. The growth of the student can be arrested by their sometimes not too considered judgment.

To further dramatize the importance of the teacher and evalua-tion, it should be noted that evaluation may produce many kinds of results. The evaluation may (a) discourage the student and cause him to feel he is a failure, (b) give him a more accurate con-cept of himself and cause him to grow on the foundation of a new and better image, (c) get him a job or promotion, (d) keep him from getting a job or even cause him to be fired.

The teacher's purpose is not that of passing judgment and categorizing the student. Rather, he works with care to encourage growth, to help the student understand where he is in the proc-ess, to guide him in positive ways, to encourage him in his strengths, and to advise him about his weaknesses.

Each teacher works with each pupil in a very complex association that involves the student's reaction to previous teachers and to teaching in general. With this awareness, and at the risk of seeming to oversimplify, an attempt will be made here to examine only the teacher and evaluation.

It has been noted that teachers as a rule do not enjoy having to make specific evaluations. This may be true because either a positive or negative grade given by a teacher can serve to arrest the progress of a student and the process of his growth by creating a momentary image to which he becomes committed. The teacher is aware of this possibility. However, "To everything there is a season." Just so, there is a time for evaluating, a time for summing up. It is hoped that no matter what progress the student has made (since all proceed at different rates of speed and on different levels), the teacher will, in his evaluating, be able to praise and to encourage the student in terms of the student's own success. "Wherefore I perceive that there is nothing better, than that a man should rejoice in his own works." In the learning process, any individual builds on whatever foundation has been laid. The budding actor engages in certain basic training of the spirit and of the body which will make it possible for him to take his place as a professional in the field. Just as the student of history or English or mathematics periodically needs an objective test or an essay test which will give him some idea of how he is achieving, the actor, as he achieves bits and pieces of knowledge and insight, periodically needs an audience or a testing ground where he can prove himself. The early performance may not even meet minimum standards, and the audience reaction may seem cold and very critical. The director, or teacher, is placed in the very awkward but important position of being able at the same time to praise the student in the process and to point out his potential success to him without giving him a distorted view of himself and of a finished product which will not meet minimum standards.

When a baby is born, the doctor holds it up to the light and makes first an observation and then a pronouncement, "It's a boy" or "It's a girl," "It is healthy," "It is weak and needs oxygen," or "It is well-formed and has all its fingers and toes," or "It is in some way not complete!" Whatever its condition, the doctor can only suggest to the parents what kinds of things can be done to help the child achieve its potential, and he can only predict possibilities in terms of what he sees. In no case does he reject or throw out a baby simply because it does not measure up to expected and hoped-for standards. The child is fed and cared for in such a way that he will at least have an opportunity to grow.

The teacher, like the doctor, looks at the child and in some way arrives at decisions concerning his potential. He does a certain amount of objective testing. The results are not used in isolation, but fit into a pattern that develops as a result of other kinds of testing. He listens carefully to the student in order to help determine whether or not he is ready for the kind of work which will be expected of him. After all, it is a part of evaluation to know "where the trip begins" and to be able to predict the probable success the traveler will have in making the trip.

He listens to the (a) lack of direction, (b) the anxiety, (c) the desperation, (d) the need for acceptance, (e) the fear that may be revealed in the voice, the quick glance, or the simple statement of such questions as: "Is this what you want me to do?" "Look at this!" "How do you like it?" "See me?" "See me?" The teacher listens to and understands the hurt student who either says or shows by his actions that he is saying "Go away. Don't look." "Don't say anything to me." "I don't believe you."

The teacher is constantly evaluating the speed and the direction of the student's learning and is keenly aware of the need to change pace, to bring pressure or to ease pressure on the student. He is flexible and is ready to make instantaneous changes when they seem to be needed.

He constantly evaluates himself to see how he relates to the process and periodically checks his own mental and emotional state to be sure his own excitement does not subside.

Perhaps one of the most deadly dangers to good teaching is

that it can become routine to the extent that the teacher works by formula instead of in terms of the evaluation to which each student is entitled. The danger of giving in to working by formula is ever present because the first exciting and spontaneous days cannot really be duplicated and there is a tendency for the human being to try to recall first experiences instead of moving on to new ones.

An awareness of these dangers will help the teacher to determine the appropriateness of certain kinds of work for specific students in his classroom. The teacher is in no way wishing to convict his students nor is he attempting to forgive. His commitment is to the conservation of the best qualities each of his students possesses. Therefore, he tries to discover potential, to excite growth without smothering or killing it, and to help the student know how to do the most with what he possesses.

In planning and executing evaluation, the teacher gives constant care to the standards he uses. If he is evaluating a social concept, he measures it against current standards if that is his reason for evaluating it. If he is interested in the social concept historically, he measures it against the period which is being examined. If he is evaluating a linear measurement, he notes whether he is measuring with a meter or a mile. If he is evaluating the worth of an American dollar, he measures it against the currency in use in the country where he will spend it. If he is evaluating a student, he is seeking to measure that student against a "norm" which has been produced by previous evaluation and standards provided by many students who have been tested and grouped according to physical age, mental age, social background, financial background, etc.

Once the student is identified by all the means possible, the teacher then constantly measures him against himself, realizing that the information provided by tests and other forms of evaluation is only reference material which will serve as a guideline to the student's potential. The goal, of course, is that the student eventually achieves the ability to continue an objective and accurate evaluation of his own growth and development, leaving his teachers to guide others on the path to self-development and maturity.

J. D. Y.

Questions for discussion

1 What are some precautions a teacher should take in preparing to evaluate students?
2 Is it possible that a teacher has prejudged and made mental evaluations which will affect a final grade obtained by objective testing?
3 In evaluating a student, does the teacher ever do so in the light of what he knows about the student's parents?
4 How does the administrator of a school fit into the evaluation of the student body?
5 Discuss all the information a teacher needs when approaching the subject of evaluation, such as, environment, social backgrounds, and other criterion.
6 What effects can evaluation have on a child? What desired effects do we seek?
7 What are the effects of an evaluation made by a person who is not equipped to make the evaluation?
8 Why must a teacher constantly evaluate himself to see how he relates to the process?
9 What tools must a teacher use in evaluation? Against what does he measure the student?
10 Discuss: "Once the student is identified by all the means possible, he is then constantly measured against himself."

... and the Lord said, I have surely seen the affliction
of my people which are in Egypt and have heard
their cry by reason of their taskmasters; for I know their
sorrows; and I am come down to deliver them out
of the hand of the Egyptians. .... Come now therefore,
and I will send thee to Pharaoh, that thou mayest bring forth
my people the children of Israel out of Egypt.
—*Exodus 3:7-10*

22

A teacher is

a conserver: one
who redeems or saves

Moses was chosen by his God to lead the children of
Israel from their bondage in Egypt. His personal sacrifices as a
redeemer were many. He had to give up wealth, position, and
power in the world that ruled his beloved people; he had to become one of them in order to teach and to lead them to the land
"flowing with milk and honey." He maintained a direct contact
with his God and followed His instructions, and throughout his
forty years in the wilderness, strove to make peace between his
people and their God. He had to save them from the grumbling

and dissatisfaction and greed and worship of idols that would have destroyed them.

The task of leading, conserving, or saving is complex. A teacher cannot just walk into a classroom, say to a group of students, "I am here to tell you what you need to know," and expect learning to follow. It is evident to anyone who has been in a classroom for even a few minutes that this will not be a good learning situation.

The curriculum, of course, is planned. The elementary school child goes to the classroom and to a curriculum that is established without consulting him. The high school student does the same but he does have an opportunity to do some selection from the curriculum. The college student has a wider selection of courses. He chooses a major or a field of concentration. However, the curriculum for the major is already established, and often there are courses within these structures which are there, not by the student's choice, but as the result of study and decisions made by established groups. When he agrees to enter a curriculum, he accepts all the prerequisites and requirements.

As the individual moves toward maturity, he makes more and more of his own decisions about learning and the curriculum he wishes to follow. Although advanced degrees may include hurdles of various kinds, which he would not have planned had he been consulted about the curriculum, he at least has the option of whether or not he wishes to enter it.

Even after he has voluntarily entered the curriculum, he may become disillusioned as did the children of Israel with their predicament and wish to change his goal. There are those who have entered teacher education programs and, having completed all the hurdles but student teaching, have become disillusioned in the actual classroom situation. Sometimes in their impatience with their master teachers and the teaching situation, they have left the field of teaching, having only glimpsed the rewards and dangers, joys and fears, work and fun of teaching. The master teacher, the supervising teacher, and the academic department in which the candidate did his major work, all bend their efforts to save such a person for a work that really needs him and for which he is suited.

Powerful nonessentials seem to hover at every level of learning and these must be made ineffective by the teachers. For example, the students need a reassurance of their ability and their worth. They need encouragement and help when their high ideals do not seem to mesh with the reality they see around them. As in the case of the person who, disillusioned by various means, gives up a career just when he is on the threshold of entering it, he needs a guide or a teacher who can help him to realize that the best he has to offer is needed by the world he is about to enter and that he cannot be effective unless he accepts the challenge.

As he becomes able to separate those powerful and smothering nonessentials that can overwhelm, from the best that is in him as a person, he will be better able to learn. Even the material in which he is most interested will stand out in sharper relief and will be more meaningful if he develops this perspective. A portion of the teacher's function is to save or to conserve the best that is in his students.

The Israelites were given many promises. Their redemption came after many trials: (1) their enduring the separation from the security of their slavery under which, even though it was oppressive, they knew what to expect; (2) their wandering and struggling and starving in the wilderness; (3) their turning against their leader and their God because of loss of faith; (4) their fightings and warrings among themselves. Yet Moses, sustained by God, had to endure their displeasure and at times had to save them from themselves.

The teacher sometimes finds himself in the position of having to save the student from himself. Alice came into my office and stood apologetically, hesitantly—something about her made me realize that I should set aside some important correspondence time which I had scheduled with the department secretary. "Alice, come in and sit down."

Alice was a political science major in need of elective units to finish her degree requirements. She had been hesitant about entering a drama class because she thought drama people were "arty," because she felt she had no talent, because she considered herself an *honest* person who did not need to act. Whether fate works in these matters or not, by the time Alice could register for her classes, all other courses were filled and, because she had to meet a graduation deadline, she very reluctantly entered the class.

She began hesitantly, "I feel terrible about last night. . . ."

"Do you mean the show, Alice? It was a terrific success. I am very proud of your first performance on television. You seemed very poised. You read intelligently. Oh, if you mean you feel terrible about questioning me on the interpretation, don't worry about that. Directors and actors must work that way. They seek understanding of each other and sometimes when they become frustrated, or even disagree for that matter, they have words. Please don't worry about that incident. I had forgotten it. . . ."

"Why did you cast me as Lady Bracknell? You were trying to tell me something, weren't you? You know all that about me and this was your way of telling me. I am so embarrassed . . . and as we kept retaping that scene I got more panicky and afraid. Why I *am* Lady Bracknell! I am impressed with style and surface and the way things *look*! I *need* to impress people and I never realized it till I was saying those lines . . . rather they were saying me. I felt as if they were being lifted right out of me. I disliked saying them in the first place, but then when we had to repeat and repeat, I felt you were probing into my whole life and background, and I became so afraid . . . so afraid. Couldn't you have found a nicer way to tell me? Why did I have to keep saying those lines over and over and over and over and over and over . . . !"

She began to quiet, and after several minutes of dabbing at her eyes, she relaxed even more and very shortly said, "I feel so clean. Almost as if I'd taken a bath."

At the end of a week, Alice came by my office.

"I haven't been to school this past week until today."

"We missed you."

"Really?"

"Yes, I need you to continue the role of Lady Bracknell."

"But you could have gotten someone else. Aren't you through with that play? I hate Lady Bracknell, I hate pretense. I want to get into something that has depth and beauty and value. . . ."

Her voice trailed off when I made no response to her outburst.

"Alice, you cannot reject Lady Bracknell. You cannot dislike her, nor can you *like* her too much if you are going to do justice to her. The only way for you to be really *free* of her is to let her borrow your physical mechanism and with it say what she has to say. You must let her stand or fall in the presence of her audience on her own and make no personal evaluation or commentary. You will experience real freedom if you can become so objective about any role you play that you do not reveal any personal attitudes in the performance. This will help you to become objective about all the kinds of people there are in the world."

It would be an easy matter, perhaps, for a teacher to be totally impatient with such a student. It would be possible to give an order and expect the student to carry it out. It would be possible for a student to recite the lines of Lady Bracknell without ever being touched by them. It would have been possible, too, for the children of Israel simply to leave the land of the Egyptians, accepting all the trials and tribulations which followed as a part of the trip to the promised land. Or, they could even have stayed in that land! But they needed to emerge from national bondage just as Alice needed to emerge from personal bondage.

Moses brought the Ten Commandments to his people in the wilderness. The teacher provided Alice with one commandment, "You can't reject Lady Bracknell." The Ten Commandments made the children of Israel free of idolatry and prepared them to enter the promised land. Alice's objective acceptance of Lady Bracknell freed her from her judgmental pose, her revulsion, and her hatred for that kind of person and preserved her talent for more useful purposes. She became able to allow for the type of person Lady Bracknell represents in society and to accept them for what they are. She was no longer bound by the power of hatred and rejection.

People are enslaved in so many different ways. Jerry was a severe stutterer. He was an intelligent, discriminating boy whose environment penetrated deeply into his sensitive nature. He needed the teacher to release him from the bondage of silence and the fear to speak. He was born eighteen months after his sister and received a football for his first Christmas. Since he did not develop as rapidly as his sister did, his father became very impatient and disillusioned with the son who was to bear his name and make him proud. When Jerry was two and one-half years old, David was born. David developed rapidly and became the "apple of his father's eye." Jerry tended to become quiet and to spend much time alone. His father hardly ever spoke to him and it even seemed at times that he had forgotten about him. Jerry was just as glad, because when his father did speak to him and he tried to answer, it was with great difficulty and embarrassment because he stuttered.

When Jerry was in fifth grade, a teacher decided to do an adaptation of Shakespeare's *Merchant of Venice* with the class. It was difficult, at first, getting Jerry to read, but he eventually did read the role of Shylock. He read it beautifully, with understanding, and with no stuttering! He was not cured at the moment, but his teacher complimented him, the other students were surprised and proud of him, and from that turning point he began to achieve in school. When he graduated from high school, he did so with high honors.

There is more to this success story and the telling of it is much oversimplified. There was, of course, much struggle and doubt and fear and despair. Success was not an end product but a part of the total process of recognizing something of worth and salvaging or reclaiming it. Therefore, perhaps the point is made here. What seemed to be a human being of little value was redeemed by a teacher who helped him find his way out of a wilderness.

Not every success story is this dramatic, nor is every story as successful as this one was, but no doubt one of the functions of the teacher is to discover and to redeem that quality in the student which may be embedded in confusion and lack of understanding.

There are many among the physically handicapped who need attention and encouragement. Nancy, a spastic girl, daughter of a very wealthy Kansas doctor, was asked to stay in her room when her mother's college girl friends came to visit and to play bridge. Nancy was reared largely by a nurse who helped to keep her out of her mother's way.

A teacher took a great deal of time working with Nancy, helping her to learn to talk. Another teacher helped her learn to walk. Still another helped her learn to type and to play the piano. One day a teacher told her she was pretty! Nancy is married now, her coordination is still a little slow, but she has a sense of pride and personal worth because into her darkness and confusion, teachers have cast rays of hope. On these, she has emerged from her wilderness of confusion and rejection. She will continue to grow, and to emerge from all the bonds and fears that seem to hover, ready to smother humanity. She will need more teaching, as does everyone. Among the most cherished gifts a person can receive are, a sense of worth, an open door, a ray of hope, a word of encouragement at a time of despair, hopelessness, or bondage.

None of this is as easy to accomplish as it is to tell. There is often much struggling and pain and embarrassment for both the student and the teacher. In one college classroom, the teacher was in the midst of a lecture. The air was tense as the teacher talked about controversial matters. The spirit in the room was divided. Some agreed with the teacher, and some did not. Suddenly, in the quietest moment, a woman approximately forty years old, stood up in her chair and shouted at the teacher, "You're crazy!" The class, of course, was very tense. The immediate reaction of the class was to side with the symbol of authority, the teacher. In that moment, the teacher could have ordered the student from the room and would have received the support of the entire class. However, he said, "You're right." After a long pause, and with the class in a state of semi-shock, he added, "Because it seems that way to you." The student began to sob, and soon was weeping violently. The class was dismissed and the teacher stopped by her desk to assure her that what she did was not wrong. She was disturbed and this one incident gave her the hope she needed. The following Monday, the student was admitted for psychiatric care at the Camarillo state hospital. During her two-year stay there, she often talked to her doctors and nurses of that moment in the classroom which became a kind of turning point out of her darkness into light. She would repeat over and over again, "I said he was crazy, and he said I was right!" It was the first time she hadn't been driven deeper into her wilderness of despair. Some hope and re-assurance were needed before she could begin developing a sense of personal worth.

Sometimes the teacher must save individual students from the outside pressures of a self-satisfied group. This can be illustrated by two examples which resulted from the casting of plays. Kenny, a boy from Iran, was cast as the merchant in *Oklahoma!* He wasn't doing well in the role and the students were worried. They would go out for cokes and hamburgers and would talk about the situa-tion. They felt that it was obviously the director's fault and that Kenny should be replaced. Kenny always went alone during break time and returned early to wait for the rehearsal to continue. When the cast returned from the break they would ignore the "menace" to their production and would reluctantly rehearse with him. Kenny was sensitive to the treatment they were giving him and only despaired more. The director noted that the portion of the play in which Kenny was on stage was the weakest and slow-est point of every rehearsal. He noted, too, that Kenny needed a sense of worth. He needed to feel that he was contributing some-thing unique and valuable to the production. Instead, he felt he was not wanted. The director then talked with the cast and re-minded them their play would be a success if they wanted it to be but that for this to happen they would need to make Kenny feel that he was important and doing well. From that point, Kenny was invited to go along when they went out to eat and rehearsals began to improve as he began to develop a sense of worth from his colleagues. He began to laugh, his timing was excellent as he developed a rhythm of playing scenes with his friends. At all the showings, his was an outstanding performance. His audience stopped the show with applause for him and the other performers were justly proud of their fellow actor. The teacher saved what could have been a disastrous performance. Not only was the show saved, but the performers were saved from embarrassment because they were a part of a successful venture in which they could be proud.

The next illustration did not have such a happy ending. Too many forces were at work and there wasn't time to accomplish what needed to be done in order to save the students from a disastrous performance.

The list of plays had been posted for the season, but before this was done a general negative attitude had already begun to develop in the college drama department. The students had gotten together and decided to parcel out the roles among themselves. They agreed that they would try for certain roles and not try for others, feeling certain that the directors would have to cast the plays according to the students' decisions.

The play that was being cast was *Androcles and the Lion* by George Bernard Shaw. The girl whom the group had decided was to play Lavinia merely showed up at the casting but did not really try for the role. She assumed that she would be given it. Another girl, not in the "in" group, did an excellent tryout for the play. The entire student body of the drama department was shocked when the cast list was posted and the director had not cast the role as the students had decided he should. Antagonism developed immediately in the cast. There were deliberate attempts to make Lavinia look foolish. They isolated her from their society, indicating that she had no right to try out for the role in the first place, and certainly not to accept it if she were offered it. The cast fought the director all the way and was bent on self-destruction. Rehearsals, which are hard work but which should also be fulfilling and rewarding periods of adjustment and growth and developing insights, became dreaded endurance tests for the director and Lavinia, who were trying to establish some rapport with the cast. However, there was only grudging cooperation in which the cast tolerated directing and then distorted with deliberate attempts to misunderstand what the director was trying to do. The director made every attempt to lead the cast out of the confusion that had developed but the students were like the Israelites as they worshipped the golden calf in the wilderness. The result was that, as they attempted to destroy, they were also caught in the destruction. The play was not a success. Though it is assigned to the teacher to conserve and redeem, the students cannot be saved if they will not listen. They must possess the desire to grow and to be led out.

To compare the two drama experiences, then, it can be seen in the case of Kenny that the teacher redeemed what was best in loyalty and acceptance within the cast members, and redeemed a boy from despair by helping him to achieve a personal sense of worth with his colleagues and with his audiences. It can also be seen that it is not always possible for the teacher to succeed at redeeming or conserving. Perhaps this is the essence of the greatness of tragedy. The goal is illuminated but the teacher fails. Sometimes the teacher continues the effort in the face of defeat, almost knowing he will be defeated, but bearing the eternal hope that he will be able to save the person. This becomes increasingly difficult when he is trying to save a group because of the momentum which can be generated by a group—for destruction as well as for positive action.

As was stated, the play, *Androcles and the Lion*, was not a success. The director was embarrassed. The students were embarrassed. Perhaps the director was needed by the students at that time more than at any other and the director had to emotionally accept and implement with action what he understood intellectually. It was not a time when he could indulge in the feelings of a person who had been affronted. It was not a time when he could say, "I told you so." It was not a time when he could feel sorry for himself for being let down by the students. This would have put the entire project on a personal basis. He had to work to understand and exhibit the role of conserver and redeemer. He worked and talked with the students about the experience. He helped restore in each of them the idea that the performances of the show were not expected to be the end product, but that it had a place in their own growing and learning. He helped them to restructure relationships that had deteriorated during the development of the play, and perhaps most valuable of all, he helped each person to realize to a degree his own potential. He helped each to realize what he had done and to realize that he is always at the fringes of darkness. He helped each to realize that he must develop his potential, aware always that no matter how far he progresses, he is always in a state of emerging, growing, achieving levels of enlightenment and growth. He did not tell them they were wrong to act as they had done. He did help them to realize that there will be experiences for every person in which he will slip back, and at these times people should penetrate to the best of themselves and bring that best to the fore with the humble awareness that every man's feet are in clay.

The teacher, then, is one who redeems, saves, and conserves. As such, he does some of the following: remains forgiving and selfless, no matter what mistakes the students make; perceives the strengths of the students; develops patience with their weaknesses; makes them aware of the dangers to which they are all subject; helps them to rebuild and restructure what they destroy; develops their desire to continue to grow; helps them to be patient with situations that matter little so they can be effective in situations that do; helps them to meet and to cope with disappointment; helps them to differentiate between what is essential and what is not; gives them a sense of ability and worth; frees them from preconceptions and unbalanced likes and dislikes; helps them emerge from personal bondage, whether it is physical or mental or otherwise; builds in them a sense of pride and personal worth, challenging them with their responsibilities as members of society.

J. D. Y.

Questions for discussion

1 Why must a teacher or a leader redeem? Why can't people save themselves?
2 To be redeemed, is it necessary to be lost?
3 Why do people turn against a redeemer?
4 How can a person become really free from that which he deplores and despises? How can he become really free from that which he likes too much?
5 Discuss "When one is in a wilderness, he must be led out by at least one ray of hope."
6 Discuss "It becomes more difficult to redeem that which is eternal about humanity as society preoccupies itself more and more with that which will rust and decay."
7 Discuss "If higher education promises only better jobs, social status, financial ease, power and possession, it will provide only more tools which in and of themselves will destroy."
8 Should teachers allow students to complain and to disagree with them?
9 How can teachers drive students deeper into darkness?
10 What is the teacher's place in redeeming individual students from the outside pressures of a self-satisfied group?
11 Can a teacher save or redeem a person who does not wish to be saved?

The end crowns all;
And that old common arbitrator,
    Time,
Will one day end it.
—*William Shakespeare*

23

A teacher is

a culminator

No one knows for sure at exactly what point life for the individual begins. It is before conception? Is it at conception? Is it at birth? No one knows for sure when life ends. Is it when the individual expires physically? Is it when he ceases to grow and mature mentally or spiritually? Is it when he is no longer remembered by those who knew him?

In learning there is no real beginning, and no end. We do not know the day and the moment a child learns to walk. We do not know the day and the moment he learns to speak. We do not know the day and the moment our own concepts are completed.

What we think we know and what we think we believe are subject to constant change as they relate to different circumstances.
There is a point, however, where we need to try to summarize, to
take inventory, to find where we are in our development so we can
evaluate our progress, take a focus on new goals, and determine
how we will achieve the new goals we establish from time to time.

If we do not terminate our progress for a time in order to take
inventory and to summarize, it is possible for us to dissipate
our energy by falling into a ritual of living where we may cease
to grow and mature both mentally and spiritually. We may lose
our personal sense of identification as we become part of a mass
of existence. We may never sense the satisfying feeling of having
completed a task, of having summarized, or of having taken inventory and, thus, as individuals to have assumed responsibility
for a point of view.

For the individual who is not part of a particular society, who
does not wish to become part of a society, and who has no particular goals, incidental or random learning may be adequate. His
experiences provide incidental bits of knowledge that may have
specific uses for him. General knowledge, however, can be useful
and it can be dangerous. If an individual possesses only partial
knowledge that is not related to larger concepts, he may act in a
distorted manner, much as an individual who jumps to conclusions
from stimulation by nothing more than inadequate clues. The
teacher is sometimes questioned by the student before all the
evidence concerning a subject is in. The student will sometimes
close his mind before the termination of a unit of study. The
teacher tries to help the student to keep an open mind, to set a
period of time in which a study can be completed, and to complete the study so the student will know a unit has been terminated
and is ready to stand the judgment of evaluation. In this way the
teacher is able to illuminate goals and to bring a focus and relatedness to learning.

The individual who does not wish to be part of a community

and who engages only in random learning will learn his lessons from and do battle with the world as he meets it and will adjust to the demands made on him at the moment. This will be difficult for him because he cannot benefit by the experiences of others. He will not have studied them in context and will have no conclusions or experiences on which to base future learning or action. The individual who never concludes, from having stood up suddenly and bumped his head on a window sill, that he should not stand up suddenly under that or any other window sill like it, will have to suffer the pain it will cost him each time he suddenly stands up under such a window sill. His unit of knowledge concerning this kind of experience will never be complete because he has not come to any conclusions based on the evidence he has received in the forms of a window sill, a sudden standing up, and a resulting aching head.

The individual who wishes to be part of a community lives in a situation that requires organization, planning and efficiency, summation and termination so that new and fresh projects can be begun and pursued on the basis of what has been learned in previously completed work. To take his place in a culture that has a head start on him, he must develop skills and learn the rules by which the people live. He must learn a systematic language and he must learn the manners and customs and laws by which the community guides itself, first in the small family unit and later in the wider community relationships. He must act out and in some ways prepare to live some scenes which he may never live in reality, but for which he is prepared if the need should ever arise. He must know, and the rest of the community must know, that he has achieved certain competencies at certain stages of his development so that predictions can be made concerning his possible performance of certain tasks, should the occasion require it of him.

It is necessary for him to be guided by a curriculum or course of study which will prepare him to act out some of the actual scenes he will have to play when the time comes. He avails himself of many kinds of experience and builds a reservoir of knowledge and emotional experience from which to draw so that he can make appropriate decisions and relationships.

Learning in the formal classroom is not random—it is planned, it is artificial, it is very selective. Time limits must be imposed so that goals can be established. The teacher must be able to terminate certain units of work and to move on to others. The only way he can do this is to provide some kind of culmination or ending to a specific unit of learning and this is done by giving tests, by promotion from one class to the next, by graduations, by play performances, by the spelling bee, by a night of the best speeches, or by a theme or term paper. In this way, classroom learning also becomes competitive because those who achieve wish to do so within time limits and at levels superior to those of their peers. Competition is the subject for another chapter, but suffice it to say here that the teacher works to get the student to compete against himself rather than against his colleagues. If he tries to better his own record or performance, his reasons for learning will be born of a better spirit. Learning, merely to better the record of someone else, is wrongly motivated. The dangers inherent in competition in learning far outweigh the possible values.

The teacher is one who brings focus to the process of learning periodically by providing a sense of completion and achievement. He designs the learning situation in such a way that there are culminations, terminations, or endings. They are markings, or mileposts, by which the student and those in his society can measure his development and can know that he is ready to move into more complex selective learning situations.

The teacher contrives the endings of study units and contrives to bring them about deliberately so that they will be most effective. To be more meaningful for students, it is better to effect an ending at the height of their involvement in the learning moment. If they become tired of a process before it ends, they can only be glad that it is over, and there will be very little residue of pleasure or learning for them.

The teacher establishes goals for the students until he can teach them how to establish goals for themselves. He develops in them a sense of responsibility. When they learn to require of themselves efficient performance, they will have greater satisfaction, pride, and self-respect. The teacher teaches them to work with a speed that is controlled by the time limit established, teaches them to finally let go of a unit of study, and to use it only as a springboard to further and more complex study.

I have worked with dramatic groups in the mounting and presenting of plays. There is an excitement and an enthusiasm in the process because everyone is aware of an established opening night and curtain time. This is the time when all the energies of the company have been brought to focus and the presentation of opening night is one of the most exhilarating experiences a person can have. This is heightened if the play is a success and if there is overt response. As the company then continues in a long run of performances, it is usually not until the very last performance, when the company knows that they will be breaking up and will no longer be working together, that they realize how much the play, the mutual experiences both good and bad, have meant to all of them. The ending is good, though, because it illuminates the pleasant associations even as they are brought to an end and helps people to realize what they have had.

Utter chaos, frustration, and failure would be the result of a decision by a group of people to "do a show sometime." In fact, an individual who "plans" to write a book, or to go around the world sometime, or to bake a cake will never accomplish anything unless the target date for accomplishment is established. If a child is told in a classroom, "You must learn to read sometime," only luck and happenstance will ever cause him to learn to read. There must be a need and there must be a time when it is necessary for him to know how to read in order for him to progress appropriately. One good reason for his learning to read within certain time limits is that he will be respected by others in his small community, and, of course, he will be in competition to maintain a place in the society which he uses as his standard for development. He may not choose to compete with the top reader, but he will at least compete, for a time, with someone in his own "class" or "grouping." He must know at a certain point that, to the satisfaction of his peers, his teacher, and himself, he has achieved the goals which are within his grasp. Therefore, the teacher establishes certain target dates for testing the progress of the entire class to find out which ones are moving more rapidly than others, and to see if his own teaching is effective. If no one in the group has achieved the goal that was established, it could be that the goal is too high, or the teacher is ineffective, or the "curtain time" or deadlines were not respected by the students.

The schedule of learning that takes place in an ordinary classroom is comparable to the planning and performing of a play. If a group of people should decide "someday we'll do a play," it will never be done. The termination or performance date of the play must be established by the director and announced to the cast, the crew, and the prospective audience. In order to be able to measure the progress of the production and to insure that it will be ready on time, interim target or termination dates are established. It is necessary that those tasks which have been planned for completion on specific dates be done so that the group can make an efficient and organized move into the next phase of the production, building on the foundation which has been established, on each of the days listed.

Many people are involved in the total production, and in many different ways. Each has a "curtain time" or termination date on which his work must be done. Among the kinds of work that must be done are publicity and posters, ticket sales, house managing and ushering, acting, directing, dancing, singing, scene designing, construction and painting, lighting, costume design, costume construction, properties, stage managing, makeup, and others. Each has a particular task and a prescribed amount of time in which to complete the task. Any one person who does not meet his "curtain time," will cause the entire production to be in jeopardy. It is only by complete cooperation that the play will be ready for the audience and opening night.

When the preparation time is over, and the play is presented to an audience, there is a new dimension of accomplishment for all who participated in the production from the ushers to the leading players. There is a feeling of achievement and success. There is the possibility of a long run. The hard work, the personal problems, the antagonisms, all fade into relative meaninglessness at the last performance when the cast is suddenly confronted with having to let go of a process that has demanded so much of them. The successes, the mistakes, the fun, the problems, the challenges, the lines of the play begin to stand out in bold relief. The final letting go, the curtain calls, the laughter, the tears, and emotional intensity cause the entire experience to take on new dimensions of meaning.

The ending is valuable. Although we say, "In learning there is no end," in the classroom we must artificially plan endings or culminations. The nearness of the end or the actual ending of anything gives it much more meaning. A child may not realize how much he is enjoying his day until the time comes when he must let go of it. Though there may be quarreling and some disappointment and disputing with his peers, he will suddenly realize the joy of play and companionship and all that they can mean to him when someone outside his association removes him from the company of others and causes his games to cease. Had he known there would be an end, or had he been able to comprehend the meaning of ending, he may have indulged himself in fuller enjoyment. People say frequently, "If I had know then what I know now, I'd have done things differently." A person must know that he has achieved a certain level and although he may not wish a series of experiences to end, they begin to have more value for him as he lets go of them.

The ending of a unit of study, or the ending of a school year, or the ending of any unit of time has been compared to the ending of a day. A person can absorb only so much, and there comes a time when there is a need to rest. There is a need to sleep, to recuperate, to review and evaluate a day, to put the achievements and failures of that day in the proper perspective. There is a need to be able to let go and to know that a day is done. There is a need for an ending. The person who allows for an ending and lets go of a day provides himself with a yesterday that he can use for a springboard into tomorrow.

J. D. Y.

Questions for discussion

1 Why is it necessary to summarize or evaluate progress? How can a teacher help in the process?
2 What dangers are inherent in the students' coming to conclusions before a unit of study is complete?
3 Should it be necessary for individuals to learn the rules by which the people of a community live? How does this relate to knowledge and learning?
4 Is it enough to learn rules? Should the reasons for the rules be studied?
5 Discuss the values of competition and cooperation in the learning process.
6 Discuss "The nearness of the end, or the actual ending of anything gives it much more meaning."
7 What values are there in planned culminations? What dangers should be considered?
8 Is there a point in teaching where the teacher no longer establishes goals, but gets the student involved in establishing goals for himself?
9 Discuss the place of speed and time limits in learning. Why are deadlines important?
10 Should learning periods be rigidly adhered to?

If only I may grow: firmer, simpler—quieter, warmer.

Do what you can—and the task will rest lightly in your hand, so lightly that you will be able to look forward to the more difficult tests which may be awaiting you.
—*Dag Hammarskjold*

24

A teacher is

a person

Teaching as described in this book is intimately related to personality. Although the nature of the book did not permit a direct study of the relation of the teacher's personality to teaching, implications from the close relation between the two are on almost every page. The varied activities of the teacher described in this book have reality and meaning only as they are expressed by an individual personality; further, these activities work back upon and profoundly influence that personality. This chapter is a brief analysis of the relation between teaching and personality, together with some suggested avenues for personality growth through teaching.

A. *Personality and Teaching*

If one tries to understand the power of the world's greatest teachers, he is steadily led toward the conclusion that life and meaning were given to their teaching by a special quality of their personalities. These personalities are greatly varied, but a common thread seems to run through all examples of powerful teaching: that which is to be considered or learned, mediated through the teacher, becomes alive and meaningful in a special way and reaches the learner as vital, direct experience. The essence of the teaching art lies in the character of the person.

There is a serious occupational hazard in teaching. Every person who enters teaching as a profession must face the danger of personality damage through his work. Some students of this problem conclude that many persons choose teaching because of basic personality defects and inadequacies, and that the strains of teaching tend merely to magnify these tendencies. Others feel that the major causes of the personality type often considered typical of the teacher are the very special strains that accompany teaching, together with undesirable mental and physical health practices.[1]

Whatever the basic causes, it seems to be clear that teachers tend to develop two widely divergent types of personality and character as a result of prolonged teaching. There is no scientific proof of this bimodal distribution of teacher personality, but long experience with and observation of teachers lead me to suggest this situation as a hypothesis. Perhaps, in time, research will throw further light on the problem.

One group of teachers under the special stresses and demands that accompany teaching develops markedly less desirable traits with increased experience. In these cases, teaching, instead of being a means to positive personality development or to full self-actualization, produces progressive personality damage. As these teachers grow older they come more and more to typify the common stereotype of the school teacher: harassed, irritable, inse-cure, defensive, punitive, opinionated, garrulous, condescending, lonely, infantile. Development of such personality is a professional hazard of the first magnitude.

No one is immune to this danger. To refuse to see what happens to a very large proportion of teachers at all levels is not to be loyal to the profession nor to serve it best. If teachers could see them-selves as they often are and as others see them, this self-under-standing might be an important step toward finding the cause and changing the results.

Often when this point is discussed, defensive teachers urge that the negative picture of the teacher is an old stereotype, stem-ming from the days of the bespectacled, lonely spinster with fierce countenance and severe hairdo, bound by Puritan habits, or the awkward, fear-ridden man for whom teaching was the last resort for a livelihood. And, it is urged, none of these things is true of the modern teacher.

The problem is infinitely deeper. Surface sophistication mani-fested in various frenetic attempts to be "free" and like "everyone else" is no evidence of wholesome personality. A distorted person-ality may manifest itself in the classroom, in faculty activities, and in the wider community, in those who dress in the latest fashion, who sport the latest hairdo or haircut, who travel, who pride themselves in being "unbound" in personal habits and beliefs. In fact, it seems that the most unattractive defenses against the great demands of the teacher's life often appear under a heavy layer of "modern" sophistication. The point is that the problem presented here is not solved by saying that the teacher of today is accepted in the most up-to-date society. Rather we must look squarely at what we all too often are and how we behave.

Teaching does not always damage or distort personality. There is the other group of teachers (let us hope increasing in numbers) who are continuously enriched by their teaching experience. Each year of teaching makes their personalities more desired and more desirable. For reasons not yet altogether clear, the stresses and special demands of the life of a teacher are the means of growth. As these teachers grow older (and even old) they come to typify the teacher at his best: kindly, stimulating, inquiring, mature, thoughtful, objective, confident, joyful, sincere, creative. Such a personality is a professional satisfaction and reward of the first magnitude.

These men and women are in the beloved and honored tradition of the great teachers of mankind in all the phases of man's effort at civilization on this planet. They usually have not been well rewarded materially. Often they have felt it necessary to avoid material affluence in order to be free, for perhaps above everything a teacher must be free.

For the teacher, teaching may be either a way to personality ruin or to personality enrichment and fulfillment. It is as if there were a divide, as on a roof or on land. If the personality is slanted in one way, the blows and demands which come upon it carry it further and further in an undesirable direction. If the same or almost the same circumstances come upon a personality slanted in another direction, the very obstacles and demands become a means of carrying it to richer and fuller realization.

Every student of the psychology of personality would like to know the major causes for the difference between these two groups. Of course, this question does not apply only to teachers, for all people are either enriched or impoverished by the living of life. However, teachers are perhaps more subject to the working of the principle (that the hammer blows of life produce the extremes of desirable and undesirable personality) than most other groups because of the very special demands of teaching.

The nature of these demands and their particular threat to personality are not fully understood. The key to the matter may be found in the emotional strain that comes from continuous interaction with numerous and varied personalities in a fluid relation that is characterized by strongly ambivalent feelings and by inescapable responsibility. Whatever the cause, everyone who has taught surely knows that the emotional, physical, and intellectual strain is very great. Stated in another and more positive way, the experiences involved in teaching tend to be intimate, direct, intense, and unpredictable.

If these experiences or interactions are received constructively or wisely, the personality will be remarkably enriched and stimulated to growth. If, for any of a variety of reasons, they are received negatively or unwisely, the personality must develop defenses or ways of reacting that make the demands bearable. These negative defensive reactions become harmful and unattractive personality traits often associated with the teacher stereotype.

But the important problem for us as teachers is what seems to make the difference and what can be done about it. Evidently the problem is very complex. The varied literature on mental hygiene which has grown up in the last fifty years bears on this issue.[2] Because of the complexity of the problems of personality healing and growth, it is risky to give brief and relatively simple answers to the question of what makes the difference between the teacher who is damaged by teaching and the one who is healed and enriched by it. Nevertheless, a few simple and practical suggestions are offered.

The key is continuous growth. In every person there is a deep and urgent need to come to rest, to find the answer, to arrive, to culminate the struggle. Perhaps it was this longing in its essence that Freud was suggesting in the "death instinct." Be that as it may, it seems that individuals and the varied groups of individuals which compose organized society live under the illusion that just over the brow of this next hill the top will be reached, or at least a top where gains can be consolidated, interests can be hedged in and shored up, and the desperate quality can go out of struggle.

The desire for culmination, for rest, for final balance, is so great that both individuals and groups strive to produce the reality by pretending to themselves and others that they have arrived. If the pretense is strong enough, growth stops and in a deep sense the death need begins to be satisfied, for death sets in whenever growth ceases. Such evidence as is available suggests that in the universe as we know it there is no point of equilibrium or balance; there is progressive unfolding and differentiation which we call growth, or there is deterioration in the direction of the full disintegration of death.

If this is a truth, it is one of the big truths with almost limitless implications for the management of human life. In relation to our problem of "through teaching to personality development" it simply means that the teacher either is growing toward the full actualization of himself or he is dying. This sort of death process is accompanied by all the painful psychological defenses which our generation has read so much about. The teacher who ceases to grow, as a matter of self-defense in an attempt to make life bearable, fights a rear guard action against deterioration. The unattractive traits developed by so many teachers are the practical manifestation of this struggle against the most frightening of all threats: the frustration of unfulfilled potential and the loss of such integrity of self as may have been achieved.

The growth side of the picture is as bright as the deterioration side is dark. There is a strong persistent need for all human beings to realize their full potential. Life can be made up primarily of the deep satisfactions of a growth process which leads steadily to the full realization of the self. For such persons, the circumstances of life varying from joy to sorrow, from triumph to failure, from pleasure to great suffering, become grist for the mill of this growth that leads to a fuller and fuller life. This is an ideal, a goal, that is rarely reached in individual lives, but the potential exists and the potential seems to produce a longing for its fulfillment.

The working teacher who wishes to avoid the evil of crystallization and consequent deterioration and to achieve that measure of growing maturity which is the only meaningful protection of personality would like to have some practical help. What does this growth involve and how can it be encouraged? Full development which sustains and continuously re-creates life in the human personality is constituted of growth in *knowledge* and growth in *being*.

Thus the teacher who would achieve the fullest personality growth through teaching must find the means in these two phases of the self. A brief analysis of each may be helpful.

B. *Growth in Knowledge*

To be alive in any genuine sense is to be learning. The odyssey which leads to ever-widening areas of knowing is lifelong. It seems to be in the very nature of man to extend the self through a fuller comprehension of the nature of things.[3] This need to know and to understand (which is an aspect of knowing) is strongest when life is strongest, i.e., in childhood and youth, and decreases only under the pressure of fear, routine, and other life-inhibiting forces. Let us examine briefly five aspects of this growth in knowing which are essential to the life of the personality.

1. The self. Of all the doctrines of religion and philosophy there are few more important to health of personality than the ancient Delphic admonition, "Know thyself." The self is the basic instrument with which life is lived. To be ignorant of either strengths or weaknesses of that instrument is to invite trouble or even disaster.

No one can hope to acquire full understanding of the vast uncharted land which is a human self, but everyone can enter upon the path to self-knowledge. Every teacher should set increasing self-knowledge as a prime goal of his personal and professional life. The study can be divided in many ways for convenience in observation. For example, one who must by the nature of his work be under considerable physical and psychological tensions needs to have a good knowledge of his body. Relatively simple information about energy supply and renewal, optimum diet, fatigue level, stress tolerance, exercise need, and other such body peculiarities may enable the teacher to use his body more effectively. Fatigue narrows perspective and distorts perception and judgment. It seems that many of the foolish things teachers do are a direct or indirect result of overfatigue. And it may be that lack of imagination and general "dead-headedness" in teaching are due in a great measure to a low energy level.[4]

Equally important is a growing knowledge of what is usually termed the mind. What are its innate or acquired tender spots? Under what conditions, at what rate, and on what type of tasks does it perform best? What are its major natural or at least deeply embedded interests or concerns? How much stress can this particular mind take before it begins to produce protective symptoms? Most important of all, what are this mind's special qualities or abilities that have distinctive promise for cultivation?

These are merely a few of the questions that the seeker for self-knowledge asks and attempts to answer about his individual mind: its nature, potential, limits, weaknesses, and strengths. At its best, this instrument is one of the remarkable phenomena in a universe of complex and remarkable things. Distorted by malfunction or limited by failure in normal growth, the mind presents an example of extreme ineffectiveness and unattractiveness. The typical person takes his mind for granted, leaving great areas of it fallow, and using it badly. Too much concern might become morbid, but to understand something of the delicate complexity of a fine machine or organism is not necessarily to become pathologically preoccupied about its care.

The third large phase of the self is so complex and unavailable for study through the methods to which we are accustomed that there is a hesitancy to speak about the spirit of man. Yet the witness of the most thoughtful men of every age is that the quality called spirit is the central essence of man as man. The evidence is strong that he denies or negates this part of himself at great peril. Man is a biological organism with very special mental equipment, but when either as an individual or in social organizations he is only that, he rapidly loses his distinctively human qualities and becomes an ineffective and unattractive animal. The distortion of human personality which results from the high development of physical and mental abilities and the neglect of spiritual potential produces a horrible being.

This subject is clearly very complex. It will suffice to suggest here that if a teacher hopes to understand his full self, he should free himself as rapidly as possible from childishly negative attitudes (often rooted in early unwise religious training) toward problems of the spirit of man which so frequently have caused a thin sophisticated blindness in modern man, and set himself to a study of this most intriguing part of himself.[5]

In the search for growth in the understanding of self, the complex human personality should not be broken into segments except perhaps for convenience in study. The self, particularly the healthy self, is a whole. The teacher is urged to seek understanding, by all available means, of this entity which determines the quality and meaning of a human life.

2. Nature of man. Man is a social animal, as Aristotle observed long ago. The wide implications of this fact still are being examined through the various disciplines that make man as individual and as organization or institution the center of their study. One thinks especially of anthropology, psychology, and sociology; but economics, political science, biology, history, literature cannot be omitted. A great proportion of man's intellectual effort has gone into the study of himself and his institutions.

The teacher, of course, cannot hope to become expert in all these areas. He need not do so. But the teacher's effectiveness depends much upon his understanding of man: his achievements, foibles, powers, institutions. Neglect to grow in this intriguing area of knowledge is not only to court failure in one's work but, equally important, is to cut oneself off from one of life's greatest pleasures.

One is tempted to offer suggestions for reading, observation, and record keeping that have been helpful for some who are seeking means of growth toward the deeper understanding of other selves. Perhaps it is better that each seek his own most satisfying and rewarding avenues. Certainly the search should not be limited to formal study through reading and thought about the behavior and achievements of man in general.

A teacher's life by its very nature is in constant relation with a wide variety of people. A habit of careful observation, with some recording and analysis, contributes greatly to understanding of others. That is, a teacher lives in the best of all psychological and sociological laboratories. Viewed in one way, these close and continuous relations with people are irritating and boring—a situation to be borne with fortitude and escaped as soon as possible; but approached differently, they are a rich and abiding source of learning. It seems strange that a person would feel the need to go away to some special place to study the behavior of people when every classroom, every college or university as a community is at hand for study.

Whatever the means used, the goal suggested is a steadily enlarging knowledge of other selves, as individuals and as groups.

3. The achievements of man. There is much that is dark and ugly about man's experience on this planet. He seems to learn extremely slowly, and in some areas almost not at all, except over long periods. However man's experience during the historical period of approximately five thousand years may be viewed, his achievements have been great. His strangely restless spirit never ceases to probe, to search, to build, to invent, to discover. More than two thousand years ago the poet Sophocles (*Antigone*, 332-365) spoke of the powers and achievements of man in this way:

Many a wonder lives and moves, but the wonder of all is man,
. . . Wise utterance and wind-swift thought, and city-moulding mind,
. . . Inventive beyond wildest hope, endowed with boundless skill.

Shakespeare (*Hamlet*, II, 2) expressed the same estimate of potential:

What a piece of work is a man! How noble in reason! how infinite in faculties! in form, in moving, how express and admirable! in action, how like an angel! in apprehension, how like a god! the beauty of the world! the paragon of animals!

Surely all of us in this culture are acquainted with the Psalmist's words (8:4, 5-6):

What is man, that thou art mindful of him? . . . For thou hast made him a little lower than the angels, and hast crowned him with glory and honour. Thou madest him to have dominion over the works of thy hands; thou hast put all things under his feet.

A chief function of the teacher is to bring each rising generation into appreciative and imaginative relation with the varied achievements of man. It is the teacher's task to guide the young into a journey of exploration that will acquaint them in some measure at least with the heritage of mankind in thought and deed. It is true that the teacher's immediate responsibility usually will be limited to a small area of this heritage, but in view of the very close relationship among all phases of knowlege and achievement a particular subject can be greatly enriched if the teacher can place it in the framework of all of man's knowledge.

A constantly growing knowledge of the achievements of man has an even greater value for the teacher in its effect on him as a person. Through breadth of experience the teacher overcomes a dangerous tendency to overspecialize. Further, he may be able to rise above the narrow provincialism of time, nationality, race, culture, or civilization. He comes to be a genuine citizen of the world, a worthy member of the human race, and thus gradually achieves the freedom of mind and tolerance of spirit which accompany growth toward wisdom.

The teacher freed of tribal and other fetters draws freely from all peoples of all times and places. His life is given breadth, depth, and joy as he shares freely in the efforts and achievements of the human race. In a sense, only through this wide experience can man become genuinely man, that is, man at his best. There is nothing mystical or sentimental implied here. The very practical suggestion is that the teacher grow in knowledge of the magnificent achievements of man: art, literature, science, architecture, government, religion, law, music—the list is long, and ever grows longer.

This is an age of specialization—a time when one cannot know even a narrow area well. Practical success seems to depend on a limited and constantly narrowing specialization. This situation with its threatening consequences offers a major support to the plea for breadth in the teachers of our time. Growth in knowledge of the wide achievements of man will make the teacher a better teacher and a better person.

4. Nature and her processes. Man is, of course, an intimate part of the natural world. In spite of his relatively great achievements, he is actually a very small part of the mammoth scheme of nature. In the course of history man has often succumbed to the temptation to forget his smallness and his limitations, and has developed what might be called a "cosmic irreverence." It is good to take proper pride in significant achievement; it is dangerous to forget limitations. Such forgetting may lead man to engage in what the Greeks called *hubris* (a prideful, irresponsible, self-centered drive for power) which is followed by *nemesis* (the deterioration and eventual destruction consequent upon unbalanced arrogant striving).

Modern man seems to be in danger of such arrogance. Often he speaks of conquering Nature when he might better speak of understanding and cooperating with her. Man's current space achievements are significant, but they need to be put in proper perspective by a meditative look into a clear night sky, or perhaps better by a view now and then through a great telescope. The point is that nature is vast and unspeakably complex both as macrocosm and microcosm.

Reverence for nature and her processes does not suggest fear, superstition, or ignorance. The teacher who seeks the best personality development will make a lifetime study, at least as an amateur, of the natural world. Such study not only enriches the teacher's knowledge, but can be a great source of pleasure even into old age. Wherever such a teacher is or goes he is in the midst of phenomena and processes that are a boundless means of learning It is a self-engendered curse to walk blind, deaf, and without feeling through the wonders of the natural world. No teacher even in a great modern city should so curse himself.

For many years a strong belief has been growing in my mind that man long cut off from nature or improperly related to her becomes distorted and tends to grow sick, although there is no proof for that belief. Whatever the truth may be, many seekers for effectiveness in life have found regular, interested, and respectful contact with natural things both healing and growth-producing.

5. One's subject or special area of competence. The teacher who seeks the fullest self-actualization or the best in personality development will find that expert knowledge of a limited area of human experience (called a subject) will be very helpful. In truth, there is no such thing as full mastery of even the most limited area of knowledge. All things are so interrelated that a *full* knowledge of even the smallest area (even Tennyson's "flower in a crannied wall") would mean a knowledge of all things.

Yet the idea of "mastery" of one's subject is a valuable one. We all know mastery is used in a relative sense. One can and should have a relative mastery of his subject at certain levels. Thus he will know more of it than most of those who are learners with him as students, and probably more than most other people. Such knowledge will give him confidence and a precious freedom of imagination.

Where one is, however, is not nearly so important as the direction one is traveling. That is, what one knows about his subject may be important, but of greater importance is constant *growth* in the knowledge of the area of one's special competence. By this means, depth is added to the dimension of breadth previously emphasized. This steady increase in depth in a single area gives special life and meaning to the whole spectrum of growth in knowledge so vital to the personality development of the teacher.

All these phases of growth in knowledge of self, of other selves, of man's achievement, of the natural world, and of one's special area of competence are a means toward the development of that degree of maturity which is the only effective guarantee that the person will be enriched by the experiences of life—even the special demands of a teacher's life. It should be clear that the absolute amount of knowledge is probably not very important—at best, it is very little—but continuous growth in knowledge is the crucial matter.

C. *Growth in Being*

Growth in knowledge cannot be separated from growth in being, for both growth and the self that grows are basically a whole. What one knows affects the quality of one's being; and also what one is influences the nature and quality of one's knowing and knowledge. Further, overt behavior is a manifestation of knowledge and being, and at the same time constanly molds both of them. Thus the intricate web of life is constituted of what one knows and is learning, of what one is and is becoming, and of what one does and is planning.

It is true that one may be well supplied in live, meaningful knowledge and not achieve optimum growth in being or becoming. Hence, it may be helpful to suggest a few avenues of growth in being. The hope is that, as teachers, what we are will not contradict what we know and what we say, but will support our verbal professions. More important, growth in being is a crucial means to the quality of personality that is enriched by the demands of teaching.

1. Sensitivity. Quality of being is indicated in large measure by breadth and depth of sensitivity. There is a kind of sensitivity involved in knowing, but here we are concerned with an aspect of personality which permeates the whole self and has strong conative, cognitive, and affective tones. It manifests itself in numerous ways.

John Donne expressed one aspect of this sensitivity when, at the end of his famous words about man's relatedness (*Devotions*, XVII), he said, "And therefore never send to know for whom the *boll tolls*; It tolls for *thee*." This is an example of one's feelings reaching out to all everywhere who experience death. The principle holds with equal force in other phases of existence, including triumph and joy. In theory, the self extends to wider and wider reaches until it tends to partake of all experience, and in this sense partakes of the nature of the Infinite.

There is another phase of sensitivity which relates perhaps more apparently to personality growth and maturity. The widely sensitive person perceives with increasing rapidity the meaning of situations involving things or people. Technically speaking, he is able to assess the factors in a situation with a minimum of cues. Or put more practically, he does not have to know all the details in order to grasp the problem as a whole. Perhaps this sensitivity is manifested most meaningfully in a teacher in his ability to put himself in the place of others, and thus perceive their feelings.

Growth in sensitivity greatly strengthens and enriches the self, but there is latent danger here, against which a warning should be given. Sensitivity must be balanced by other qualities of knowing and being or the personality may find itself with a load it cannot carry. Man is finite and cannot bear an infinite burden. It is true that every hungry child in the world is in reality my child, but a high level of maturity is required if that type of sensitivity is to be carried wisely. The young poet Edna St. Vincent Millay in "Renascence" expressed the awful burden in these lines:

> No hurt I did not feel, no death
> That was not mine; mine each last breath
> That, crying, met an answering cry,
> From the compassion that was I.[6]

She found it a burden sufficient to crush the heart until she had moved upward by a new birth. As the teacher grows in sensitivity he grows in other dimensions of personality, and is not only able to bear this breadth of feeling but feels himself only part man without it.

Teachers who have the desire and courage to plunge deeper into the intriguing problem of the relation between the growing self and the nonself, and the effect of that relation on personality health, will find a brilliant analysis by the novelist Richard Hughes in chapters 26-28 of *The Fox in the Attic*.[7] This author presents excellent psychological insights, particularly on the dangers of the irresponsible overextension of the self, in the clear and interesting language of a great novelist.

2. Interest and curiosity. In her sensitive book, *The Journey*, Lillian Smith asks the question, "What is this stubborn thing in man that keeps him forever picking the lock of time?"[8] It seems to be in his basic nature to do so. We call this part of his complex nature interest and curiosity.

Much of man's probing and searching has been in an attempt to solve practical problems. Much more of the unceasing search is to try to satisfy his insatiable need to explore, to experience, to understand. These qualities are a part of the essence of man, of what keeps him alive and growing as man. When routine, fear, illness, or habit destroys interest and curiosity, the vibrant quality of life tends to go out of the person.

The teacher who desires to continue growing and hence to actualize his personality through teaching cultivates the roots of wide interests and restless curiosity. Like the most "alive" people who have lived, he spends his "time in nothing else, but either to tell, or to hear some new thing." But interest is a greater joy and profit than curiosity. To see every object and event in life with the fresh attention of a wholesome child is to have at hand an inexhaustible source of mental stimulation.

Narrowed interests mean a narrowed self. The overnarrowed self, however expert it may be in a limited field, will fulfill the prophecy of the poet: "And he whose soul is flat—the sky / Will cave in on him by and by."[9]

Fortunately, interest and curiosity are such positive forces in personality that they need a minimum of cultivation; usually they need only to be protected and given a chance to express themselves. But the wise teacher will be alert to the symptoms of dying interest, will strive to avoid undue fatigue, and will seek varied and new experiences to whet interest and nourish curiosity. New places, different problems, new associates, varied challenges (even if self-set) help to keep interest alive.

The point of these observations is that interest and curiosity are both a symptom and a cause of life and growth in the working teacher. It is balanced growth that enables the teacher to take the demands of life in a way that brings continuing personality development.

3. Love. This great word (one is tempted to say this greatest of words) has been so loosely and badly used that many are hesitant to use it, or use it largely cynically. I find that many teachers and other advanced graduate students are embarrassed when love is discussed. They seem to be afraid of the subject, yet evidently many in our world are love-starved and would profit from a frank expression of their need.

Perhaps nearly all of us have been wounded more or less deeply in our love relations. This fact may not be the fault of anyone or even of the culture (although doubtless grievous individual and cultural mistakes are made), but may arise from the extremely complex nature of love in all its myriad expressions. Yet I am convinced that there is a common essence in every manifestation of love, both giving and receiving.

In love we come to, or at least near, the ultimate in all the phases of existence: physical, mental, and spiritual. What is the relation between the love of the professional prostitute and that of the service-centered saint? Of the self-sacrificing mother and the adolescent afire with first physical infatuation? Of the friend for friend, and the seasoned husband and wife? Of course, I do not know. But the relation is there, and the implications are profound for human life. It may be that running through all of love is the losing of self and the concerns of self in a concern for the welfare and happiness of another. However misguided this quality may be, within it, if it is genuine, lie healing and creativity.[10]

The nature and meaning of love have been a major concern of the best minds of mankind from Plato's justly famous "Symposium" and Paul the Apostle's Corinthian poem to the insightful analysis of C. S. Lewis or the modern psychiatrists. It is not necessary to fathom this thought and analysis to conclude that the ability to give and receive love is crucial to personality health and growth. The evidence from every source available, including the best in psychological theory and research, supports this conclusion. Indeed it seems true that man must love and be loved or perish.

The teacher should know that there are many kinds of love to be given and received. There is a wide variety of human temperaments which seem to deal with love in different ways. Our present knowledge about this problem is sketchy, and the problem is of great complexity. Thus there is serious danger of false, harmful generalizations. For example, many single teachers have been advised by self-styled experts that they cannot be wholesome and well without the giving and receiving of physical love, and have been urged to seek such experience without regard to other needs of the personality. Such irresponsible advice acted upon usually compounds the original problem. Many types of temperament seem to be able to live a full creative life without certain manifestations of love. Even the deep need for love can be satisfied wisely only in terms of the values held by the whole self. To violate this principle is to court disaster.

Be that as it may, the teacher who would grow in love—the ability to give and receive self-forgetting concern—must seek and find healthy and growth-producing love expressions. The particular manifestations differ with individual temperament and are as varied as life itself. Each growing teacher will seek appropriate experiences of love, but he will seek them as the pearl of great price.

4. Self-determination. It is reported that the last words of Buddha to his disciples were that they must make their own environment. In an important sense, no man is truly free until he can produce his own environment whatever his apparent circumstances may be. Slavery to changing conditions tends to enslave all of life. A person so dependent may lose self-respect unless he is

flattered or is overtly successful; he may be overwhelmed with fear or beside himself with pride at the loss or gain of economic security or affluence; he may lose courage when things go against him.

Few things are more important to the growth toward maturity which we as teachers are seeking to understand, and perhaps in a measure achieve, than self-determination. Growth in this quality means an increasing ability to feel and behave in terms of resources which are within the self. These resources are always available, and strengthened and guided by them, the individual's thought and behavior are not subject to every chance change of fate. His standards and the strength to live by them come more and more to be in himself, and hence ever present and dependable.

A few illustrations may make the principle of self-determination clearer. The maturity of a class is indicated by the extent that external events influence its behavior. A slight change in the room, such as a simple accident or the appearance of an animal often will produce disorder in a group of less mature children. As they grow the controls of their behavior become internalized and if they are reasonably healthy emotionally, they will be less and less influenced by external events. The more mature class will behave about the same whether or not the teacher is present or the environmental circumstances favorable. The reactions of its members are not primarily determined by external conditions but by principle that centers in the self.

The behavior of many adults is guided chiefly by external requirements. They follow regulations in regard to traffic or litter or business ethics if they feel there is a likelihood they will be seen or in some way brought to account for the violations. Others reach that level of maturity where the standards for their actions are little or not at all dependent upon sanctions from without, but rest upon a flexible, growing body of principle—essentially a philosophy of life—that is based in truth as they are able to perceive it.

One other example closely related to the teaching-learning process will suffice. A discouragingly large number of students come, through their formal education, to conceive of learning primarily as meeting the requirements set by the teacher. This is the "lesson-learning attitude" referred to earlier which is so destructive of genuine learning. Teachers may develop the same attitude when caught in the whirl of too much "publish or perish" or some other similar pressure. The key to understanding this attitude in oneself or others is to see that the activity involved has lost its meaning or significance except as a means of satisfying an external authority or surmounting what seems to be an artificial hurdle. The person involved is not self-determined and, to the degree that he is not, is essentially a slave.

Most important of all, the self-determined person is free in one of the most meaningful senses of that great concept. He is free from the vexing caprice of varied and rapidly changing circumstances. He is able to view failure or success, praise or blame, flattery or abuse with equal poise because he has developed an increasingly stable and dependable process by which to judge the reality of the situation. Such freedom is in no sense irresponsible, or determined by impulse or personal whim. It is controlled and guided by the limits of truth or reality, and such wisdom as the person has been able to acquire, but the crucial point is that the limits are self-accepted and self-imposed in the case of the self-determined person.[11]

The teacher who desires to find the fullest development of personality for himself and his students through teaching will strive to grow in self-determination. The poise and flexible stability thus achieved can do much to make teaching a growth-producing experience.

5. Humility. Does one dare speak of humility in a world which is very nearly mad for power, prestige, honor? I think so. The truth, the nature of things, is not changed by any particular madness that arises at a particular place or time. It may be that humility is not the best word to use, for its deepest meanings have been lost or distorted by caricatures of genuine humility. Perhaps reverence or awe in the presence of the Universe comes nearer to the meaning we seek. Professor Whitehead says: "And the foun-

dation of reverence is this perception, that the present holds within itself the complete sum of existence, backwards and forwards, that whole amplitude of time, which is eternity."[12] Two great men of this age, Albert Einstein and Albert Schweitzer, have given emphasis to this point in both word and manner of life.

Humility as used here is the opposite of an overwhelming pride. It helps one to understand his proper place in the larger scheme of things. Such humility of mind is the foundation of respect for other people and their varying abilities. It is a stimulation and support to growing interest and curiosity: the very heart of the lifelong learning attitude. The teacher who is achieving this reverence is recognized by students and fellow-teachers as another learner in life's unending school. Few traits open up the gates of continuous and cooperative learning more effectively than a genuine spirit of humble reverence before what is to be learned and the process of learning.

This spirit should not be confused with lack of confidence, self-effacement, or fear. These things are often overt manifestations of unrequited pride or distorted self-centeredness. Genuine humility or reverence is crucial to the most creative self-confidence. I believe no one would consider Albert Einstein or Helen Keller or Abraham Lincoln either proud or groveling; rather they had the incomparable strength of genuine humility and the wholesome awe that accompanies it.

What a relief it is to perceive one's small but important place in the universe with some accuracy! To be able to say to oneself, and believe it—here I am, small but growing, ignorant but learning, petty but achieving greater perspective, hostile and afraid but growing in love and confidence—is to be on the road to magnificent freedom. It is to do much to establish a new relation between teacher and student and between teacher and teacher. If I observe correctly, nearly all institutions of learning are seriously poisoned now by a web of pretense—an attempt to protect and sustain false notions of status and prestige which are rooted in meaningless pride. Probably large numbers of teachers long to escape this meaningless game and in reverence and humility grow from where they are. Here then is a profoundly rewarding avenue for personality growth through teaching.

6. Peace. When peace is suggested as a crucial component of a healing growth, a fundamental question arises, Is not peace in contradiction to the dynamic quality which is the essence of growth? Peace as the term is used here is at the very core of optimum growth. In the deepest sense, it is both the end and the means of growth.

It is essentially a philosophy of life that gives unity and meaning to the search and struggle. Such peace is not political peace or even lack of tension between persons. It arises from an individual's basic beliefs—what he holds to be true. It is a result of the complex of ideas, feelings, and beliefs by which a man lives. Although there is a certain quality of quiet about this peace, it is the most fully living thing in all the world for it makes the fullest unfolding life possible. It becomes a core of stability from which never-ending growth flows.

There are many examples of this quality in the history of man, but let us think here of only two, the two that have most profoundly influenced the development of the best in Western civilization: Socrates of Athens and Jesus of Nazareth. A little book called *Socrates: The Man and His Thought,* written by Alfred Taylor, would be helpful to any teacher interested in seeing the results of a unified philosophy by which to live. The Christian scriptures are everywhere available, but I fear often neglected and distorted. A growing teacher cannot afford to neglect them, and will find genuine study of them, free from distortion, an exercise of much profit and satisfaction.[13]

The present world is full of fear, confusion, and tension. To a degree man's world has always been such, but many factors make current life more threatening and disturbing than ever before. We are suggesting that if the modern teacher would fulfill his privileges and responsibilities well he must be developing a body of principle by which he lives that progressively gives him the poise and strength of peace in the midst of great struggle. In short, he must be growing in peace if he would develop optimum personality (his own and his students') through teaching.

There is a danger that all of this will seem abstract and little related to life. What are some of the practical implications of growth in this quality?

A unified but ever-growing philosophy of life assists one to learn the great lesson of acceptance—not the acceptance of despair or slavery or death, but that of hope, of freedom, and of continuous rebirth. Through understanding, which perhaps approaches wisdom, the person learns to accept, and thus deal with creatively, the nature of himself, of others, and of the wider Universe. He thus may gradually escape the desperate scratching at life (including self, others, and the nature of things) that arises from fear and its evil child, hatred, and enter the province of satisfying growth. In this province there is struggle often of profound and far-reaching significance, but the personality's reaction to it is not fearful defense but self-fulfilling growth—a growth that instead of producing a steadily increasing weight of harmful armor frees and strengthens for the next encounter.

An important aspect of acceptance is some understanding of the nature and place of tragedy in human life. Many seem to confuse widespread misery and the various manifestations of man's inhumanity to man with the profound principle of tragedy. Misery and suffering often accompany tragedy, but they are in no sense its essence. The central meaning of tragedy lies in the gap between man's aspirations or dreams and his performance or accomplishments, and in his struggle to close this gap. He is forever dreaming—perhaps nothing is more fundamental to his nature—forever falling far short of his vision, and forever striving to come up to his dreams.

Clearly this process has built into it a kind of failure, for the vision always outruns the performance, however good the accomplishment. Thus, in a sense, every individual life and every organized society is a tragedy; but in this process seems to lie the source of man's creativeness. Of course, the struggle is often small and petty and manifests little of the classic quality which is so related to potential-releasing growth. Indeed, as we have tried to show, the teacher's attempt to deal with this tragic aspect of life all too frequently results in a web of ineffective and unattractive personality traits. Some understanding and acceptance of the tragic nature that includes profound creative promise is of great value to the teacher.

A coherent philosophy places one's life in a framework infinitely larger than himself. The growing person puts his life in an ever-extending frame of place, time, and thought. Spinoza suggested that the best character is set in a framework of eternity. In this way the individual life escapes the petty limitations of its narrowly personal concerns and achieves some unity with larger and more meaningful concerns of man and God.

One of the greatest evils of man is unwholesome self-reference. The theme of most of the great teachers of mankind has been the need of a growth beyond self. This long-time view is of special importance to the person who aspires to greatness in teaching. The most important aspects of the teacher's work reach far beyond the immediate into the long continuous processes of generations. Much of the best he achieves appears too late for him to see; thus he rarely is overtly commended or rewarded for his efforts. History more often shows him neglected, misunderstood, and not infrequently done to death.

One illustration on the positive side makes the nature and power of the long view clearer. Some years ago I went back to visit on a farm in my home community. My friend who owned the small farm was now old—in his early eighties—and not very well. I found him working along a fence line behind the old house. After a brief greeting, I inquired what he was doing. He was planting young apple trees. As the mind will do, in a twinkling my mind surveyed the situation: an old man even now short of breath from a heart ailment; family grown and gone, uninterested in the farm that nourished and supported their education; very young apple trees that at best would not bear fruit for many years. Evidently this man could not enjoy or even see the fruit of this afternoon's labor.

Of course, I did not raise this question. But he sensed my thought and said that it was his chief joy to plant for tomorrow. The satisfaction did not seem to flow from an anticipation of anything that might come to him or his family now or later, but chiefly from a widely based concern for the enrichment and betterment of life in all its varied manifestations. Certainly my farmer friend would not have expressed his feeling and faith so formally, but the crucial sense of the ongoing nature of life and his vital role in it apart from self-centered preoccupations was there. A great teacher needs something of this conception of life.

The peace of which we speak is a great support for a faith that gives meaning and zest to the living of life. To believe deeply that life is worthwhile one must believe in himself, in others, and in the ultimate goodness of the large processes of the Universe. Without such faith the entire process tends to become a painful, meaningless, losing struggle. At the end of Hamlet's speech on the magnificent qualities of men, quoted earlier, he concludes, "And yet, to me, what is this quintessence of dust? man delights not me; no, nor woman neither, though by your smiling you seem to say so." Or a self-destroyed Macbeth describes life as being "a tale told by an idiot, full of sound and fury, signifying nothing."

The loss of this basic belief in life, this zest for life, this faith in its significance often results in a panic of activity designed to deceive oneself and others by pretending almost violently that life is good and meaningful. Caught in this trap the individual pursues all the empty symbols so publicized in our time: sophistication, material accoutrements, conformity, activity, status, tawdry honors. Pretense may be built mountain high, but the self remains empty, directionless, and anxious.

The teacher who would grow through teaching must cultivate the roots of peace—a philosophy of life based upon the fullest truth he can perceive. He will be growing in the ability to look squarely at every part of life, particularly its tragic nature, and yet be in-spired and challenged by its processes and its promise for the gradual fulfillment and enrichment of human life.

So we come, for the moment, to the end of our thoughts together about the relation of teaching to personality development. Teach-ers will know that these thoughts are merely hints of what might be said, and also only the suggestions of one fellow-teacher whose sole claim to authority is that he is a searcher after truth and wis-dom. The hope is that other thoughts will be stirred and a more widespread search stimulated.

The thesis of this chapter is not that every teacher must be a *great* teacher or a *great* person in order to achieve full personality development through teaching or to avoid serious personality damage. The central idea is that the teacher must be *growing toward* excellence in every phase of his life that relates to teach-ing. An increasingly clear vision of the goal and a steady growth toward it do not seem beyond reasonable hope.

E. V. P.

Notes and selected readings

Part I *Background*

1. What is teaching?

1. A perceptive modern novelist expressed this complexity with its paradoxes in this way:

> It had been made abundantly clear in the last hour that teaching is first of all teaching a person. . . . Was anyone safe from the perils of such responsibility? How carelessly she had criticized her own professors down the years! How little she had known or understood what tensions drove them on and tore them apart, what never-ending conflict they must weigh and balance each day. For she had come to see that it was possible, if one worked hard enough at it, to be prepared as far as subject matter went—though Lucy herself could not imagine such a blessed state—but it was not possible to be prepared to meet the twenty or more individuals of each class, each struggling to grow, each bringing into the room a different

279

human background, each—Lucy felt now—in a state of peril where a too-rigorous demand or an instantaneous flash of anger might fatally turn the inner direction. . . . How did one know? How did one learn a sense of proportion, where to withdraw, where to yield?

And she guessed, not for the first time, that there could be no answer ever, that every teacher in relation to every single student must ask these questions over and over, and answer them differently in each instance, because the relationship is as various, as unpredictable as a love affair.

May Sarton, *The Small Room* (New York: W. W. Norton, 1961), pp. 104-5.

Although in one sense teaching is like a love affair, in perhaps a profounder sense it is like a friendship. For reasons not clear to me, the subject of friendship has been neglected in modern times. See C. S. Lewis, *The Four Loves* (New York: Harcourt, Brace & World, 1960), for a discussion of friendship.

2. *The Book of Tao,* translated by Frank J. MacHovec (Mount Vernon, N.Y.: Peter Pauper Press, 1962), pp.5,7.

3. This statement about human potential is taken almost verbatim from an earlier publication: Earl V. Pullias, "The Education of the Whole Man," *A Search for Understanding* (Dubuque, Iowa: William C. Brown, 1965), pp.12,14.

4. Alfred North Whitehead, *The Aims of Education and Other Essays* (New York: Macmillan, 1959), p.10.

5. See Gilbert Highet, *The Art of Teaching* (New York: Alfred A. Knopf, 1950), for further discussion of this problem.

2. Some obstacles to growth toward excellence in teaching

1. Dr. Erich Fromm put the case dramatically in a recent address:

A man sits in front of a bad television program and does not know that he is bored; he reads of Viet Cong casualties in the newspaper and does not recall the teachings of his religion; he learns of the dangers of nuclear holocaust and does not feel fear; he joins the rat race of commerce, where personal worth is measured in terms of market values, and is not aware of his anxiety. Ulcers speak louder than the mind.

Theologians and philosophers have been saying for a century that God is dead, but what we confront now is the possibility that man is dead, transformed into a thing, a producer, a consumer, an idolator of other things.

New York Times, April 17, 1966. A report of his address to the 43rd annual meeting of the American Orthopsychiatric Association in San Francisco.

2. See *The Republic of Plato*, translated by Benjamin Jowett (Oxford: Clarendon Press, 1908).

3. For a clear and provocative attack on the foundations of pedantry, see J. Abner Peddiwell, *The Saber-Tooth Curriculum* (New York: McGraw-Hill, 1939).

4. See Catherine Drinker Bowen, *Yankee from Olympus* (Boston: Little, Brown, 1944), for a stirring account of this dilemma.

5. *The Thoughts of Thoreau*, selected with a biographical foreword and introduction by Edwin Way Teale (New York: Dodd, Mead, 1962), p.73.

6. Based upon material originally presented in Earl V. Pullias, Aileene Lockhart, and others, *Toward Excellence in College Teaching* (Dubuque, Iowa: William C. Brown, 1963), ch.4.

Part II A teacher is many things

3. A teacher is a guide

1. Nikos Kazantzakis, *The Odyssey: A Modern Sequel*, translated by Kimon Friar (New York: Simon and Schuster, 1958); Lillian Smith, *The Journey* (Cleveland: World Publishing Co., 1954); Johann Wolfgang von Goethe, *Wilhelm Meister*, Everyman's Library nos.599,600 (New York: E. P. Dutton); Miguel de Cervantes, *Don Quixote of La Mancha*, translated and edited by Walter Starkie (New York: New American Library, 1963); A. N. Whitehead, *Adventures of Ideas* (New York: Macmillan, 1933); J. R. R. Tolkien, *The Hobbit* (Boston: Houghton Mifflin, 1938); John Steinbeck, *Travels with Charley in Search of America* (New York: Viking Press, 1962). In a sense, it seems to me, the best of history always has the flavor of an odyssey. The same is true of the great dramas of Shakespeare and the Greeks, especially the tragedies such as *Macbeth, Hamlet, Antigone*.

2. These tasks are discussed in a somewhat different way in Earl V. Pullias, Aileene Lockhart, and others, *Toward Excellence in College Teaching*, ch.2.

3. Perhaps the best technical analysis of objectives available is *The Taxonomy of Educational Objectives*: Handbook I, *Cognitive Domain*, edited by Benjamin S. Bloom; Handbook II, *Affective Domain* by David

R. Krathwohl, Benjamin S. Bloom, and Bertram B. Masia (New York: David McKay, 1956, 1964).

4. See Nathan Pusey, *The Age of the Scholar* (Cambridge, Mass.: Harvard University Press, 1963), p.36, for an insightful statement concerning the nature and meaning of high skill in reading.

5. The philosopher, teacher, and journalist, José Ortega y Gasset, in his delightful essay, *Mission of the University* (London: Routledge & Kegan Paul, 1952), ch.3, states the problem of economy very well.

6. See Edward D. Eddy, Jr., *The College Influence on Student Character* (Washington, D.C.: American Council on Education, 1959); Philip E. Jacob, *Changing Values in College* (New York: Harper & Brothers, 1957); and Nevitt Sanford, ed., *The American College: A Psychological and Social Interpretation of the Higher Learning* (New York: John Wiley & Sons, 1962), for further discussion of this problem.

7. See Houston Peterson, ed., *Great Teachers* (New Brunswick, N.J.: Rutgers University Press, 1964), for brief sketches of noted teachers.

8. A. N. Whitehead, *The Aims of Education*, p.147.

9. There is an extensive literature on testing. Unfortunately, most of it deals with the technical aspects of test making and measurement, relatively little with the crucial problem of the relation of testing to learning.

4. A teacher is a teacher

1. Many of Helen Keller's books touch on the power of her teacher. Perhaps *Teacher: Anne Sullivan Macy* (Garden City, N.Y.: Doubleday, 1955), remains the simplest and most convincing.

2. Gilbert Highet in his *The Art of Teaching*, pp.74-173, has much of value to say on this aspect of teaching. Much of the power of Madame Montessori's work results from her skill in these processes. See E. Mortimer Standing, *Maria Montessori, Her Life and Work* (London: Hollis & Carter, 1957).

3. See Lane Cooper, *Louis Agassiz as a Teacher*, rev. ed. (Ithaca, N.Y.: Comstock Publishing Associates, Cornell University Press, 1945); and Milton Mayer, *Young Man in a Hurry* (Chicago: University of Chicago Alumni Association, 1957).

4. See Ronald Gross, ed., *The Teacher and the Taught: Education in Theory and Practice from Plato to James B. Conant* (New York: Dell, 1963), for historical descriptions of the teacher in action.

5. Perhaps this is the reason that students oftentimes learn best from

fellow students who are themselves in or near the difficulties of the learning. Probably one of the most promising developments in the future will be a more systematic use of students for certain levels of teaching.

5. A teacher is a modernizer: a bridge between generations

1. See Bruno Bettelheim, "The Problem of Generations," *Daedalus*, Proceedings of the American Academy of Arts and Sciences, 91(1962): 68-96.
2. Edward D. Myers, *Education in the Perspective of History*, with a concluding chapter by Arnold J. Toynbee (New York: Harper & Brothers, 1960), p.273.
3. Oliver Wendell Holmes, "The Deacon's Masterpiece," *The Oxford Book of American Verse* (New York: Oxford University Press, 1950), p.196.
4. William Ernest Hocking, *Human Nature and Its Remaking* (New Haven, Conn.: Yale University Press, 1923).

6. A teacher is a model: an example

1. This thoughtful distinction is mentioned in *The Autobiography of Robert A. Millikan* (New York: Prentice-Hall, 1950), p.287.
2. See Sylvia Ashton-Warner, *Teacher* (New York: Simon and Schuster, 1963), for the most vivid and readable of these descriptions. *Teacher* will be more meaningful if *Spinster* (New York: Simon and Schuster, 1959) by the same author is read first. See also Gardner Murphy, *Freeing Intelligence Through Teaching* (New York: Harper & Brothers, 1961).
3. An extensive technical and semi-technical literature is developing in this area. For concerns expressed by teachers, perhaps the periodical literature is most useful.
4. A. N. Whitehead, *The Aims of Education and Other Essays*, pp. 139-40.
5. William Ernest Hocking, *The Coming World Civilization* (New York: Harper & Brothers, 1956), p.9.
6. Charles Lamb, "Hester," *The Oxford Book of English Verse* (Oxford: At the Clarendon Press, 1955), p.688.

7. Earl V. Pullias, "How Do You Behave When the Children Misbehave?" *Childhood Education,* 10(1934):230-37.

8. It does not follow, of course, that a "good" or "wise" example will always be followed. Often what seem to be good teachers have very bad students. The teacher is one influence in many. See Gilbert Highet, *The Art of Teaching,* ch.IV, for interesting historical examples.

See Nevitt Sanford, *The American College,* and current literature on adolescence for evidence concerning the influence of peers. One wonders if the power of the peer group does not increase in proportion to the teachers' and parents' refusal to accept their full responsibility.

9. Robert Browning, "Saul," in *Poems of Robert Browning* (New York: Oxford University Press, 1920).

10. *The Works of Plato,* selected and edited by Irwin Edman (New York: Tudor, 1928), p.315.

7. A teacher is a searcher: one who does not know

1. *The Works of Plato,* p.314.

2. See John Henry Newman, *The Idea of a University* (New York: Longmans, Green & Co., 1947), for a classical statement and Karl Jaspers, *The Idea of the University* (Boston: Beacon Press, 1959), for a more recent analysis.

3. Edwin Markham, "The Man With the Hoe," in *Great Poems of the English Language,* compiled by Walter Briggs (New York: Tudor, 1933), p.1106.

4. Readers interested in pursuing this thought further should see Gardner Murphy, *Freeing Intelligence Through Teaching,* for an analysis by a distinguished psychologist.

5. See George Orwell, *Nineteen Eighty-Four* (New York: Harcourt, Brace, 1949), and Aldous Huxley, *Brave New World Revisited* (New York: Harper & Brothers, 1958).

6. I personally am convinced that this quality deep in man will eventually unhinge any dictatorship that persistently obstructs this search.

7. See Pierre Teilhard de Chardin, *The Phenomenon of Man* (New York: Harper and Brothers, 1959); also, Gerard Piel, "The Acceleration of History," *Current Issues in Higher Education* (Washington, D.C.: Association for Higher Education, National Education Association, 1964), pp.22-32.

8. For a very thoughtful recent discussion of this process, see Jerome S. Bruner's books, *The Process of Education* (Cambridge, Mass.: Harvard University Press, 1961), and *On Knowing: Essays for the Left Hand* (Cambridge, Mass.: Harvard University Press, 1962).

9. The famed science teacher Louis Agassiz is the classic example of a teacher who emphasized this approach.

10. See William Ernest Hocking, *The Coming World Civilization*, Study III.

11. *Sayings of Buddha* (Mount Vernon, N.Y.: Peter Pauper Press, 1957), pp.37-38.

12. See Huston Smith, *The Purposes of Higher Education* (New York: Harper & Brothers, 1955), ch.III, for a thoughtful discussion of this complex problem.

8. A teacher is a counselor: a confidant and friend

1. The author of this chapter is trained as a counselor and has engaged in various types of counseling throughout his professional career. The term "counselor" or "counseling" may be used in many senses. What is said in this discussion in no way is intended to deprecate counseling in the more technical and professional sense. This discussion is pointed to the needs and interests of the classroom teacher. Many technical problems that concern those interested in the theory of counseling are touched lightly or not at all. For those interested, there is a fine literature on counseling and guidance available at any reasonably good library.

2. See any of the better books on personality and mental hygiene for the simplest evidence on this point. For example, Harold W. Bernard, *Mental Hygiene for Classroom Teachers*, 2nd ed. (New York: McGraw-Hill, 1961); Helen Leland Witmer and Ruth Kotinsky, eds., *Personality in the Making: The Fact-Finding Report of the Midcentury White House Conference on Children and Youth* (New York: Harper & Brothers, 1952); Louis P. Thorpe, *The Psychology of Mental Health*, 2nd ed. (New York: Ronald Press, 1960); and Karen Horney, *The Neurotic Personality of Our Time* (New York: W. W. Norton, 1937).

3. Clifford Geertz, "The Impact of the Concept of Culture on the Concept of Man," in *New Views of the Nature of Man*, edited by John R. Platt (Chicago: University of Chicago Press, 1965), p.108.

4. See Erich Fromm, *Escape from Freedom* (New York: Henry Holt, 1941).

5. See Lewis Mumford, *The Conduct of Life* (New York: Harcourt, Brace, 1951), for a very insightful if somewhat discouraging analysis.

6. Many teachers have found Arthur T. Jersild, *When Teachers Face Themselves* (New York: Teachers College Press, 1955), and George Williams, *Some of My Best Friends Are Professors* (New York: Abelard-Schuman, 1958), interesting and helpful because of their analyses of the special problems of teachers.

7. Any one of his many books presents this idea. The basic theory is well stated in Alfred Adler, *The Neurotic Constitution* (New York: Dodd, Mead, 1926).

8. See Abraham H. Maslow, *Toward a Psychology of Being* (Princeton, N.J.: D. Van Nostrand, 1962), for interesting evidence on this point.

9. Sylvia Ashton-Warner, *Spinster*, p.9.

9. A teacher is a creator: a stimulator of creativity

1. Willard F. Libby, "Man's Place in the Physical Universe," in *New Views of the Nature of Man*, p.9.

2. Sylvia Ashton-Warner, *Teacher*, pp.11,33.

10. A teacher is an authority: one who knows

1. See J. Abner Peddiwell, *The Sage of Petaluma: Autobiography of a Teacher* (New York: McGraw-Hill, 1965), ch.V.

2. President Charles de Gaulle is one of the most interesting and thoughtful of contemporary political figures. His career and his writings throw light on the relation of personality to leadership. See François Mauriac, *De Gaulle* (Garden City, N.Y.: Doubleday, 1966), for a literary biography. De Gaulle's own writings, particularly *The War Memoirs of Charles De Gaulle* (New York: vol. 1: Viking Press, 1955; vols. 2-3: Simon and Schuster, 1959-60), and his much earlier book, *The Edge of the Sword* (New York: Criterion Books, 1960), present another type of analysis.

3. See Earl V. Pullias, Aileene Lockhart, and others, *Toward Excellence in College Teaching*, ch.4.

4. Lord Chesterfield, *Letters to His Son and Others*, Everyman's Library no. 823 (New York: E. P. Dutton, 1951), p.47.
5. Catherine Drinker Bowen, *Yankee from Olympus*, p.128.

11. A teacher is an inspirer of vision

1. See A. N. Whitehead, *Adventures of Ideas*, ch. II and III, for a brilliant analysis of the nature and meaning of this fact.
2. Interested teachers may find the following books of help: Henry B. Parkes, *Gods and Men: The Origins of Western Culture* (New York: Alfred A. Knopf, 1959); Crane Brinton, *Ideas and Men: The Story of Western Thought*, 2nd ed. (Englewood Cliffs, N.J.: Prentice-Hall, 1963); Bertrand Russell, *A History of Western Philosophy* (New York: Simon and Schuster, Inc., 1945); and Arnold J. Toynbee, *A Study of History*, 12 vols. (New York: Oxford University Press, 1935-1961).
3. William Ernest Hocking, *Experiment in Education* (Chicago: Henry Regnery Company, 1954), p.271.
4. The concluding chapters of Loren Eiseley, *The Immense Journey* (New York: Random House, 1957), touch interestingly on this problem.
5. Sidney Cox, *A Swinger of Birches: A Portrait of Robert Frost* (New York: New York University Press, 1957), p.14.
6. See Robert Graves, *Mammon and the Black Goddess* (Garden City, N.Y.: Doubleday, 1965).
7. Some perhaps will recall in this connection John Dewey's essay, *Interest and Effort in Education* (Boston: Houghton Mifflin, 1913).
8. A few most influential examples are Homer and the rich Greek mythology, most of the classic dramatists and poets, the Bible, Dante, Goethe, Shakespeare, and very nearly the whole body of English literature, and the nineteenth-century American writers.
9. See Sean O'Casey, "The Bald Primaqueera," *Atlantic Monthly*, September, 1965:69-74.
10. Malcolm Cowley, *The Faulkner-Cowley File: Letters and Memories, 1944-1962* (New York: Viking Press, 1966), p.15.
11. Sir Arthur Quiller-Couch, ed., *The Oxford Book of English Verse*, new ed. (Oxford: At the Clarendon Press, 1955), p.xiii.
12. See A. N. Whitehead, *Science and the Modern World* (New York: Macmillan, 1926), for a fine analysis of this problem.

13. For a delightful statement of this principle, see Albert Schweitzer, *The Teaching of Reverence for Life* (New York: Holt, Rinehart and Winston, 1965), a little book published toward the end of his life.

12. A teacher is a doer of routine

1. For an excellent analysis of this relation at a somewhat technical level, see A. N. Whitehead, *Adventures of Ideas*, ch.VII; for a more popular analysis see Edith Hamilton, *The Echo of Greece* (New York: W. W. Norton, 1957). See also Huston Smith, *The Purposes of Higher Education*, ch.II.

13. A teacher is a breaker of camp

1. See John W. Gardner, *Self-Renewal: The Individual and the Innovative Society* (New York: Harper & Row, 1964); and Arnold J. Toynbee, *A Study of History*. For a less formal but perhaps even more convincing statement of this principle, see Robert Lawson, *Rabbit Hill* (New York: Viking Press, 1944).

2. See Alfred Adler, *Understanding Human Nature* (New York: Greenberg, 1927).

3. See William Ernest Hocking, *The Coming World Civilization*, Studies IV and V, for an analysis of this point. See also Samuel H. Miller, *The Dilemma of Modern Belief* (New York: Harper & Row, 1963), and Paul Tillich, *Morality and Beyond* (New York: Harper & Row, 1963).

4. Austin Tappan Wright, *Islandia* (New York: Farrar & Rinehart [Holt, Rinehart and Winston], 1942), p.405.

5. Sidney Cox, *A Swinger of Birches: A Portrait of Robert Frost*.

6. Alfred, Lord Tennyson, *The Idylls of the King: The Passing of Arthur*, l.407.

14. A teacher is a storyteller

1. Lillian Smith, *The Journey*, pp.122-27.

2. Nora Waln, "The Singer of Noonday Rest," *Atlantic Monthly*, March,1058·35-40.

3. Ruth Sawyer, *The Enchanted Schoolhouse* (New York: Viking Press, 1956), p.78.

15. A teacher is an actor

1. Thomas Mann, *The Confessions of Felix Krull, Confidence Man* (New York: Alfred A. Knopf, 1955), p.384.

17. A teacher is a builder of community

1. John Dos Passos, "P.S. to Dean Briggs," in *College in a Yard: Minutes by Thirty-nine Harvard Men,* edited by Brooks Atkinson (Cambridge, Mass.: Harvard University Press, 1957), p.63.
2. Virginia Sorensen, *Plain Girl* (New York: Harcourt, Brace, 1955).

18. A teacher is a learner

1. Alice Lee Humphreys, *Heaven in My Hand* (Richmond, Va.: John Knox Press, 1955), p.12.
2. Antoine de Saint-Exupéry, *The Little Prince* (New York: Harcourt, Brace & World, 1943).
3. Sylvia Ashton-Warner, *Teacher,* p.31.

19. A teacher is a facer of reality

1. Roark Bradford, *How Come Christmas: A Modern Morality* (New York: Harper & Brothers, 1948).
2. Antoine de Saint-Exupéry, *The Little Prince,* p.70.

20. A teacher is an emancipator

1. Irving Stone, *The Agony and the Ecstasy* (Garden City, N.Y.: Doubleday, 1961), p.211.

2. Marguerite de Angeli, *Door in the Wall* (Garden City, N.Y.: Doubleday, 1949).

3. Virginia Sorensen, *Plain Girl.*

24. A teacher is a person

1. See George Williams, *Some of My Best Friends Are Professors,* and Arthur Jersild, *When Teachers Face Themselves.*

2. For an especially thoughtful discussion, see Abraham H. Maslow, *Motivation and Personality* (New York: Harper and Brothers, 1954), and *Toward a Psychology of Being* (Princeton, N.J.: D. Van Nostrand, 1962).

3. Gardner Murphy expresses this thought convincingly in *Freeing Intelligence Through Teaching.*

4. Many teachers have found the work of the Canadian physician, Hans Selye, *Stress of Life* (New York: McGraw-Hill, 1956), helpful in understanding and dealing with stress.

5. For further reference, see Franz Winkler, *Man: The Bridge Between Two Worlds* (New York: Harper & Brothers, 1960)—the approach of a psychiatrist; Aldous Huxley, *The Perennial Philosophy* (New York: Harper and Brothers, 1945)—a more philosophic and mystical view; and Paul Tillich, *The Dynamics of Faith* (New York: Harper and Brothers, 1957)—a theological view.

6. Edna St. Vincent Millay, from "Renascence" in *Collected Poems* (New York: Harper & Brothers, copyright, 1912, 1940, by Edna St. Vincent Millay). By permission of Norma Millay Ellis.

7. Richard Hughes, *The Fox in the Attic* (New York: Harper & Brothers, 1961).

8. Lillian Smith, *The Journey*, p.7.

9. Edna St. Vincent Millay, "Renascence," in *Collected Poems.*

10. Those interested in pursuing this point may find the introduction to the book, *Saviors of God* (New York: Simon and Schuster, 1960), by the Greek poet, Nikos Kazantzakis, stimulating.

11. See Edith Hamilton, *The Echo of Greece*, particularly the first chapter.

12. A. N. Whitehead, *The Aims of Education*, p. 23.

13. A. E. Taylor, *Socrates: The Man and His Thought*, Doubleday Anchor Book A9 (Garden City, N.Y.: Doubleday, 1953); many persons have found special pleasure in *The New English Bible: New Testament*, a recent translation (published jointly by Cambridge and Oxford University Press, 1961).

Index